Cultural Diversity, Liberal Pluralism and Schools

Culturally diverse liberal democracies on both sides of the Atlantic are currently faced with serious questions about the education of their future citizens. What is the balance between the need for social cohesion, and at the same time dealing justly with the demands for exemptions and accommodations from cultural and religious minorities? In contemporary Britain, the importance of this question has been recently highlighted by the concern to develop political and educational strategies capable of countering the influence of extremist voices, in both the majority and minority communities.

Starting from recent debates in North America about possible accommodations to meet the concerns of non-liberal religious groups, the book goes on to examine several issues centred on education in culturally-diverse societies. Neil Burtonwood argues persuasively that the work of Isaiah Berlin, the British philosopher and historian of ideas, has considerable potential for illuminating questions about a properly liberal response to pluralism, and the education of cultural minority children in a liberal democracy.

This is the first book to bring his writing to bear on education. Berlin's liberalism is distinctive in attending to the benefits that individuals gain from their memberships of cultural identity groups and religious communities, while remaining committed to Enlightenment values based on individual freedom. Yet his need to find compromises to balance the claims of individuals and groups makes Berlin's version of liberal pluralism so relevant to many vital questions of education policy and practice that concern philosophers of education today.

Neil Burtonwood is Senior Lecturer in Educational Studies at the University of Leeds; he previously taught in high schools and at Bretton Hall College of Higher Education. He is the author of *The Culture Concept in Educational Studies*.

Routledge international studies in the philosophy of education

Cultural Diversity, Liberal Pluralism and Schools

Isaiah Berlin and education

Neil Burtonwood

Routledge
Taylor & Francis Group

LONDON AND NEW YORK

First published 2006
by Routledge
2 Park Square, Milton Park, Abingdon, Oxon OX14 4RN

Simultaneously published in the USA and Canada
by Routledge
270 Madison Ave, New York, NY 10016

Routledge is an imprint of the Taylor & Francis Group, an informa business

© 2006 Neil Burtonwood

Typeset in Times by Wearset Ltd, Boldon, Tyne and Wear
Printed and bound in Great Britain by TJI Digital, Padstow, Cornwall

British Library Cataloguing in Publication Data
A catalogue record for this book is available from the British Library

Library of Congress Cataloging in Publication Data
A catalog record for this book has been requested

ISBN10: 0-415-36501-5 (hbk)
ISBN10: 0-203-01604-1 (ebk)

ISBN13: 978-0-415-36501-7 (hbk}
ISBN13: 978-0-203-01604-6 (ebk)

For Jean, Tom and Matthew

After the ruinous experiments of the lately deceased century, after so much vile behaviour, so many deaths, a queasy agnosticism has settled around these matters of justice and redistributed wealth. No more big ideas. The world must improve, if at all, by tiny steps.

(McEwan, 2005: 74)

Contents

Preface

While there has been considerable attention given to the intellectual legacy of Sir Isaiah Berlin since his death in 1997, relatively little has been said so far about the implications of his work in philosophy and the history of ideas for education. Although he says little directly about education, it is the thesis of this book that Berlin's writing on the subjects of liberalism, pluralism and, not least, his abiding concern to avoid cruelty and suffering, has relevance to several key debates in the philosophy of education. In discussing some of the questions around contemporary issues such as civic education, faith-based schools, values education and education for citizenship and national identity I hope to show the relevance of Berlin to the philosophy of education and to contribute to the wider debate about the way that the claims of liberalism and pluralism are best reconciled in the interests of both liberty and identity in culturally diverse societies.

Acknowledgements

I am grateful to my colleagues in the Inclusive Education Research Group in the School of Education at the University of Leeds for the opportunity to share some of the ideas that eventually came to be formulated as the proposal for this book. Colleagues beyond Leeds have also been very helpful either in responding to the original proposal, in reading and commenting on various drafts of chapters or in corresponding with me about their own work. In each case I am grateful for the collegiality shown and I wish to extend my thanks especially to Harry Brighouse, Mike Degenhardt, Henry Hardy, Stephen Macedo, Michael Merry, Paul Standish, Jack Weinstein and Colin Wringe. I am also grateful to Terry Clague and his colleagues at Routledge for editorial guidance throughout the writing process.

Versions of some sections of the book have appeared in an earlier form as articles or were presented as conference papers. I am grateful to members of the Philosophy of Education Society of Great Britain for their response to parts of Chapter 6 which were presented as a conference paper at the Annual Conference in April 2005; in particular I would like to thank Mark Olssen for his comments on that occasion. Parts of Chapter 4 were published in an earlier form in 'Social cohesion, autonomy, and the liberal defence of faith schools' in *Journal of Philosophy of Education*, Volume 37, 2003 and I am grateful to Blackwell Publishing for permission to reproduce this material. In Chapters 2 and 5 I have used extracts from 'Isaiah Berlin, diversity liberalism, and education' originally published in *Educational Review*, Volume 55, 2003 and I am grateful to Taylor & Francis Ltd (www. tandf. co. uk) for permission to reproduce this material.

The quotation from Ian McEwan's book *Saturday*, published in 2005 by Jonathan Cape, is reprinted by permission of The Random House Group Limited and Rogers, Coleridge and White Ltd. While preparing my manuscript I read that Ian McEwan had been reflecting on Isaiah Berlin while writing *Saturday* and it is not difficult to see the influence of Berlin, not least in the quotation I have selected to appear at the beginning of this work.

Neil Burtonwood
Leeds

Abbreviations

CRE	Commission for Racial Equality
DES	Department of Education and Science
DfEE	Department for Education and Employment
DfES	Department for Education and Skills
NCC	National Curriculum Council
NFVEC	National Forum for Values in Education and the Community
OfSTED	Office for Standards in Education
QCA	Qualifications and Curriculum Authority
SCAA	School Curriculum and Assessment Authority

1 Isaiah Berlin and liberalism

Introduction

Recent literature from the United States of America and Canada reveals that for liberal educators solutions to some key questions regarding the appropriate educational arrangements for children belonging to cultural minorities are to be found in the kind of political philosophy that is being written by liberal philosophers and their communitarian critics. While educators in the United Kingdom have only recently begun to draw on this detailed philosophical work, there is no doubt that the issues, questions and themes that dominate recent political and moral philosophy in North America have a significant bearing on educational issues in an increasingly culturally diverse United Kingdom. It is the thesis of this book that the work of Sir Isaiah Berlin, British philosopher and historian of ideas, has considerable potential for illuminating questions about the education of cultural minority children in a liberal democracy. Despite a considerable literature on the intellectual legacy of Berlin since his death in 1997 little has been said about the relevance of this work to education. This book will attempt to fill this gap.

Consider some of the questions that dominate recent thinking about education and cultural diversity in liberal and democratic societies. Communitarian critics of liberalism doubt the justification for an expansive liberal civic education in societies that are increasingly culturally diverse. While liberals might argue that cultural and religious diversity within society underlines the importance of an extensive civic education designed to cement diverse elements within the polity, their communitarian opponents are more likely to be disturbed by the apparently oppressive nature of a liberal civic education at odds with the cultural and religious commitments of non-liberal minorities. Are there limits to diversity that liberals must feel obliged to set and how are religious fundamentalists to be accommodated when their chosen lives follow currents that run against the liberal mainstream? Liberals committed to individual autonomy as *the* defining feature of liberalism are challenged by the question as to whether there is a credible version of autonomy that can accommodate the choice of a non-autonomous life. Recently some liberals appear to have been persuaded by the claims of cultural and religious diversity over those of individual autonomy. These 'diversity liberals' find themselves in the seemingly illiberal position of supporting the claims of cultural groups to control the lives of their own members. Feminist critics have demonstrated the ways in which this leaves particular members, especially women and children, vulnerable to oppression. Is that threat realistically ameliorated by making right of exit a condition of liberal support for extending group rights to communities and, if so, what kind of education is necessary and sufficient to make such a right meaningful? One kind of community that has particularly exercised the thinking of liberals and communitarians alike is the national community. Can liberalism be reconciled with nationalism in such a way that traditionally cosmopolitan liberals can feel comfortable with an education for national identity?

This is a formidable set of questions and one that has generated a considerable North American literature particularly over the last five years. The chapters of this book will address each of these questions both in terms of what has been said of the North American context and also the implications for the United Kingdom. What these questions share is a tension within liberalism between commitments to individual autonomy and to societies characterised by diversity. This same tension permeates Berlin's writing on liberal societies and cultural minorities because Berlin's distinctive, some would say communitarian, liberalism demonstrates commitments both to a liberal ideal of individual freedom and to a communitarian emphasis on the value of group identity and a sense of belonging.

Isaiah Berlin: background and philosophy

This chapter will focus on Berlin's life and work, exploring those aspects of his liberal pluralism that are relevant to the education of cultural minority children in liberal democratic societies. In this section I will say something by way of introduction about how Berlin has been located within the liberal tradition before going on to note the impact of his work on British academic life.

Berlin and liberalism

It has been argued by John Gray (2000) that liberalism has 'two faces'. One is represented by an Enlightenment tradition that privileges reason and values personal autonomy in the form of individual choice-making above all else. Berlin is perhaps best known for his espousal of this kind of liberalism as 'negative freedom' or freedom from external constraint; in fact, Berlin's essays on liberty are regarded by supporters and critics alike as a definitive statement of this kind of liberalism (see especially Berlin, 2002a).[1] Gray, however, identifies another face of liberalism, one that is more concerned with social and cultural diversity. Here the key value is not individual autonomy but tolerance, a tolerance that needs to be extended to those communities where members choose not to live their lives with individual autonomy as a central value. In the light of his commitment to cultural groups and the sense of belonging that membership of such groups engenders Berlin has been championed as a major contributor to this second version of liberalism (Tamir, 1998).

Jacob Levy (2000) starts from a rather different theme in Berlin's writing and, as a result, he offers a quite different interpretation. It is because of the fact of diversity that Levy chooses to emphasize Berlin's concerns about the violence, cruelty and terror that can occur when individuals commit totally to the identities of nation or cultural group. Chapter 1 will conclude by placing these fears within the context of Berlin's early life in what he often described as a terrifying century. Berlin's sometimes autobiographical writing will provide a context for examining what Levy, following Judith Shklar, calls a 'multiculturalism of fear'. This version of what Shklar (1998) referred to as the 'liberalism of fear' encourages recognition of the importance that individuals give to their group affiliations but without losing sight of the dangers that these particular identities can represent. This tension between the merits and dangers of strong group identities is especially evident in those parts of Berlin's writing that deal with nationalism, Jewish identity and the role that the nation-state of Israel plays in the lives of all Jews.

Berlin's life and work is often associated with paradox; he has been characterized as a supremely successful immigrant who assimilated into the English elite while remaining a critic of cosmopolitan rootlessness and an advocate of minority cultural identity. While his defence of liberty is widely regarded as one of the most important accounts of liberal individualism, his valuing of group belongingness appears to suggest a liberalism that owes at least something to the communitarian critique of liberal commitments to individual rights. In his widely known articulation of value pluralism as the recognition of diverse and incompatible human goods, Berlin often speaks of the inability to reduce such goods to any kind of rank order, and yet any reading of Berlin's work suggests that his equally strong rejection of determinism demands some prioritization for individual choice-making. While it will be shown that what makes Berlin's liberalism so distinctive is the attention he gives to Counter-Enlightenment thinkers and their Romantic successors, it is also true that he always saw these thinkers as the enemies of the kind of freedom to which he was fundamentally committed. I will conclude this chapter by arguing that it is the 'third face of liberalism', the overwhelming desire to avoid cruelty and human suffering together with a recognition of the importance of universal human rights that underpin decent societies, that enables Berlin to combine liberalism and pluralism in such a way that neither is allowed to exclude the other.

Berlin and British academic life

Berlin was born in 1909 into a prosperous Jewish family in Riga, Latvia.[2] In 1916 the family moved to St Petersburg where the young Isaiah witnessed the Russian Revolution. After the November Revolution the family returned to Riga before emigration to England in 1920. After being a pupil at St Paul's School Berlin entered Corpus Christi College, Oxford, as an undergraduate in 1928.

Oxford was to be Berlin's academic home for the rest of his life. Lecturing at New College was followed by a fellowship at All Souls before taking up the Chichele Chair in Social and Political Theory in 1958. Berlin eventually resigned his Chair to become founding President of Wolfson College, a role that he occupied from 1966 to 1975. After 1975 Berlin was re-elected to All Souls where he remained a fellow until his death in 1997.

In his 1953 essay *The Hedgehog and the Fox* Berlin (1994a) famously quotes the Greek poet Archilochus who said that the fox knows many things while the hedgehog knows one big thing. This reference regularly appears as part of evaluations of Berlin's own contribution to social and political philosophy; was Berlin himself hedgehog or fox? On one view Berlin is a hedgehog whose big idea is value pluralism; the view that human values are many and, contrary to Enlightenment thinking, these values, often incommensurable, cannot be combined into some utopian society that delivers all that human beings regard as good. Given the plurality and incommensurability of goods, individuals and societies must recognise that fulfilling certain values will inevitably mean that others must be sacrificed. This is the value pluralist version of Berlin associated most closely with Gray (1995, 2000).[3] Other commentators reject what Daniel Weinstock (1997) has called the 'Graying of Berlin' and prefer a version of Berlin as an eclectic fox who manages to combine the essentially liberal ideas and commitment to reason shared by Enlightenment thinkers with the psychological insights of their Counter-Enlightenment and Romantic critics (Lukes, 2001).

Whether the focus is on value pluralism or the many other strands in his thought there can be no doubt about the influence of Berlin on twentieth-century political and moral thought.[4] Stefan Collini (1999: 195, 198) refers to Berlin as the 'academic equivalent of a saint ... with more admirers than any figure in recent British academic life' while James Cracraft (2002) regards Berlin as the most eloquent advocate of liberalism and pluralism of his era. For others it is the originality of his understanding of the relationship between the liberal Enlightenment and its Romantic critics that sets Berlin apart from other historians of ideas (Honneth, 1999); an understanding which, according to Noel Annan (1997: xv), allows Berlin to provide 'the truest and most moving of all the interpretations of life that [his] generation has made'. In a set of reflections on what ought to be valued in higher education Robin Barrow (1999: 139) concurs with these views and he attributes Berlin's greatness as a thinker to the fact of his being steeped in a cultural tradition. These positive evaluations of Berlin's contribution to academic life were recognized through election to the British Academy, the award of the Order of Merit and a knighthood. Fellow academics have recognized Berlin's contribution in two *Festschriften* (Dworkin, Lilla and Silvers, 2001; Ulmann-Margalit and Margalit, 1991) and in the many tributes that have been published since Berlin's death in 1997.[5] The continuing significance of Berlin's contribution to anti-totalitarian scholarship has recently been noted by Cecile Hatier (2004) who sees in twenty-first century religious fundamentalism a form of monism that threatens individual freedoms no less than the political tyrannies of Berlin's century.

The focus of this book is the value of Berlin's work in understanding the tensions between the requirements of civic education in liberal democracies and the demands of cultural minorities for forms of education that support cultural identity. Two aspects of Berlin's writing make him particularly interesting from this perspective of cultural diversity and education. First, Berlin's own life story suggests the potential for creativity that sociologists in the early part of the twentieth century associated with individuals characterized as 'marginal' (Park, 1928) or as 'strangers' (Simmel, 1908). In his own 1952 essay on Jewish identity, *Jewish Slavery and Emancipation*,[6] Berlin comments on the ability of the outsider to perceive aspects of the native culture hidden from its own members. It has been said of Berlin that however successfully he appeared to be assimilated into English culture he could still be described as 'remaining an exile all his life' (Collini, 1999).[7] In his many essays on Russian thinkers Berlin again and again associates creativity with those who find themselves in some way detached from their society. It is this quality of detachment that Robert Park and Georg Simmel considered so important in allowing the stranger to see what remains hidden from the native. In what he had to say about education it was always this creativity, so often associated with culture contact situations, that Berlin took to offer such a rich model for education in culturally diverse societies.

Second, Berlin's own explorations of other cultures in his essays in the history of ideas provide a model for this kind of education. Berlin is often credited with a remarkable ability to get into the worlds of the thinkers whose ideas he chooses to explore. Steven Lukes (1994) likens this ability to what Giambattista Vico called the quality of *'fantasia'* which involves reconstructing the world of the thinker whose ideas are being examined; a quality that provides a psychological and historical context that contemporary political philosophy often lacks (Lilla, 2001). Patrick Gardiner puts this very clearly in introducing the collection *The Sense of Reality* (Berlin, 1996) when he emphasizes how:

> [Berlin] sought to understand from within the problems that obsessed those who had propounded them; the ideas of the past (he felt) could only be brought to life by 'entering into' the minds and viewpoints of the persons who held them and the social or cultural contexts to which they belonged.
>
> (Gardiner, 1996: xiv)

The three faces of liberalism

Enlightenment liberalism

In an interview with Rahan Jahanbegloo (2000: 70) Berlin sums up his view of the Enlightenment with these words: 'The values of the Enlightenment, what people like Voltaire, Helvetius, Holbach, Condorcet preached, are deeply sympathetic to me ... They liberated people from horrors, obscurantism, fanaticism, monstrous views'. This is why Roger Hausheer (2003: 48), despite acknowledging Berlin's critique of the Enlightenment, still regards Berlin as a 'patron saint of the Enlightenment' and so, while there are some aspects of Enlightenment thinking that Berlin clearly resists, I begin my account of Berlin's distinctive liberalism with a focus on those Enlightenment ideas to which Berlin always remained committed. These are an emphasis on freedom from external constraint, what Berlin came to call 'negative freedom'; the rejection of determinism and a view of individual choice-making as being definitive of human life; the recognition of certain universal values that underpin decent societies; and finally the valuing of reason. Whatever the conditions made and qualifications entered Berlin declares: 'Fundamentally I am a liberal rationalist' (Jahanbegloo, 2000: 70–71).

Negative and positive liberty

Berlin's famous account of negative and positive liberty is undoubtedly the best known and most hotly debated element in his work. It has been variously evaluated as 'the standard point of departure for analyses of political freedom in contemporary political theory' (Crowder, 2004: 64) and as 'inflated, obscure, irrelevant, confused' (Cohen, 1960: 216–218).[8] It was in his lectures given to undergraduates at Bryn Mawr College, Pennsylvania, in February and March of 1952 that Berlin first set out the distinction between what at this time he referred to as the 'liberal' and 'romantic' versions of liberty. Liberal freedom is about the absence of constraints so that individuals are able to formulate and pursue their own projects. The Romantics added to this version of liberty the idea that individuals might be unaware of their own true natures and would therefore benefit from the guidance of those better equipped to know this true nature. Only on reaching their true, hitherto hidden, nature can individuals really become free. It is this idea that others might know better a person's 'true' nature that disturbed Berlin so much. In this he saw the excuse given by so many totalitarian leaders and social engineers for constraining or 'educating' individuals so that they might be 'free'. This is what George Crowder (2004: 57) refers to as Berlin's 'inversion thesis' whereby the Romantic version of liberty becomes 'twisted into the very opposite of what freedom ordinarily means'. This inversion of liberty Berlin largely attributed to Rousseau's view of real liberty as conformity with the 'General Will'.

   In October 1958 the distinction between what he had called liberal and Romantic notions of liberty was re-stated in Berlin's lecture *Two Concepts of Liberty*.[9] The same distinction was now referred to as that between negative and positive liberty. Negative liberty is properly liberal in seeking to free individuals to follow their own direction subject only to not harming others; this can be stated in the form: liberty as 'freedom from'. As Berlin (2002a: 169) puts it, 'I am normally said to be free to the degree which no man or body of men interferes with my activity'. Positive liberty is the version favoured by those who want to provide the means by which individuals can be free; that is liberty expressed in the form of 'freedom to'. Herein, says Berlin, lies a great danger. This is the Romantic desire to free those who fail to see what is in their own good; those unable to control their weaker selves so that a better self can emerge. It is in positive liberty and in the determination to achieve this at any cost that Berlin sees the seeds of despotism and tyranny.

For Graeme Garrard (1997) it is the 'Counter-Enlightenment' element in Berlin's liberalism that makes him so original and important. While he remained committed to what the Enlightenment delivered in terms of freedom from the constraints of custom and tradition, Berlin most significantly provided the corrective to those Enlightenment *philosophes* such as Rousseau who inverted freedom in such a way as to allow the social engineers to argue that the state can know the real selves of its individual members better than they themselves. According to Garrard the Enlightenment project was essentially about individual freedom and by drawing attention to the totalitarian implications of positive liberty Berlin re-aligns this project with its central liberal purpose. Far from administering its death blow as Gray argues, Berlin actually rescues the Enlightenment for its central liberal purpose.[10]

There have been criticisms from some commentators that Berlin neglects the shortcomings of negative liberty while failing to see any benefit in positive liberty.[11] Bhikuh Parekh (1982), for example, sees in negative liberty what for him is the typically a-social liberal view of humankind with its undeveloped view of the relationship between the individual and her community. In the same communitarian vein Parekh notes how certain forms of liberty, for example the spiritual kind, require an authoritarian context. For Parekh it is inappropriate to express regret, in the way that he claims Berlin does, for losses of liberty that are quite proper. In fact Berlin is always clear that liberty is one human value among many and that there will be occasions when, in the interests of another value, it is quite proper to limit liberty. The fact that parents might quite properly have their freedom to choose private education constrained in the interests of social equality is one such example. All that Berlin would add is the need to record that in such cases there has been loss of liberty. By the same token Berlin does register concern that negative liberty, taken to extremes, can result in the kind of laissez-faire politics and economics of which he disapproved.

Liberty and the rejection of determinism

Throughout his writing Berlin insists that it is choice-making that is definitive of being human; this is consistent with the rejection of determinism in all its forms. For Berlin the simple fact that we speak so often of human behaviour in terms of praise and blame suggests the fundamental nature of our belief in the free actions of individuals. If it were the case that we are constrained by some aspect of our identity or history to act in a particular way then it would make no sense to speak of these actions as either praiseworthy or blameworthy. In using this vocabulary we accept responsibility for our behaviour. Berlin would share with Seyla Benhabib (2002) the rejection of cultural determinist defences in courts of law when minority culture individuals claim a 'cultural defence' for behaviour that falls outside the legal norms sanctioned by the majority society. Although the rejection of determinism underpins much of Berlin's writing I will focus here on the essays *Political Ideas in the Twentieth Century* and *Historical Inevitability* which appear in the original *Four Essays on Liberty* (Berlin, 1969)[12] and a further two publications that appear in *Liberty* (Berlin, 2002a); the first is the essay *From Hope and Fear Set Free*,[13] and the second *A Letter to George Kennan*.

At the root of twentieth-century totalitarian doctrines Berlin identifies the idea that the inner conflicts that free individuals experience ought to be removed, not only for the benefit of society, but in the interests of these troubled individuals themselves. In *Political Ideas in the Twentieth Century* Berlin states his preference for individual variation to the most delicately fashioned, but imposed, pattern. It is a reification of the worst kind to attribute active properties to such entities as races or cultures because the idea that individuals act only on the basis of a group identity robs individuals of freedom of choice and eliminates the idea of individual responsibility. In *Historical Inevitability* Berlin (2002a: 158 n. 1) criticizes sociologists of knowledge for reifying culture in this way.[14] In *From Hope and Fear Set Free* Berlin speaks of freedom as the possibility of choosing between options so that 'the measure of the liberty of a man or a group is, to a large degree, determined by the range of choosable possibilities' (Berlin, 2002a: 272). Berlin goes on to identify freedom with the range of avenues open to an individual, the broadness of those avenues and the further avenues to which they lead. The idea that freedom is increased by removing desires that cannot be fulfilled is explicitly rejected; ignorance as an obstacle to choice may lead to serenity but this is not freedom.[15]

In his *Letter to George Kennan* Berlin re-states most clearly his rejection of determinism by insisting that however constrained an individual may be it is the possibility of choosing that makes that individual human. Our entire system of categories for assessing human actions requires an acceptance that human activity is the outcome of choice. In Berlin's own words:

> [A]ll these notions in terms of which we think of others and ourselves, in terms of which conduct is assessed, purposes adopted – all this becomes meaningless unless we think of human beings as capable of pursuing ends for their own sakes by deliberate acts of choice – which alone makes nobility noble and sacrifices sacrifices.
>
> (Berlin, 2002a: 337)

The ultimate crime of the Nazi and Soviet era was to deny individuals the knowledge of their own situation thus denying them the opportunity to choose how to live – and die. The individual might be happier to be denied choice, and therefore responsibility, but only at the cost of the destruction of all self-respect. For Berlin choosing badly is better than not choosing at all because 'we believe that unless they choose they cannot be either happy or unhappy in any sense in which these conditions are worth having' (*ibid:* 342). It is because he believes that a liberal society affords individuals the greatest range of options from which to choose that Berlin is a liberal. In a letter written in 1952 Berlin described liberal society as one where:

> The largest number of persons are allowed to pursue the largest number of ends as freely as possible [and] in which these ends are themselves criticised as little as possible and the fervour with which such ends are held is not required to be bolstered up by some bogus rational or supernatural argument to prove the universal validity of the end.
>
> (cited in Hughes, 2005: 204)

Two recent publications point to Berlin's anti-determinism as a key source for arguing against the use of the methodologies of the natural sciences in disciplines concerned to understand human beings. In political science Ryan Hanley (2004) regards Berlin as crucial to highlighting the dangers of applying the methods of natural science to understanding political behaviour and in avoiding the positivism that denies individual agency and responsibility. Hanley (*ibid:* 329) sees 'Berlin's defense of free choice via negative liberty [as] itself an element of [a] larger project to re-establish an appreciation of the moral responsibility and agency of individual political actors'. In education Gary Thomas and Georgina Glenny (2002: 348)) draw on Berlin to argue against applying scientific methods outside the field of natural science. Education, they say, is concerned with the kind of human affairs identified by Berlin as not given to explanations through scientific method.

Human universals and decent societies

It has been regularly suggested that Berlin's thesis that human values are many, often incommensurable, and beyond ranking must open him to the charge of relativism (for example Kateb, 1999). This will be discussed at greater length in subsequent chapters; here I restrict myself to introducing Berlin's frequent assertion of human universals without which, in his view, no decent society can survive. In his interview with Rahan Jahanbegloo Berlin puts the matter thus:

> The idea of human rights rests on the true belief that there are certain goods – freedom, justice, pursuit of happiness, honesty, love – that are in the interest of all human beings, as such, not as members of this or that nationality, religion, profession, character, and that it is right to meet these claims and to protect people against those who ignore or deny them. There are certain things which human beings require as such, not because they are Frenchmen, Germans or medieval scholars or grocers but because they lead human lives as men and women.
>
> (Jahanbegloo, 2000: 39)[16]

For Berlin (1991a: 11) these common values serve as a bridge between cultures, the means by which we can understand other ways of life. This expression of support for the idea of human universals leads Richard Wollheim (1991: 77) to conclude that Berlin's concerns with national identity and other cultural expressions of community belonging are no more than 'a set of nuances that colour the surface of life ... in no way incompatible with the idea of a common human nature'. Berlin's pluralism is constrained by his observation that although human ends are various there is a limit to this diversity and that limit is determined by a 'common moral horizon' based on the protection of individual interests. It is this insistence on a 'common moral horizon' that allows Berlin to set limits to the 'goods' that human beings can meaningfully value and therefore the kinds of cultures that liberals can legitimately support (see Kenny, 2000; Riley, 2000, 2001, 2002; Weinstock, 1997; Zakaras, 2003). Values may be plural but not in such a way that barbaric and irrational cultures must be tolerated let alone protected.[17]

Reason

With Jonathan Riley (2001, 2002) and against the views of George Kateb and John Gray previously cited I will argue in what follows that, despite his fears that too much faith in reason leads to utopian beliefs about the perfect society and thus starts us on the road to totalitarianism, Berlin remains a rationalist first and foremost. Reason may not always provide the basis for making choices between values that clash but reason does prescribe limits to the kinds of choices that members of decent human societies can make. These limits are determined by a set of minimal human rights which no liberal can choose to ignore. According to Riley's interpretation Berlin's constrained pluralism provides legitimacy for a range of liberal cultures choosing different values that fall within a common moral horizon; excluded is any illiberal culture where the minimal core of universal values is compromised. No liberal society, for example, can allow slavery or the killing of the innocent; the right to life supports political systems that seek a redistribution of wealth that provides sustenance for all; and the right to freedom from attack must always have priority over an illiberal right to racial purity.

The Counter-Enlightenment and modern communitarianism

> My claim is that there is a distinctive form of liberalism that has its genesis in the reaction *against* the Enlightenment, and that Berlin is the most prominent and important representative of this form of liberalism.
>
> (Garrard, 1997: 282 original emphasis)

John Gray, Avishai Margalit and Yael Tamir all present Berlin as a kind of proto-communitarian thinker. This interpretation is based on Berlin's writing about the importance of community identity and belonging which he derives both from the engagement with Counter-Enlightenment thinkers that has characterized much of his writing in the history of ideas and from his own experience of being a member of a minority cultural group in England.[18]

Berlin's experience of his own identity sensitized him to what the Counter-Enlightenment had to say and this served, says Hausheer (2003: 34), to give Berlin 'an early existential jolt out of any comfortable rut'. Tamir suggests that it is Berlin's experience in England of membership of a marginal group that sensitizes him to belongingness as a human need when she recalls Berlin responding to a comment she made to him about his apparent easy adaptation and acceptance into English life. Berlin replied:

> I know that I am still a Russian Jew from Riga, and all my years in England cannot change this. I love England, it has become my home, I have been well treated here and I cherish many features of English life, but I am a Russian Jew; that is how I was born and that is who I will be to the end of my life.
>
> (Tamir, 1991: 186)

Cracraft (2002) concurs with this view of Berlin as remaining to some extent an outsider despite his success and status within English academic and public life and asserts that Berlin is always attentive to Jewish identity when he is writing about his own life or about others. For Tamir (1998) this is what makes Berlin such an important writer for those who champion the interests of the marginalized and disenfranchised.

There is some support for this view in what Berlin himself has to say about identity and belonging. In his essay *Rabindranath Tagore and the Consciousness of Nationality* Berlin (1996) applauds the Bengali writer's acknowledgement of the human need for belonging; this is a need, says Berlin, as significant as that for food and shelter. What individuals gain from their membership of a group is not only the affection of their fellow members but also a sense of loyalty and common purpose shared with others. There is a sense of solidarity or fraternity that only membership of such a group can provide and there is bound to be considerable discontent should this close-knit group be threatened. And so when Berlin (1998: 258) reflects on the strands within his own identity and the influences on his writing he says: 'I have never been tempted, despite my long devotion to individual liberty, to march with those who, in its name, reject adherence to a particular nation, community, culture tradition, language – the myriad unanalysable strands that bind men into groups'. In this address to an Israeli audience Berlin attributed his own version of liberalism, one that sought to correct the Enlightenment neglect of the human value of belonging, to his Jewish identity.[19]

Margalit (2001) recalls how for Berlin belongingness was about feeling at home, feeling able to act spontaneously without fear of how others might react. It is about being understood by one's fellow members – effortlessly. One does not need to explain everything in the way that this is necessary when talking to strangers. Most importantly membership cannot be refused by the group because one is a member by birth not as a result of any achievement. Elsewhere Margalit (1999) says that although Berlin is best remembered for his commitment to the values of liberty and equality, in fact it was fraternity that Berlin valued above these others; for Margalit this concern for solidarity came from Berlin's own solidarity with Jews everywhere.

Without doubt Berlin's liberalism is characterized by a feeling for group membership that is unusual among liberals. There is therefore some basis for the way that Tamir, Margalit and others choose to present a communitarian Berlin, a liberal who avoids the communitarian criticism that liberalism fails to do justice to the social nature of human living. That said, in what follows I will conclude like Garrard (1997) that Berlin's communitarianism retains a strong liberal dimension with its outer limits defined by the freedom of the individual. While Margalit is right to note that membership of the group cannot be denied to a member who chooses membership, it is also the case that Berlin was very clear that there was no obligation on members to choose in this way.[20] Berlin serves as a challenge to those liberals who deny the communal dimension to individual well-being and as a corrective to those communitarians who fail to recognize the complex and plural nature of individual identity.

Value pluralism

It is to his reading of Giambattista Vico and Johann Gottfried Herder that Berlin (2000a: 13) attributes his own pluralism. Against monism which is the utopian idea that all good things are compatible thus making the perfect society possible, Berlin argues for pluralism which says that, far from being compatible in the way that monists require, the many and diverse goods that humans value do often come into conflict.[21] When conflict between values occurs choices have to be made, choices that are often tragic insofar as the achievement of one human good can require the sacrifice of another; for example, more equality, less liberty (Berlin, 2002a: 212–217). Berlin's version of pluralism is regularly taken to mean cultural pluralism, which is the often made observation that values differ between cultures, an observation that is sometimes extended to cultural relativism, which is the idea that each human culture has its own set of values and is to be judged only in its own terms. It should be clear from what has already been said about Berlin's commitment to universal human values that set limits to what decent societies can value that Berlin is no relativist. In fact the pluralism that Berlin asserts goes beyond the conflict of values between cultures to acknowledge that conflict also occurs between individual members of cultural groups and even within individuals themselves.

In his essay *The Originality of Machiavelli* Berlin (2000b)[22] attributes to Machiavelli the initial blow that begins to take apart the monism that dominated Western rationalist thought. Machiavelli challenged the idea that there could be one version of the perfect society because he identified two sets of virtues that are incompatible, Christian humility and pagan ambition. Thus Machiavelli discovered the 'uncomfortable truth ... that not all ultimate values are necessarily compatible with one another – that there might be a conceptual ... and not merely material obstacle to the notion of the single ultimate solution which, if only it were realised, would establish the perfect society' (*ibid*: 316). Berlin (1991a) returns to Machiavelli in *The Pursuit of the Ideal*[23] before going on to relate how his further studies of the works of Vico and Herder support this value pluralist outlook by identifying how moral systems vary between historical periods and between geographical areas.

The central significance of value pluralism to Berlin's thought is made evident by his own attempts to correct any misinterpretation of his commitment to negative liberty. In a footnote to his 'Introduction' to *Four Essays on Liberty* Berlin (2002a: 50 n. 1) says that interpretations of his essays on liberty that suggest support for negative freedom to the exclusion of other human values fail to recognize how fundamental value pluralism is to his thought. To privilege negative freedom above all other values would be a form of monism that he is concerned to challenge. It is the combination of pluralism and negative liberty that Berlin regards as the proper basis for a humane liberalism.

An important consequence of value pluralism is the recognition that where values are incommensurable and, because it is desirable to avoid destructive conflict, compromises have to be achieved: 'Some among the Great Goods cannot live together. This is a conceptual truth' (Berlin, 1991a: 13). This suggests the need for a minimum degree of toleration so that trade-offs can be achieved. Although collisions of goods cannot be completely avoided, they can be softened by examining a particular situation and arriving at a trade-off that achieves a balance of goods. In coming to this conclusion towards the end of *The Pursuit of the Ideal* Berlin notes that although this answer is unlikely to inspire idealists it does have a tragic quality that rings true with the kinds of gains and losses that choices between courses of action involve. It is in this context that Perry Anderson (1992: 243) identifies Berlin's (1998: 24–33) discussion of, and approval for, President Roosevelt's New Deal as an example of how Berlin used the minimization of suffering as the means for adjudicating the necessary trade-offs between the competing goods of individual liberty and social justice.

Belonging, nationalism and multiculturalism: the search for status

According to Engin Isin and Patricia Wood (1999) Berlin provides the essential starting point for an account of group rights in what they refer to as Berlin's 'third concept of liberty': the recognition of cultural groups. For Isin and Wood, Berlin's recognition of group rights would extend to non-liberal groups and they recommend Berlin as a corrective to liberal defenders of group rights (for example, Kymlicka, 1996a) who stop short of supporting rights for non-liberal groups. The attribution of group rights theory to Berlin is often based on his account of what he referred to as the search for status by oppressed groups. In 1959 Berlin gave a radio talk on this search for status.[24] This was based on a passage in *Two Concepts of Liberty* where Berlin (2002a: 200–208) seeks to explain the psychology involved when individuals show a willingness to give up some of their negative liberty in exchange for government by members of their own group. He begins with an account of two kinds of 'unfreedom'. To experience a lack of recognition as a self-governing individual is one kind of loss of freedom; to be aware that one's group is neither recognized nor respected is another. The response to the latter is often to wish for the freedom of the group: 'Although I may not get "negative liberty" at the hands of members of my own society, yet they are members of my own group; they understand me, as I understand them; and this understanding creates within me the sense of being somebody in the world' (Berlin, 2002a: 203). This is a search for status rather than liberty.[25] In another essay Berlin expresses the same thought when he says that individuals prefer to be ordered about by members of their own group than be ruled, however well, by foreigners (Berlin, 1991a: 251). It was a trip to Palestine in 1934 that led Berlin to the conclusion that the Arabs preferred to be ruled by their own people (even if badly) rather than be well governed by Jews (Ignatieff, 1998a: 81; Berlin, 2004a: 120).

Much of what Berlin has to say about this search for status and the human need for belonging appears in his writing about nationalism. It was the thinkers of the Counter-Enlightenment and their Romantic followers who struck Berlin as recognizing the human psychological need to belong; one of Berlin's close associates notes how he often remarked how the philosophers of the Enlightenment under-estimated the power of national attachment (Hampshire, 1991). In *My Intellectual Path*[26] Berlin (2000a: 13) himself has this to say:

> The sense of belonging to a nation seems to me quite natural and not in itself to be condemned, or even criticised ... But in its inflamed condition ... it is totally incompatible with the kind of pluralism I have tried to describe.

While Berlin recognizes the way that national identity might provide the sense of belonging that humans require, he is equally aware of the dangers such identification can bring. It is because Tagore's nationalism looks both inwards towards Bengali cultural identity and language but also outwards on the wider world that Berlin finds this version so satisfying. Without this balance nationalism is capable of giving rise to the most appalling consequences. Berlin's nationalism is liberal because, although he wants people to be able to sustain strong relationships with their co-nationals, he also wants members of other nations to retain the same right. And so for Michael Walzer (2001) Berlin's nationalism allows, for example, Iraqi nationalism as long as Iraqis respect the national ambitions of the Kurds. When Ignatieff follows Berlin in putting 'belonging' at the centre of his own version of liberal nationalism he draws a line when the sense of belonging becomes so strong as to produce violence: 'My journeys have made me re-think the nature of belonging ... I have been to places where belonging is so strong, so intense that I now recoil from it in fear' (Ignatieff, 1994a: 188).

Commentators are divided about the extent to which Berlin's writing is supportive of what has come to be known generally as multiculturalism. I have already identified Tamir as one source for the view that Berlin's sensitivity towards cultural identity makes him an important ally of minority groups claiming recognition from the liberal mainstream in democratic societies. This view is shared by O'Sullivan who argues that the contemporary relevance of Berlin is highlighted by the centrality that identity politics has taken up within political theory. According to O'Sullivan (2003: 85) it is Berlin's studies of Herder in particular that have led liberals to abandon their previous assumption of cultural uniformity and which now provide 'the foundation for a revised version of pluralism capable of accommodating a multicultural society'. Other commentators appear less confident about the implications of Berlin on nationalism for multicultural society. Pierre Birnbaum (1996) argues that that Berlin neglects the internal diversity within national cultures. Whereas Stuart Hampshire (1991) relates how Berlin remained persuaded by John Stuart Mill's argument for tolerance of diversity as a basis for supporting important experiments in living, Lukes (1998) reports that when pressed in interview Berlin expressed little optimism about diversity in the twentieth century, citing Ireland, India, Belgium and Spain as societies torn apart by cultural division.

One of Berlin's letters to his parents from his war-time period working in New York provides an interesting insight into Berlin's thoughts about multiculturalism (Berlin, 2004a: 394–395). He reports how he used to pass some of his time in New York visiting Jewish religious courts hearing cases brought by individuals who he describes as appearing to be straight out of 1880s Russia. In one case a Jewish beggar protests that his surgeon failed to bury his amputated leg in consecrated ground thus condemning this man to walk on one leg throughout eternity in the next life. In another a woman protested her brother-in-law's refusal to release her from her marriage vows thus condemning her husband's soul to lie face down for eternity. Berlin reflects with some amusement on such cases being treated with such gravity in 1942 New York and expresses the view that he is unimpressed by attempts to get English Jews to remain true to their faith in much the same way.[27] This confirms the impression given to Lukes that despite his concern for cultural identity Berlin is no straightforward supporter of the kind of multiculturalism that was to develop from the 1970s on both sides of the Atlantic.

A fuller treatment of this question about how far Berlin's pluralism is of a multiculturalism-supporting kind must be left to later chapters but enough has been said already to afford some support for the idea of Berlin as a liberal who recognizes the value that individuals gain from their collective attachments; in doing so he can be regarded as a liberal communitarian. This dimension to Berlin's thought derives much from his reading of Counter-Enlightenment thinkers who he clearly regards as having a better sense of human psychology than the philosophers of the Enlightenment, at least insofar as the need to belong is concerned. In what follows I will argue, however, that Berlin is always clear that his concern is to separate out what is useful in Counter-Enlightenment writing from that which is very dangerous (see especially Berlin, 2002b) and he never lets his reader forget that many of the writers who fascinated him so much were the enemies of freedom and there was much in what they said that displeased him (see Lilla 2001: 37).

Liberalism as a response to cruelty and fear

According to Shklar (1998: 5)[28] cruelty is the worst of human vices and its restraint must always be the first priority of liberalism because 'liberalism's deepest grounding is in place from the first, in the conviction of the earliest defenders of toleration, born in horror, that cruelty is an absolute evil, an offense against God or humanity'. For Shklar freedom, in the Berlinian negative sense, is impossible in the presence of fear because freedom requires the willingness of citizens to hold their officials to account and fear restrains this important democratic activity leaving tyrants free to do their worst. Shklar's liberalism is protective of individual freedoms and sensitive to the vulnerability of individuals within strong communities when community 'prophets' claim group rights over individual freedoms. In her critique of Walzer's communitarian group-orientation Shklar expresses a strong preference for Berlin's version of liberalism, one that, in her view, better represents what freedom and genuine pluralism entail. Group freedom is not individual freedom and for liberals it is the latter that must prevail.

Levy (2000) begins his account of multicultural policies in democratic societies by citing Shklar's account of liberalism based on the need to avoid cruelty, the worst of human vices and the cause of fear. Levy challenges Gray's interpretation of Berlin as favouring diversity above all else. For Levy diversity has many outcomes, some of which are to be avoided. Strong communities can be cruel to some of their own members as well as to members of other communities. There are dangers as well as opportunities arising from diversity and so diversity is not to be valued in itself. While attacks on cultural minorities are to be avoided, so are attacks by minorities on each other and by minorities on their own members. Levy therefore defends multicultural policies that are designed neither to defend nor transcend ethnic boundaries but aim rather to mitigate the dangers that they present. According to Levy, Gray's privileging of a form of toleration that extends to illiberal groups is too inclusive and in citing Berlin as source Gray fails to acknowledge those aspects of Berlin's account of liberalism that derive from a concern to avoid cruelty and fear.

Crowder (2004) also challenges Gray's interpretation of Berlin's pluralism as being inclusive of a very wide range of cultural, including non-liberal, groups. For Crowder, Berlin is the kind of 'pessimistic liberal' who sees liberalism as a 'holding action against undesirable forms of human life' (*ibid*: 172–173) and maintaining the line between 'civilization and barbarism' (*ibid*: 175). In similar vein Stephen Holmes (1994) counters communitarian criticisms that liberals neglect the importance of group loyalty. Liberals, says Holmes, are only too aware of the importance that individuals place on their group loyalties; but they are also aware that the outcomes of these loyalties are not exclusively good; sometimes group loyalty can have very destructive consequences for individuals, both members and non-members.

How far are Shklar and Levy justified in grounding their versions of the liberalism of fear and the multiculturalism of fear, respectively, in the liberal pluralism of Isaiah Berlin?[29] In discussing Berlin's concern with cruelty and violence both Michael Ignatieff as biographer and Henry Hardy as editor attach considerable significance to an early experience in Berlin's life which, not surprisingly, appears to have had considerable impact. Introducing *The First and Last* (Berlin, 1999) Hardy (1999) places Berlin's lifelong concern with cruelty and violence in the context of an incident that took place in 1917 in Petrograd during the February Revolution. The seven-year-old Isaiah witnessed one of the Tsar's policemen being dragged away by a mob to be lynched. Hardy remarks on the tremendous impact on Berlin of this early experience (see Ignatieff, 1998a: 24 for an account of this incident). This experience is reflected five years later when the then 12-year-old Berlin wrote a story for a children's magazine competition that told of a Russian nobleman killing a Soviet Commissar in revenge for the murder of the nobleman's father on the orders of the commissar. Berlin chose as his title for this story *The Purpose Justifies the Ways* – the motto attributed to the commissar – and for Hardy this represents Berlin's first expression of opposition to the idea that present cruelty can never be justified by the promise of a better future.[30] The experience of seeing suffering was one that remained with Berlin throughout his life. In an interview[31] given towards the end of his life Berlin reflects on the times he has seen: 'At 82, I've lived through virtually the whole century, the worst century Europe has ever had. In my life, more dreadful things occurred than at any other time in history'.

Berlin's attitude towards cruelty and suffering is also evident in an anecdote that is remembered by several of his friends. It is often reported how Berlin liked to challenge colleagues with a thought experiment that went thus: if there was a magic lamp that when rubbed could re-invent the Jews as Scandanavians with no experience of suffering, should the lamp be rubbed? Margalit in a *Tribute*[32] to Berlin remembers one such occasion when on being asked this question by Berlin he answered quickly and negatively. Berlin, Margalit (1999: 112) recalls, was unhappy with this response: 'He did not like the speed with which I replied. He took this as an unbearable lightness toward Jewish suffering'. On another occasion Margalit[33] offered the view that, although he didn't think Berlin would rub the lamp either, he was not sure. Wollheim (2001: 166) is sure and disagrees with Margalit on this point when he recalls, '[Berlin's] often repeated sentiment that if there were a pill that Jews could take that would turn them overnight into Danes, he would favour their taking it'.[34]

For Berlin suffering is never a blessing, it is always a curse, and 'the first public obligation is to avoid extremes of human suffering' (Berlin, 1991a: 17). To fail to do so is inhumane and indecent. In his essay on Jewish emancipation, and consistent with Wollheim's memory of the thought experiment, Berlin (1952) concludes that for Jews not committed to the faith it is not obvious that suffering is justified by cultural preservation. When Lukes (1998) pressed Berlin for an example of what would mark the boundary of intelligible behaviour he answered that any human being expressing a desire to inflict pain on another being without good reason is beyond understanding.[35] Consistent with his view that present suffering never justifies future goods Berlin always condemned Jewish terrorism and for this reason famously refused to shake the hand of Prime Minister Begin.[36] It was because he wished to see an end to cruelty that Berlin, in his last words, expressed a desire to see a just and peaceful settlement in Israel with the Palestinians.[37]

This book will argue that Berlin is a pluralist who recognizes that among political systems liberalism offers the best chance of protection from cruelty and the fear of cruelty. He is an opponent of monism first and foremost because of his recognition that the certainty that goes with final solutions usually calls for huge sacrifice and comes with great violence and terror. But the preference for pluralism over monism remains liberal in Berlin's case (though not Gray's) because Berlin's is a limited pluralism that refuses approval to societies and communities that fall short of human decency by failing either to protect their own members from cruelty and fear or by preventing the threat of cruelty to others (Gutmann, 1999). What Berlin teaches, says Amy Gutmann, is that it is the pursuit of the ideal that produces inquisitions and holocausts; we should settle, she says, for non-ideal solutions that beat other 'less decent' solutions.

It is his overwhelming desire to avoid cruelty and human suffering together with his belief in universal human rights that must underpin decent societies that allows Berlin to combine liberalism and pluralism in such a way that neither excludes the other. It is this combination of concerns that likens Berlin's liberalism to Shklar's liberalism of fear; both recognizse that liberal democracy is an imperfect system but one that has proved superior to any alternative when it comes to providing a civil society capable of keeping at bay the fears and insecurities of its citizens.

Conclusion: unresolved tensions – weakness or strength?

It has been suggested that Berlin's work is permeated by conflict, by what might be called unresolved tensions between the human goods that he values. Jonny Steinberg (1996) questions how Berlin can retain a view of modernity as progress in the way that he does while continuing to give an account of the incommensurability of values. For Axel Honneth (1999) it is the conflict between a liberalism with negative liberty as its core value and a commitment to communal identity that suggests unresolved tension. After all, communities can only survive and retain their identity by denying some negative liberty to their own members. This tension between individual liberty and community identity has resulted in some quite different interpretations of Berlin's attitude towards non-liberal groups. One view is that Berlin's universalism and liberalism must require of him an opposition to non-liberal groups that deny individual rights to their own members (Kenny, 2000; Riley, 2000, 2001, 2002). Alan Ryan on the other hand sees Berlin's liberalism as sufficiently wide in scope to accommodate non-liberal groups: 'Berlin would rather see vivid, non-liberal ways of life flourish than see them suppressed for the sake of the spread of liberal principles' (Ryan, 1998: 534).

For Ira Katznelson (1999) Berlin presents the conundrum of a pluralist committed to some universal values. This, he says, follows from Berlin's prioritization of the need to avoid cruelty and fear. Pluralism is preferred to monism because of the great cruelty that has been the outcome of monist insistence on a single truth. Millions have been slaughtered in the pursuit of supposed single truths. Equally universal values are required because of the cruelties that follow when standards for judging societies are relinquished.

Joan Cocks (2002) notes how liberal nationalists claim Berlin as a key source but for her there is a tension between liberalism and nationalism and it is one that runs through Berlin's writing on nationalism and collective rights. Like Honneth, Cocks identifies a conflict between Berlin's concern for collective identities and his regard for individual freedom. The same tension is evident in his advocacy of Jewish assimilation while recognizing that no Jews were better assimilated than those of Hitler's Germany. Berlin's case for a Jewish homeland is expressed, says Cocks, both in terms of Herderian cultural identity and a Millian freedom for individual Jews to decide whether to live in Israel or not. Given all of this, Cocks is less confident than Berlin about the benign nature of Herder's cultural nationalism because she sees culture as no less exclusive than blood and therefore concludes that the Jewish treatment of the Arabs is fundamental to Israeli nationalism and not the aberration that Berlin supposes.

Ignatieff is a liberal nationalist who shares with Berlin a concern for the sense of belonging for which human beings often crave. This is most clearly brought out in *The Needs of Strangers* but, like Berlin, Ignatieff (1994b) also fears the way that belonging as a nationalist value can become warped in such a way as to threaten individual freedoms. More recently in *The Warrior's Honor* Ignatieff (1998b: 38) describes how 'Serbness' as a form of aggressive nationalism became frightening and he agrees with Berlin that a liberal form of pluralism must be constrained by a continuing commitment to a universally shared human rights culture.[38]

What, then, should we make of these apparent conflicts? Are these tensions a sign of weakness in Berlin's work or do they speak to the most important challenge facing liberals concerned with freedom and justice in culturally diverse societies? Margalit (2001) observes that Berlin himself would not feel constrained to resolve the kind of tensions described by Berlin's critics and supporters alike. If Bernard Williams is right when he says that for Berlin value pluralism means that in order to respect truth we should not try to eliminate real conflicts in our value system but remain conscious of them then these tensions can be seen as a strength rather than weakness. As Williams (1978: xvii) says, 'To deny the conflicts, indeed to try to resolve them systematically and once for all, would be to offend against something absolutely true about values'. Berlin is unwilling to commit totally to either the Enlightenment or its Romantic critics preferring to promote what is of benefit in both perspectives. In his interview with Jahanbegloo Berlin declared a commitment to both liberalism and pluralism but claimed no logical connection between the two. Referring to the Enlightenment and Romanticism Weinstock (1997: 494) concludes that, '[Berlin] recognizes the ethical outlooks we inherit are inconsistent, but insists that both of the incompatible sets of values deserve our allegiance'. One set of values is not to be totally abandoned either for the sake of the other or for the sake of consistency.

2 Political philosophy, cultural diversity and education

An overview of the *Yoder* and *Mozert* cases

In the previous chapter I drew upon what have been called contrasting faces of liberalism, one with Enlightenment origins that concerns itself with individual autonomy and relies on difference-blind individual rights, and another that is more concerned with the differences between cultural groups and the kinds of accommodations necessary to allow group members to live according to their own, possibly non-liberal, beliefs. In this chapter I will consider both perspectives by examining how liberals of both traditions respond to the widely reported *Yoder* and *Mozert* cases in the United States.

Wisconsin *v.* Yoder

The case of *Wisconsin* v. *Yoder*[1] has been described as the 'high water mark of judicial accommodationism' for religious groups in the United States (Macedo, 2000: 153). The Amish of Wisconsin sought exemption from the last two years of compulsory education for their children. They felt that this period of schooling would expose their children to worldly influences and values that were inconsistent with their own teaching and that would interfere with the religious development of the children and therefore compromise the survival of the community. After initial refusal by the Wisconsin education authorities to accommodate the Amish in this way both the Wisconsin Supreme Court (1971) and the United States Supreme Court (1972) found in favour of the Amish and, as Stephen Macedo says, this remains the furthest that any American court has gone in accommodating a religious group seeking exemption from civic requirements perceived by the group as imposing a particular burden on them and their chosen way of life.

In *Yoder* the United States Supreme Court was persuaded that the Amish way of life provided children with a decent, satisfying and productive future. The Amish were seen as law-abiding, decent and self-sufficient citizens. The vocational training that Amish children got in the period between ages 14 and 16 was seen as healthy work and very different in kind from the kind of exploitative labour that public education up to the age of 16 was intended to exclude. The court was also persuaded by the sincerity of Amish religious beliefs and the close relationship between religion and the community's way of life. Referring back to the judgement in the much earlier *Pierce* case,[2] the *Yoder* Court recognized that civic interests in education fell short of requiring all children to experience the same public education. The Amish were not regarded as presenting any kind of threat to American society; indeed their way of life, agrarian and traditional, appeared to represent what many regarded as central American values of self-sufficiency and independence.

This tendency to justify Amish educational practice in terms of the partial nature of Amish citizenship (see Spinner, 1994; Spinner-Halev, 1999) has, however, limited the value of the case as precedent for other cultural and religious groups seeking similar exemptions. As can be seen from the *Mozert* case discussed below exemptions have been denied to religious groups that do not withdraw from mainstream society in the way that the Amish do.

Support for this judgement in favour of the Amish was not unanimous; Judge Douglas sounded a dissenting voice within the *Yoder* Court when he expressed concern that the court had failed to distinguish sufficiently the interests of parents and children. For Douglas there was insufficient attention to the voices of children, with only one child, Frieda Yoder, called to witness her support for her family's way of life. Douglas wondered about the implications of the court ruling for children who might have ambitions for a life that lay outside the parameters of traditional farming. This voice of dissent has been regularly cited by liberals concerned for the future autonomy of Amish children.

Mozert *v.* Hawkins County Board of Education

Like *Yoder*, the *Mozert* case[3] has been fundamental in shaping the debate about the education of cultural and religious communities:

> It is no exaggeration to state that for more than a decade *Mozert* v. *Hawkins County Board of Education* decided by the Sixth Circuit Court of Appeals ... has shaped the legal and political landscape of discussion and debate on religious accommodation in the public schools.
>
> (Salomone, 2000: 121)

What has been thought of as a defining moment in the 'culture war' between liberal intellectuals and communities of believers (Macedo, 1995a, 1995b) came about in 1983 when a group of Christian fundamentalists launched a complaint against the local school board of Hawkins County, Tennessee. This complaint centred on the use by Hawkins County schools of a series of reading books (the Holt Series) that included material considered inappropriate and offensive to their religious beliefs by members of the Christian fundamentalist community. Parents were worried about passages in the readers that, according to them, included the following: the idea that moral values are relative, examples of disrespect towards parents, evolutionary rather than creationist theory, the false notion that salvation was possible for anyone with a belief in a supernatural being, illustrations of idolatry in prayer, and instances of magic and witchcraft (Stolzenberg, 1993). Parents argued that the lack of balance and the secular bias in these texts resulted in the denigration of their own beliefs and that the material, if studied by their children, threatened the salvation of both those children and their parents. By treating all views as equally acceptable these materials challenged the parents' own belief that their own views represented the one and only truth. These parents, therefore, requested that their children be exempted from the use of these books and the exposure to a range of other cultures that they entailed. [4]

Initially some Hawkins County schools agreed to the request to use alternative texts but the Hawkins County School Board eventually made the Holt Series mandatory and suspended a number of students who refused to use them. In a recent summary of, and response to, the *Mozert* case Vojak (2003) links the series of books to the kind of citizenship aims to which the school authorities were committed. Resisting this attempt to influence the values of the children some families opted instead for religious schools, others chose home-schooling. The *Mozert* case families appealed to the federal court that their constitutional rights of free exercise of religion were being denied. After a series of court cases the federal appeals court, with Judge Lively writing for the court, found in favour of the school board on the grounds that 'mere' exposure to materials that conflicted with the religious beliefs of parents did not amount to indoctrination and the denial of free exercise of religion. Macedo (1995b) regards Judge Lively's ruling on the right of the schools to teach tolerance as recognition of the distinction between the public and private realms to be found in political liberalism which says that, while schools ought not to comment on the truthfulness of any particular religious belief, there is a duty on schools to teach a philosophy of 'live and let live'. Judge Kennedy, in her written opinion on the case, concurred that society had an interest in schools contributing to a degree of cultural conformity in support of citizenship values and so an education for democratic living does, on this view, demand that critical thinking skills be included in the curriculum. In a note of dissent Judge Boggs regretted the failure to find a hybrid educational programme that could have been more inclusive; while this judge concurred with the court finding he did go some considerable way in acknowledging the impact of civic demands on the families concerned. In the same way Nomi Stolzenberg (1993) draws attention to the gulf between the Mozerts' understanding of neutrality and that of Judge Lively's court. For religious fundamentalists neutrality itself is an affront because it treats their beliefs as just one set alongside many others rather than the one and only truth; absolute truth, their truth that is, becomes a matter of debate. The religious fundamentalists' belief in biblical inerrancy does, for them, give their own beliefs a status that they deny to any others: 'The doctrinal treatment of a plaintiff's beliefs as that individual's belief and nothing more denies them respect, serious consideration, on their terms' (*ibid*: 630). The exposure that the Holt Series brings about would, on this view, remain damaging even where children reject all opposing views and retain the way of life of their parents; this is because of the loss of innocence entailed when children come to see that their own beliefs are contested elsewhere. Again it is Stolzenberg who grasps this when she says: 'It is one thing for beliefs to be transmitted from one generation to another. It is another to hold beliefs, knowing that those beliefs are transmitted, that they vary, and that their truth is contested' (*ibid*: 633).

Responding to *Yoder* and *Mozert*: Enlightenment liberalism and the limits to diversity

Enlightenment liberalism and the individual

'Men must think and know for themselves' said John Locke (1975 [1689]) in *An Essay on Human Understanding* (Book 1; Chapter IV, Section 23). This is a central tenet of the Enlightenment philosophy with which Isaiah Berlin identified when he said, 'I have never lost my admiration for and sense of solidarity with the Enlightenment' (Berlin, 2000a: 4). In this section of the chapter I examine arguments for civic education that cohere around Enlightenment ideas about individual autonomy and I will be particularly concerned with the implications of civic education for societies that include communities like the Amish and the fundamentalist Christians that feature in the *Yoder* and *Mozert* cases. In considering Enlightenment liberal reactions to *Yoder* and *Mozert* I aim to demonstrate the connections with those aspects of Berlin's moral and political philosophy that have their roots in his often expressed admiration for Enlightenment thinking.

According to Jeremy Waldron (1993: 43), '[t]he relationship between liberal thought and the legacy of the Enlightenment cannot be stressed too strongly'. I begin with a brief sketch of what liberal educators have taken to be the defining ideas of the Enlightenment. Central to the Enlightenment legacy is a concern for individual freedom from external constraint, what Berlin referred to as 'negative liberty'. Waldron, like Berlin, acknowledges the danger inherent in the idea of 'positive liberty' that the individual becomes her real self by identifying herself completely with her social class, cultural community, ethnic group or religious faith. While not unaware of the enjoyment and benefit that humans get from the goods of fraternity and community, Waldron insists that these goods are enjoyed by individuals as individuals. While groups are clearly necessary for the enjoyment of these goods, it is also the case that groups can operate to constrain individual choices and when this conflict occurs between the individual and his group it is individual rights that the Enlightenment liberal prioritizes. Waldron (1995, 1996) is more suspicious than Berlin of Herderian notions of culture and community, preferring a cosmopolitan outlook that relies on the individual having a range of cultures on which to build an identity rather than relying on one particular cultural identity. Although Berlin often rejected 'rootless cosmopolitanism' (for example, Berlin, 1998: 258), his account of his own intellectual development drawing on the separate strands of English empiricism,

Russian thinking and Jewish identity is not far from Waldron's own description of a cosmopolitan identity (see Waldron, 1995, 2003a: 47 n. 18).

For Macedo (2000: 275) this liberal concern with individual freedom means that liberals cannot be neutral about the characters and life plans of citizens. Those who wish to live free must acknowledge the same right in others and this demands an approach to shared living that privileges what political liberalism calls public reasonableness. Because members of some cultural groups will find it difficult to live alongside those with whom they disagree, there will be some limits to the diversity that a liberal society can tolerate.[5] Adopting what he calls 'tough-minded liberalism' Macedo (1995a) makes no apology for asserting the need for an education that focuses on the virtues that public reasonableness requires of citizens of societies that are liberal and culturally diverse. Brian Barry (2001) is also setting limits to the cultural diversity that liberal societies can tolerate when he claims the non-negotiability of the liberal commitment to individual freedom. This commitment to individual freedom is recognized by some liberals to require a fully comprehensive liberalism that refuses to sell individuals short; arguing from a feminist perspective Penny Enslin (2003), for example, is ready, like Macedo, to acknowledge the implication that cultural diversity will be subject to limits.

Following much the same theme Amy Gutmann (1989) argues that the American constitution was never intended to exempt religious groups from a civic commitment to obey just laws. Tolerance of cultural groups might buy peace between groups but buying that peace at the price of the rights of individual members of oppressive cultural groups can never be an acceptable outcome in a liberal society founded on individual rights.[6] While liberals committed to Enlightenment ideals of individual freedom do sometimes advocate the accommodation of illiberal groups this is usually a strategic rather than principled stance. Will Kymlicka's well-known version of multicultural citizenship, for example, includes accommodations designed to have a liberalizing effect on non-liberal groups; just as Catholics and Jews liberalized on being included in liberal society so will Muslims. Kymlicka (2003) calls this the 'liberal wager' and he worries that policies such as the French restrictions on the wearing of religious symbols in public schools will have exclusionary consequences rather than having the intended effect of social inclusion. In much the same way liberal commentators on the *Mozert* case have suggested that one unfortunate consequence of the court finding in favour of a liberal curriculum has been the withdrawal of religious conservatives and fundamentalists from public education and an increase in the number of children being home-schooled or sent to private religious schools.

In his book *Culture and Equality* Barry (2001: 6–7) bemoans the way that what he calls 'culturalist liberalism' has lost its moorings in the Enlightenment foundations of liberalism. For Barry the Enlightenment conception of citizenship with its commitment to the single status of each citizen sharing the same legal and political rights with none of these rights assigned on the basis of group membership, religious or otherwise, remains the best guarantee that individuals have of equal consideration. Barry regrets the 'flight from Enlightenment individualism and universalism' (*ibid*: 9) that multiculturalism represents; considerations of culture, he says, undermine considerations of equality. Berlin often used the examples of liberty and equality to demonstrate that certain goods inevitably come into conflict; achieving a degree of equality between members of society is a good, for example, that can be achieved only by accepting some limitations on liberty. In situations of value conflict we are forced to choose and any choice will involve some loss as well as gain but these situations are rarely of the 'all or nothing' kind and the best outcomes usually involve compromise – so much equality, so much liberty. Multiculturalists, says Barry, have ceded too much to cultural groups thereby undermining both equality and individual liberty. The kind of diversity that Barry favours is that between individuals rather than between groups because groups often rely upon coercion to achieve internal homogeneity and strong group identity. Groups can interfere with the individual freedoms of their own members and they often do. Where groups rely on coercion to do this, they will have to change. Barry recalls that liberalism never accepted a public–private distinction that leaves parents free to deal in whatever way they choose with their children. In fact it is liberalism that has consistently championed the right of vulnerable individuals especially women and children to be free of the authority of their groups when that authority is used against their interests.[7]

In a challenge to pluralism Barry argues that, 'because human beings are virtually identical as they come from the hand of nature ... there is nothing straightforwardly absurd about the idea that there is a single best way for human beings to live' (*ibid*: 262). This apparent monism is toned down when Barry goes on to acknowledge that there can be reasonable disagreement about the nature of what is a good life as long as basic human rights are accepted. This approximates to Berlin's limited pluralism which allows for a range, but not an unlimited range, of ways of life.

In eventually recognizing the value of a limited cultural diversity Barry stresses the importance of individual members of groups having the right and means of exit from their group. This has clear implications for education because 'children should be brought up in a way that will enable them to leave behind the groups into which they were born, if they so choose' (*ibid*: 149). In what follows I consider a number of liberal arguments for civic education. I will draw upon discussion of the *Yoder* and *Mozert* cases to assess the extent to which Enlightenment liberals are prepared to accommodate non-liberal groups and their requests for exemptions from civic education.

Brian Barry and education for life

Barry (2001) notes how most Amish claims for exemption from civil society on the basis of free exercise of religion have been rejected in the courts. The *Yoder* case is the exception and this is the reason it is often taken to represent the furthest the United States has gone in accommodating a cultural group. Barry accepts that voluntary associations must be able to retain authority over their own members; in order to continue its existence a voluntary association must even be allowed to expel apostates. For Barry the problem with the Amish is that they cannot be taken to constitute a voluntary association. Given that members are born Amish the voluntary nature of association must depend on the right of exit and given the Amish practices of the sharing of property and opting out of social security there is no clear route of exit for those who so choose. Even if these constraints were to be removed there remains an issue about the kind of education required if exit is to be a viable option. Barry starts from an Enlightenment liberal recognition of the importance of adults being able to make their own choices and draws from this the implication that education must include teaching that encourages and facilitates the capacity to make choices. Children's interests in education potentially conflict with those of parents and both sets of interests merit attention and consideration; additionally society has an interest in how children are educated. On the basis of these considerations Barry defends an education that prepares children for a future life in mainstream society. Having access to the best knowledge we have of the world is a benefit that Barry wants all children to enjoy and he opposes those who would limit access either by removing their children from school before the normal leaving age or by denying access to particular books. Because society has an interest in children learning about issues such as sexually transmitted diseases and teenage pregnancy, it follows that parents should not be able to deny their own children access to relevant education on these and similar matters.

Barry dismisses those arguments for the Amish exemption that cite the numbers of Amish individuals who do leave the community; it is voluntariness that matters, not numbers.[8] With Berlin, Barry does not believe that freedom is to be achieved by reducing desire: 'If you are locked in a room, you are not free to leave it; this is equally true whether you want to leave it or not' (*ibid*: 244).[9]

If democracy requires that children be educated to use critical reason then the attempts of the *Mozert* parents to prevent the exposure of their children to teaching about evolution becomes for Barry a matter of grave concern. Referring to what he calls the 'mind-numbing' and 'mind destroying' qualities of creationist texts, Barry describes creationism as too intellectually corrupting to be allowed in any school – public or religious: 'If there is any public stake in education, it must surely extend far enough to save children from this travesty' (*ibid*: 246, 249).

Education and autonomy

Barry notably does not seek to base his version of Enlightenment liberalism on individual autonomy although he is clearly sympathetic to education that facilitates autonomy and he does claim that autonomy facilitation (rather than autonomy promotion) represents one version of a liberal education. Autonomy considerations do feature prominently in several other widely-discussed liberal accounts of education. Berlin (2002a: 46) identified compulsory schooling as a constraint on children and therefore an infringement of liberty but he regarded this as a justifiable constraint because of the greater liberty that education eventually provides for the mature person. Given Berlin's often stated reluctance to accept restrictions in the present on the grounds of some future benefit this is a very significant argument and I will return to this when examining diversity liberal arguments for limiting civic education that claim Berlin as source.

Parents do not own their children and Enlightenment liberalism justifies parental authority not in terms of parental rights or desires but rather in terms of children's needs. In his book *Creating Citizens* Eamonn Callan (1997a) talks about the role of education in equipping children for the living of chosen lives. Such an 'education against servility' (Callan, 1997b: 221) enables children to engage with ethical beliefs at odds with those of the family home, not only as beliefs meaningful to others, but with the potential to contribute to the children's own developing conception of the good. Walter Feinberg (2003: 401) agrees when he says: 'Educating children in a way that intentionally maintains the initial dependency, and reproduces uncritically the parents' goals in the child, is a type of tyranny'. While this version of liberalism is prepared to warrant the right of parents to choose a religious education for their children (see Macedo, 2000 commenting on *Pierce* v. *Society of Sisters*, 1925) this is neither to deny the civic interest in how and what children are taught nor is it to see *Pierce* as a precedent to be taken into account in all similar cases. Parental rights are not to be allowed to trump all other legitimate interests in how children are educated. Enlightenment liberalism rejects the idea implicit in arguments for cultural preservation that children can ever become the means by which the end of community survival is achieved.[10]

Liberal responses to the *Yoder* decision often criticize the way that the truncated education experienced by Amish children impacts on the prospective autonomy of these children. Meira Levinson (1999) includes in her account of *The Demands of Liberal Education* teaching that prepares children so that when they become mature individuals they will be able to formulate and revise their own conception of a good life; on this view Amish education falls short of the demands of a liberal education. In like mind Gutmann (1980), specifically citing Berlin's 'negative liberty', argues that the *Yoder* decision in favour of the Amish undermines individual freedom by ceding authority to the community. More recently Gutmann (2000) supports the *Mozert* decision in favour of children's rights to an open future and calls for *Mozert* to be seen as the rule in this kind of dispute, with *Yoder* remaining the exception. These liberal defenders of education for autonomy are willing to extend their support for the teaching of critical thinking even when the outcome is likely to involve introducing a degree of tension into the home (Feinberg, 1995; 1998).

Rob Reich (2002: 99–112) is explicit in citing Berlin as a key source for his own account of what he calls 'minimalist autonomy'. This involves the recognition that we make choices from the basis of attachments that serve as our 'compass points' and yet also recognizes that Berlin was still able to say 'I wish to be an instrument of my own, not other men's acts of will. I wish to be a subject, not an object' (Reich, 2002: 100 citing Berlin, 2002a: 178).[11] It is the choosing that is important here, what kind of life is chosen is open; it might be one of agnosticism, one of cosmopolitan doubt, or one of faithful devotion. Like Berlin, Reich argues that we should not respect the child's wish to drop out of school because we do respect her future autonomy and we see schooling as an activity justified by the contribution it makes to that autonomy. Reich's pluralism is therefore of the Berlinian limited kind in that it clearly opposes monistic theories that claim to know what is good for all human beings. Minimalist autonomy requires that ways of life be chosen but it does not prescribe that one particular form of life be chosen.

Reich does claim that his minimalist version of autonomy requires that individuals are made aware of different ways of life and he offers multicultural education as a pedagogical strategy well suited to this purpose. Reich (2003) criticises Kymlicka for restricting the cultural materials available to the individual to those that exist within her particular culture. This 'intra-cultural navigation' appears to be unnecessarily limiting and, like Waldron, Reich considers how reviewing one's own culture can be more effectively done from a perspective that is informed by an awareness of rival conceptions. It follows that exposing children to values and beliefs different from those of the home is a function of schooling.[12] Support for this intercultural model can be found in various parts of Berlin's writing: in his claims for education about other cultures as a strategy for combating prejudice and in his own frequent observation about the way that Jewish immigrants have been able to develop accounts of their culture of habitation in ways that perceive aspects of that culture that are often less well understood by 'native' members. There is also a close parallel between Reich's critique of the cultural essentialism involved in arguments for culturally relevant pedagogy and curriculum (for example Afro-centric education as articulated by Molefi Kete Asante, 1992) and Berlin's rejection of cultural determinist accounts that make individuals simply products of their own culture. It is not surprising in the context of these arguments that Reich should consider home-schooling to be much the greatest threat to liberal education in America. The number of children who are home-schooled far outweighs those affected by the *Yoder* and *Mozert* decisions.

Autonomy and belonging

Feinberg and Callan have both amended somewhat their earlier accounts of autonomy in order to find some space for a consideration of the good of belonging. Feinberg (2004) relies on a distinction between a propositional rationality that requires of a truth claim that it survives rational scrutiny and a pragmatic rationality that is inclusive of claims that are warranted because they cohere with other beliefs and allow believers to live well rather than live true. According to Feinberg this shifts the focus from autonomy to authenticity and Feinberg's account of authenticity is very close to Berlin's view of belonging; it stresses feeling at home, being situated in a particular set of possibilities, fitting in. A commitment to reflection is maintained but this is seen as a matter of degree, not of kind, and Feinberg uses the example of the Nicene Creed to show how traditions can be shown to foster, and are themselves the outcome of, debate. Feinberg's description of the relationship between choice and tradition(s) as a 'tracking back and forth across and between traditions and strands of a single tradition that provides the tensions and material required for intellectual growth' (*ibid*: 47) comes remarkably close to Berlin's autobiographical account of intellectual development as the combination of three strands of identity – English empiricism, Russian ideas and Jewish identity.

Shelley Burtt (2003) is also concerned to demonstrate the human goods associated with lives of faith; she identifies practical reason and moral courage as virtues that are consistent with liberal autonomy and goes on to argue that these virtues can be found at the centre of 'comprehensive educations' designed to ensure that children come to share the way of life of their parents. It is inevitable, she says, that members of such groups will reflect on their own way of life because raising questions about identity is part of living an identity. It is in this way that a life comes to be lived from the inside and this is the only way to live well.

In his recent discussion of autonomy considerations Callan (2002a) draws on Nicholas Wolterstorff's autobiographical account of a life in religion[13] in order to show how autonomy might be demonstrated in adherence to a way of life because '[a]utonomous revision and adherence are twin facets of the one virtue' (*ibid*: 127). Liberals who favour exposure to ethical pluralism appear to have in mind a philosophical pluralism of the Berlinian kind, says Callan, when the reality is more the 'polymorphic nihilism' of consumerist and superficial identities that Burtt and religious citizens fear. In the face of this there is something then to be said for the rituals and habitual behaviours and other non-rational foundations of life that encourage adherence. Reflecting on Wolterstorff's account of how the austere beauty of religious buildings and ritual and the repetition of liturgy and scripture provided him with a 'fundamental hermeneutic', Callan concludes that such an individual who draws on the fulfilment and reassurance of religious practice is not simply heteronomous but a person who is adhering to faith autonomously. On this view reasoning has to be inclusive of experience and feeling and once this is accepted 'we might find that we liberals have more in common with many who cherish faith and tradition than we ever thought we had' (*ibid*: 139).

With Berlin, Callan recognizes that human goods, such as civic education and respect for particularistic religious identities, will sometimes conflict and when this happens there is a case for compromise. Also like Berlin, Callan warns against placing a burden on liberty (for example, restricting the freedom of parents to choose a religious education for their children) for the sake of some speculative future gain (a less divided society). In the spirit of compromise Callan suggests there is a case for early education in a religious school with transfer to a common school during adolescence. I will return to this strategy in the discussion of faith schooling in Chapter 4.

Citizenship and political liberalism

The *Yoder* Court ruled that Amish-style education of their children (public schooling followed by post-14 community-specific vocational training) was an adequate preparation for adult life. From an Enlightenment liberal perspective this suggests an impoverished model of citizenship, one that excludes the skills of critical thinking together with knowledge of science and of other ways of life (Arneson and Shapiro, 1996). For Macedo (2000) this becomes an issue of 'civic health' because good citizens are not born, they grow towards good citizenship through education. Against the *Mozert* families' claims Macedo argues that awareness of other ways of life is both a basic requirement of being able to choose and fundamental to learning how to live well in a diverse society. For much the same reasons Macedo, in his most recent work, regards *Yoder* as wrongly decided.[14]

Macedo, we have seen, presents Rawlsian political liberalism as a way forward in dealing with the claims of religious groups who resist particular aspects of civic education. By recognizing and separating public and private dimensions political liberalism allows the public school to focus on shared principles leaving the religious question aside. Criticality as a liberal virtue is now restricted to the public sphere of life in a liberal democracy and there is no requirement that children apply criticality to their own way of life. By leaving aside the religious question Macedo (1995a: 475–476) believes that the school door remains open to reasonable fundamentalists.

Political liberalism requires of citizens that their deliberations in the public sphere are couched in terms of reasons that other citizens can understand and appreciate. On this view the Mozerts' claims for exemption on the grounds of God's instructions to them falls short of public acceptability. While religious citizens are welcome to regard fundamentalist beliefs as having authority in the private sphere they have no authority in the public realm. It follows that political liberals restrict their support for autonomy-facilitating education to the public sphere; this is consistent with a wish to follow the later John Rawls in his shift to a theory of justice that accommodates cultural diversity and demonstrates inclusion of a variety of comprehensive ways of life (Rawls, 1993; 1999). The permeability of the boundary between the public and private spheres and the possibility of the spill-over of autonomy considerations from public to private has stimulated considerable debate. In arguing the liberalizing advantages of accommodating religious citizens so as to keep their children in public schools political liberals not only recognize the possibility of spill-over between the public and the private but appear to want to take advantage of it. I return to this in my discussion of diversity liberal responses to political liberalism.

Autonomy and children's rights

Enlightenment liberals are keen to balance the claims of children's interests in their future autonomy with the claims of families for a role in influencing their own children (Appiah, 2003). For Richard Arneson and Ian Shapiro (1996) it matters that parents cannot know the future personalities of their children and therefore cannot know what way of life will work best for their children. For many liberals this provides justification for autonomy-promoting education and reason to question whether accounts of faith-based education pay sufficient attention to the rights of children. Defenders of parental authority in choosing a religious education for their children are accused of ignoring the fact that the rational abilities of many teenage children are the equal of many adults and of sacrificing the future autonomy of children in the interests of the present autonomy of adults. Either way children's interests are neglected.[15]

James Dwyer (1998) agrees that there has been insufficient attention to children's interests in philosophical discussion about religious schools. In this context the *Yoder* decision can be seen as interpreting the free exercise clause as establishing the right to control the thoughts of others and allowing parents 'to make [children] the type of persons one wants them to be in the light of one's own religious beliefs' (*ibid*: 51). Dwyer goes on to report with regret the way that this decision has been influential in home-schooling cases where religion has been the key factor.

Harry Brighouse (2003a) makes children's interests central to his argument for autonomy-facilitating (as opposed to autonomy-promoting) education. The case for autonomy-facilitating education is made in the context of recognizing Berlin's value pluralist argument that there are many ways of living a good life. Here Brighouse is agreeing with Francis Schrag (1998) about the diversity of good lives and the need to include chosen lives of religious devotion among those recognized as worthy.[16] Where Brighouse disagrees with Schrag is in making the point that for Berlin pluralism goes beyond cultural diversity to include value conflicts between and within individuals. Individual personalities differ and so a way of life that works for one person does not work for another. A homosexual boy, for example, is not suited to a way of life that regards his sexuality as an abomination. For Brighouse it is unjust that some children will get an education that is not suited to their needs. It follows that an education that prepares all children for future living must include elements designed to facilitate choice and the capacity to live with the outcomes of that choice, including the choice to exit the group. Brighouse itemizes the content of this kind of education as follows: knowledge of the world and of the various sets of beliefs, religious and secular; a capacity to recognize fallacious argument and to understand the difference between arguments that rely on evidence and those that are founded on authority; and an awareness of the ways that believers and non-believers deal with moral problems, conversion experiences and their own doubts. This programme is likely, says Brighouse, to require children to come into contact with religious believers and the first-hand advocacy of religious beliefs. Where this programme differs from autonomy-promotion is in the way it quite deliberately draws back from inculcating in children any inclination to make use of the skills of autonomy.

Brighouse deals with a number of objections to his proposed autonomy-facilitating education. To the claim that it neglects legitimate parental influence Brighouse responds that his approach both retains a degree of parental influence and allows for the legitimate involvement of other adults in shaping the development of future citizens. To the claim that the religious liberty of parents is compromised Brighouse counters with the future religious liberty of children; furthermore autonomy-facilitating education does not preclude parents from introducing children to their own faith, for example taking children to church. Against those diversity liberals such as Galston and Burtt who worry about the impact on children of exposure to a range of religious and secular beliefs, and especially the influence of aggressive materialism, Brighouse replies that autonomy-facilitating education does not preclude children eventually coming to choose traditional ways of life; what it does do is make it more likely that children are free to choose ways of life that can be lived well from the inside.

In this section I have identified Enlightenment liberal support for education that prepares children for life in a culturally diverse and democratic society. I have shown that these concerns focus on preparing children for participation in economic, social and political life. So that children can live their lives well from the inside, Enlightenment liberals favour education for autonomy-facilitation but accept that mature adults might choose lives of religious devotion. Where Berlin is cited in support of liberal arguments of this kind it is in the context of individual liberty and the importance of choosing, whether the outcome be one of rejection of, or adherence to, a particular way of life. Although Enlightenment liberals might disagree about the exact nature of civic education there is agreement that a substantial civic education will be required if children are to be well prepared to live satisfying lives that remain well lived from the inside while tolerant of other citizens who choose to live differently. It is now time to look in more detail at diversity liberal concerns about civic education generally and education for autonomy in particular.

Responding to *Yoder* and *Mozert*: diversity liberalism and the limits of civic education

Toleration, even-handedness and respect for cultural groups

Chandran Kukathas (2003: 2) begins his account of *The Liberal Archipelago* with the question: 'How can diverse human beings live together, freely, and peacefully?' This is the question, Kukathas says, that has come to dominate political philosophy. In Chapter 1 I demonstrated that much of Berlin's thinking about moral and political philosophy is articulated in response to this very question. For diversity liberals such as Monique Deveaux (2000) the answers that are discussed in the first part of this chapter fail to provide an adequate response to diversity. They fail because they attempt to show respect for individuals as individuals without recognizing the value that individuals invest in their cultural attachments to groups.

This neglect of group identities and attachments is often attributed to the impact of early Rawlsian thinking about justice for individuals unencumbered by community memberships whose needs are considered only in terms of what is shared by all human beings such as the need for sustenance rather than those needs that are shared by members of specific human groups on the basis of particular religious and cultural attachments (Carens, 1997; Sandel, 1982). Once attention shifts to these more particularistic identity-based needs, a policy of neutrality between groups can be seen to fall short of what justice requires. An often-cited example that Joseph Carens (2000) gives is that of rest days: neutralists might respond to a complaint by Jews and Muslims that institutional support for Sunday as a rest day falls short of justice by advocating Wednesday as a rest day; this, says Carens, does nobody any good and fails to recognize an important aspect of societies with a history of Christian tradition. Much better, therefore, is a policy of even-handedness that retains Sunday as a rest day but puts in place arrangements whereby members of other faiths have rights to take alternative days as rest days.

For Carens, in finding for the Amish, the *Yoder* Court provides another example of even-handedness and as such it represents an advance on those liberal accounts that complain of the loss of individual autonomy experienced by Amish children. While it is no doubt true that Amish children experience fewer opportunities than other American children (for example Carens cites their lower representation in the university population) this is an outcome that the Amish do not complain about because they value the competing good of community belonging and the sharing of a particular form of life which does not depend on educational success beyond basic skills. The interest that Amish children have in living this way of life counts against any interest they might have in equal educational opportunity. The educational compromise that early leaving represents provides Carens with an example of even-handedness in that it recognizes both competing goods rather than insisting on full acceptance of one good at the cost of completely sacrificing the other. On the face of it this sounds very much like the kind of compromise that Berlin favours when choices have to be made between competing goods.

One diversity liberal who claims to build a case for liberal pluralism on the basis of Berlin's work is William Galston (2002). Adopting Gray's pluralistic interpretation of Berlin (Gray, 2000) Galston claims that there are two liberal traditions; one tradition identifies with Enlightenment commitments to individual autonomy and critical reason while another is concerned with the post-Reformation need for toleration of religious diversity, with religion being 'the grain of sand in the oyster of politics around which the pearl of liberalism gradually formed' (Galston, 2001: 104). While those who might be referred to as 'autonomy liberals' argue for the primacy of individual rights, diversity liberals prioritize greater tolerance of religious and cultural groups including those that do not value the individual liberty of their own members. Because Berlin is the contemporary source most closely associated with the idea that moral values are many and often irreconcilable, Galston regards him as essentially a diversity liberal and it is on this basis that Galston builds his 'diversity state'.[17]

In this 'diversity state' there is to be social space where members of illiberal groups can live their lives without interference. For Galston (1991: 249) this is consistent with a liberal tradition that is 'animated by the effort to carve out spheres that are substantially impervious to government'. Some of these members (referred to as 'resident-aliens') may even want to opt out of some of the benefits of citizenship in order to avoid some of its burdens. Galston (1995: 523) is prepared to tolerate this opting out up to the point where liberal society itself is threatened because 'properly understood liberalism is about the protection of diversity'.

This diversity liberalism is defended on three grounds. First there is the empirical reality of cultural and moral pluralism. Galston (2002: 4) regards Berlin's recognition of the plurality of human goods as the closest approximation to the moral world we actually inhabit. Second, there is John Stuart Mill's argument that diversity is instrumentally valuable because a belief held in the face of alternatives is much more meaningfully held.[18] Third, diversity is held to be intrinsically good and Galston claims Berlin as the most important contemporary source of a belief in diversity as an intrinsic good (*ibid*: 27).

Any response to Galston's defence of diversity liberalism needs to consider whether the attributions to Berlin are justified and then whether liberals can be comfortable with the kind of diversity that might have to be tolerated. In what follows I will be questioning how far Galston can call upon Berlin's version of pluralism in support of his own diversity state but first it will be useful to consider the response to this kind of defence of diversity by an author who does see Berlin as valuing diversity intrinsically. George Kateb (1994) expresses surprise that liberals like Berlin argue for some congruency between respect for cultural group membership and the negative liberty of individuals. Replying to the kind of arguments that Galston offers in defence of diversity Kateb accepts, but refuses to celebrate, the inevitability of group identity and consequent diversity: 'Let there be some regret as generation after generation, people as it were spontaneously perpetuate and often intensify cultural groups in which they have been raised or to which they convert. Let there be praise for those who resist the drive' (*ibid*: 519). For Kateb, as for Mill he claims, the real beneficiary of diversity is not the committed member (the 'impassioned partisan') but the 'disinterested bystander'. Finally, Kateb challenges the idea that pluralism is to be valued as an intrinsic good on the dubious grounds that it is in our group membership that we find our true selves. Although Kateb (1999) does seem to think that Berlin is to be associated with the notion of pluralism as intrinsically valuable, his characterization of individuals alienating themselves to an abstraction is remarkably close to what worries Berlin about positive liberty. Although Kateb and Galston both claim Berlin as source for the view that pluralism is intrinsically valuable, this is an association with Berlin that I will eventually want to qualify.

In Galston's account 'expressive liberty' refers to the right of individuals and groups to live their lives as they see fit. This includes the right to live the unexamined, non-autonomous life because '[e]xpressive liberty protects the ability of individuals and groups to live their lives in ways that others would regard as unfree' (Galston, 2002: 101). This tolerance of illiberal communities is best exemplified by Galston's treatment of *Ohio Civil Rights Commission* v. *Dayton Christian Schools Inc.*[19] In this case a Christian fundamentalist school refused to renew the contract of a pregnant married teacher who wanted to return to teaching after the birth of her child. This refusal by the school was based on the belief that women with young children should not work outside the home. While recognizing the burdens this placed on this woman, Galston (1995, 2002) regards the right of the community to exemplify its beliefs about gender roles in its employment practices as sufficiently important to override this woman's loss. In coming to this conclusion Galston makes a move that diversity liberals commonly make in these circumstances; he makes support for an illiberal practice conditional on community members enjoying a meaningful right of exit. There are, says Galston, alternative employment opportunities for this teacher and, that being so, he is prepared to support her removal from her post.

For a diversity liberal like Galston toleration is never '*mere* toleration'; this often underrated virtue is one that is essential to the avoidance of bloody conflict. A liberalism that starts from this virtue of toleration favours societies '[organized] around the principle of maximum feasible accommodation of diverse ways of life, limited only by the minimum requirements of civic unity'(Galston, 1999: 45). In his book *Liberal Pluralism* (2002) Galston identifies these limits as the protection of human life, the development of basic capacities, and the development of those skills necessary for social and economic participation. So human sacrifice and foot-binding are excluded because these fail the first two conditions but education in the skills of critical evaluation will not be required where a community deems this unnecessary and threatening to its future as a viable culture.

Galston (2001) rejects Barry's liberal egalitarianism and argues instead for legal exemptions for religious and cultural groups burdened by existing laws. Court decisions that enabled German-American parents to have their children educated in the German language (*Meyer* v. *Nebraska*, 1923), that respected the right of American Catholics to send their children to Catholic schools (*Pierce* v. *Society of Sisters*, 1925), and that exempted Amish children from public education after the age of 14 (*Wisconsin* v. *Yoder*, 1972) all find favour with Galston and all appear to him to be consistent with Berlin's pluralism, one that is characterized by 'a generous receptivity to ways of life other than one's own, and a deep commitment to making the effort to understand why others come to embrace outlooks that one regards as peculiar, even repellent' (Galston, 2002: 107).

Although it is Berlin's value pluralism on which Galston builds this most recent version of the 'diversity state' he does acknowledge the importance of 'negative liberty' defined as individual choice-making in the absence of coercion. It follows that individuals must not be coerced into communities nor forced to remain because

[t]he surest sign of unfreedom occurs when individuals are coerced to remain in ways of life they wish to leave. The politics of negative liberty seeks first and foremost, to protect the ability to leave – although not necessarily to cultivate the awareness and reflective powers that may stimulate the desire to leave.

(Galston, 2002: 51)

Eventually Galston is forced to acknowledge that the kind of education necessary to make this right of exit meaningful is not unproblematic for his version of liberalism. Making that right meaningful demands an education that goes beyond what many illiberal communities are prepared to accept, not least the Amish. Diversity liberalism is forced into a difficult balancing act of supporting an education sufficient to make exit a realistic option while refusing to support an education that might have the effect of stimulating the desire to leave. I turn to the question of how successful diversity liberalism has been in negotiating this balance in Chapter 5.

While toleration is fundamental to Galston's version of the diversity state, Deveaux (2000) argues the need for diversity liberalism to go beyond tolerance and to show respect for the values of groups. Liberals from Locke to Rawls, Raz and Kymlicka are guilty, she says, of basing a case for the tolerance of groups on the role that groups play in underpinning individual choice. Respect for groups requires listening to their members not just as individuals but as members of their own groups. Failure to have one's identity recognized in this way constitutes an inequality no less serious than material inequality and diversity liberals call for a 'politics of recognition' (Taylor, 1994a) to address this grievance. This kind of recognition takes on a particular significance when the group is an oppressed group. Berlin's account of the psychology of oppressed groups and the possibility of individual members' willingness to forego negative liberty in order to retain group self-government has already been discussed. Jeff Spinner-Halev (2001) appears to be thinking in these terms when he says that the justice of protecting individual rights must be balanced against the injustice of oppressing already disadvantaged groups: 'I will argue that avoiding the injustice of imposing reform on oppressed groups is often more important than avoiding the injustice of discrimination against women' (*ibid*: 86). Feminists such as Susan Moller Okin (2002) who criticize diversity liberal tolerance of gender discrimination are said to fail to distinguish between oppressed and non-oppressed groups. This distinction matters far more to Spinner-Halev than that which Kymlicka makes between national minorities and immigrant groups. Where Kymlicka calls upon liberals to extend minority rights to national minorities (though not necessarily to immigrants) Spinner-Halev favours extending more substantial space for illiberal groups that are oppressed irrespective of whether they are national minorities or immigrants.[20]

Belonging

In Chapter 1 I identified community belonging as a human good that Berlin acknowledged attributing its recognition to his own experience as a member of the Jewish community. Replying to cosmopolitan critics of essentialism in accounts of group identity Tariq Modood (2000) draws upon the 1997 *Fourth National Survey of Ethnic Minorities in Britain* (Modood *et al.*, 1997) for evidence that the members of minority groups strongly associate with their group identity and its associated practices. For Modood religion is the key to identities of this kind and he criticizes theorists of difference (he has Charles Taylor in mind) who, in his view, pay insufficient attention to religion as a basis for cultural identity. Where Modood does agree with Taylor is in regarding human dignity as dependent on non-members respecting the beliefs held by members of groups. Liberals are criticized then for failing to attribute worth to the value that religious citizens get from choosing to bind themselves to others within communities of obedience and mutual obligation.[21] Mills (2003) underlines this view of religious identity by caricaturing liberal religious education as a weekly diet of different religious experiences – today Shintoism, next week Islam, then whatever children choose, and so on. For Mills religion is not about choice; it is about inter-generational induction into a community of faith.

Galston's account of belonging as a human good stays close to Berlin. What Galston calls 'expressive liberty' is experienced as a close fit between what a person believes and how that same person is called upon to behave; it is about being able to live a life true to oneself. Galston wants to give parents considerable discretion in raising their children in ways consistent with their own deepest convictions. Against autonomy liberalism he argues that '[t]he greatest threat to children is not that they will believe in something too deeply, but that they will believe in nothing very deeply at all' (Galston, 1991: 255).

And so diversity liberals find themselves committed to educational environments that, at least in the early years, 'habituate' and 'constrain' children in a particular way of life (Spinner-Halev, 2000: 64, 77). But this is an 'enabling constraint' in the sense that future choices are best made from the context of a secure cultural framework. Spinner-Halev's argument at this point is consistent with future autonomy. Deveaux, on the other hand, contrasts the goods of security and well-being with individual autonomy. Traditional communities like the Amish, she says, provide sources of comfort and refuge from which members gain a sense of direction and place. The autonomy that traditional group members seek is autonomy for their community rather than for their individual selves (Deveaux, 2000: 132). Reflecting on Berlinian value pluralism Michael Ignatieff notes the conflict between the goods of private agency and community belonging when he warns against attributing false consciousness to those who choose lives of obedience because '[religious] adherents may believe that participation in their religious traditions enables them to enjoy forms of belonging that are more valuable to them than the negative freedom of private agency' (Ignatieff, 2003: 74). On this view cultural belonging is an intrinsic good rather than an instrumental good justified by its role in future choice-making.[22]

Democratic pluralism and good citizenship

It has been argued that the existence of a plurality of civil associations contributes to the healthy life of a democracy and that citizens will feel better dis-
posed to the wider democracy when their own sub-cultural identities are
respected. For example, Andrew Wright (2004) makes the claim that Roman
Catholics and Jews have been all the more enthusiastic about United Kingdom
citizenship since their specific identities came to be properly respected by the
state. Michael McConnell (2000) makes much the same point about the United
States when he recalls how the Philadelphia public feast to celebrate the Constitution in 1789 included the provision of a kosher table.[23] On this view a democratic society allows a Catholic to be a Catholic and a Jew to live as a Jew.
McConnell expresses this in terms of Berlin's favourite metaphor for belonging
which is that all citizens must be allowed to feel that they are at home.

There are, say diversity liberals, many ways to be a good citizen. Regular participation in critical reflection on public matters is one important contribution that
citizens of a democracy can be expected to make but diversity liberals point to
other ways that citizens who are not enthusiastic deliberative democrats can serve
their society. The Amish have been described as 'partial citizens', in that they are
in America but not of America according to Spinner (1994: 108) who describes
the Amish as 'quiet partial citizens, content to pursue salvation in their own distinctive, if illiberal, way'. Kymlicka (2001) accepts this description of the Amish
and endorses the view that their partial status justifies exemptions from civic
burdens as long as the Amish remain isolated from the public domain.[24]

It has already been noted how the *Yoder* Court made much of Amish law-
abidingness and community self-sufficiency and Galston (1999) points to social
co-operation and law-abidingness as examples of civic virtues demonstrated by
non-liberal religious citizens. Rosemary Salomone (2000: 88) applauds the court
for recognizing the role that cultural groups can play in fostering social stability:
'Nowhere before or since has the [Supreme] Court articulated such insight into
the role that religious sub-groups play as sources of values and control over their
members that, in the end, benefits and stabilizes the larger society'.

Democracy, say diversity liberals, benefits from cultural options in the form
of different ways of life being available to citizens. In a materialistic world, says
Stephen Carter (1993), it is religion that provides secular society's dissenters,
the modern equivalent of the bold atheists that John Stuart Mill wanted to ensure
the internal diversity of society. But Mill, as Berlin observed, was concerned
with individual choice while diversity liberals such as Spinner-Halev and Carter
recognize that the availability of religious conservatism as an option within
society might well depend on the lack of options within the religious community
itself. In his response to diversity liberal arguments for pluralism as a safeguard
against tyranny and societal conformity Dwyer (1998: 98) counters that this
argument is only credible 'when divergent factions confront one another in the
public arena, not when factions that are petty tyrannies themselves vilify one
another and segregate themselves from the mainstream'.

Diversity and the private sphere

According to Rawls:

> Justice as fairness honors, as far as it can, the claims of those who wish to withdraw from the modern world in accordance with the injunctions of their religion provided only that they acknowledge the principles of the political conception of justice and appreciate its political ideals of person and society.
>
> (Rawls, 1988: 268)

Arneson and Shapiro (1996) assume that Rawls has *Yoder* in mind here. The distinction that Rawlsian political liberalism[25] relies upon between a public realm where citizens can be expected to operate in terms of public reasonableness and a private realm where citizens are free to pursue their own conceptions of the good proves problematic for diversity liberalism in a number of ways. I have already noted that doubts are often expressed about the security of the boundary between these two realms; isn't there a likelihood that critical skills honed in the pursuit of public debate about political issues will spill over as children begin to apply these skills in thinking about their own ways of life? Clearly many do recognize this possibility and in some cases, as we have seen, go so far as to argue for accommodating non-liberal parents in public schools so as to ensure their children remain in the public sector where this spill-over is an inevitable outcome of spending time in a liberal environment. Spinner-Halev takes this line in relation to accommodating the *Mozert* parents, many of whom sent their children to religious fundamentalist schools on losing their case against Hawkins County. For Spinner-Halev an accommodation that involved using alternative texts in the classroom was to be preferred to the exit of children from public education; in much the same way Spinner-Halev argues for public funding of Islamic schools in the United Kingdom so that Muslim children will be exposed to the liberalism of the national curriculum.

While some liberals want to exploit the permeability of the public–private boundary religious citizens themselves often reject the boundary altogether claiming instead that their religious identity cannot be compartmentalized in this way. On this view social inclusion requires that religious citizens be allowed to bring their private perspectives into the public domain. John Tomasi urges political liberals to acknowledge the burden that political liberalism places on religious citizens when the public culture spills over into the private domain while denying these citizens the right to bring their religious perspective into public debate. In cases like *Mozert* Tomasi (2001: 91–95) calls for greater accommodation of religious non-liberal citizens in order to reduce these burdens. While Tomasi acknowledges that these children must be involved in a civic education that teaches about justice, this must be done, he says, in a way that allows 'citizens of faith' to link this civic education to their own world. This means paying attention to the non-public lives of the children in a way that enables the children to make a success of these lives. Tomasi uses the term 'compass concepts' to refer to important defining elements of private lives that children ought to be able to bring into public education so that they can make sense of the public sphere but do so on their own terms.

Rights to culture and to free association

Another version of diversity liberalism starts from a right to a particular culture, one's own. This is most famously expressed by Avishai Margalit and Moshe Halbertal (1994). I have already discussed the way that Margalit emphasizes those parts of Berlin's work that focus on community belonging, specifically Berlin's writing about Israel and Jewish identity. Margalit and Halbertal begin from the premiss that individual personality is shaped by membership of one's own culture. It follows that denial of the right of an individual to her culture is to interfere with her formation of personality. Kymlicka, it will be recalled, defended the right to culture in terms of the role that culture plays in choice-making; this defence bound Kymlicka to a refusal to support cultural groups that denied choice-making to their own members, what Kymlicka calls internal restrictions. Margalit and Halbertal resist being bound in this way and argue that their own defence of a right to culture applies equally to liberal and illiberal groups. They give the example of the Ultra-Orthodox Jews of Israel, a community that is characterized by illiberal practices that discriminate against some of their own members, most notably women. The Ultra-Othodox are quite willing to resort to coercive measures and constraint when required as a means both of ensuring conformity among their own members and to control the behaviour of non-members visiting Orthodox neighbourhoods.

This 'right to culture' argument fails to take account of the way that cultures evolve in ways that cannot be predicted (Brighouse, 2003a). It follows that any state support for aspects of cultural identity will tend to have a conservative influence that privileges those in the group who currently hold power. The outcome is that the future direction of the culture is taken out of the hands of some members, particularly younger members whose influence is yet to be brought to bear. Brighouse goes on to question whether children, still unable to articulate their own view of culture, can properly be said to 'have a culture', and therefore a right to that culture. Our obligation to children is therefore 'to ensure that they are able to function effectively in whatever culture turns out to be theirs when they reach adulthood' (*ibid*: 101). It is extremely doubtful that the gender-specific education that Margalit and Halbertal accept as appropriate for the children of Ultra-Orthodox Jews comes anywhere close to this requirement.[26]

Enlightenment liberals such as Reich (2003: 302–307) point to the possible illiberal treatment of individuals that follows from the group rights argument whereas Galston (2002: 101) is prepared to accept these illiberal consequences, as we have seen, on the grounds that '[e]xpressive liberty protects the ability of individuals and groups to live in ways that others would regard as unfree'. By conflating the freedom of individuals and groups in this way Galston underplays the part that groups can play in constraining the freedom of their individual members.

Theorists of group rights to culture such as Margalit and Halbertal have tended to support the *Yoder* decision; in his book *The Liberal Archipelago* Kukathas (2003) reaches the same conclusion but by a somewhat different route. Kukathas offers a libertarian argument for diversity based not on group rights but on individual rights of association. The fundamental right in a liberal society is, on this argument, the right to association and to its corollary which is the right of disassociation. A liberal society is no more than an association of associations, with each association being left alone providing that its members retain the right of disassociation – the right of exit. For Kukathas the Amish should be free to live as they choose; if ever Amish leave in such numbers as to make the community unviable – so be it. There is no right of cultural preservation, so only the acquiescence of its members will sustain a cultural group, and for Kukathas, this is exactly as it should be.

Kukathas regards as free those individuals who have neither chosen to be members of a group nor ever conceived the possibility of exit as an option.[27] Unlike Reich and other Enlightenment liberals Kukathas is willing to accept the oppression that can occur within cultural groups. In defence of this position Kukathas points to: the dubious historical record of interference with other cultures; the often inaccurate versions of other cultures that provide the basis for interference; and finally he observes, like Berlin, the psychology that drives oppressed members to rally behind their oppressive fellow members when faced by foreigners determined to intervene in their way of life. Against Barry, Kukathas (2002) expresses doubts about the benign nature of the outcomes when the state chooses to intervene in the ways that parents bring up their children. Acknowledging that his own defence of (parents') rights of association will inevitably result in some harms done to children by their parents, Kukathas insists that the only way this differs from Barry's recommended policy is that, unlike Barry, he is prepared to acknowledge this 'downside' of his own position.

Conclusion: Berlin and education

I have referred already to Gray's identification of 'two faces' of liberalism. Galston's diversity liberalism inspired by Berlin's value pluralism represents one of those 'faces'. Galston has been very supportive of American religious parents who criticize public education for making available to their children forms of critical reasoning with the potential for reflection and review of their own way of life. Whether it be the Amish seeking to withdraw their children from school two years earlier than other American children or Protestant fundamentalists seeking to prevent their children coming into contact with alternative world views, Galston supports these parents in their battles with what Enlightenment liberals regard as the proper aims of education in a liberal and culturally diverse society. Yet Galston claims that it is his position that is liberal because, for him, liberalism is primarily about toleration of the widest possible range of communities within a society. On this view the real test of a liberal society is its willingness to accommodate the wishes of illiberal communities. For this version of diversity liberalism Galston claims Berlin's pluralism as the most important intellectual source.

Given Galston's claim for the liberal credentials of his accommodationist stance towards illiberal groups it is pertinent to note how John White (2003) records with regret what, for him, appears to be the declining influence of liberalism in philosophy of education. Core liberal ideas such as personal autonomy are, he notes, out of favour. This is because liberalism, as White understands it, stands charged by its critics with having an 'atomistic' view of persons that privileges individual autonomy and denies social attachments. According to White some of these critics would prefer a collective version of autonomy that recognizes the value that individuals place on their community attachments; others want to recognize the value to individuals of lives that do not involve autonomy at all. Making the case for the kind of liberalism I have referred to as Enlightenment liberalism White worries about the pressure that collective identities can, and often do, place on individuals and he doubts that non-autonomous lives can go as well as autonomous ones, at least in the context of living in modern societies. White goes on to suggest that advocates of the right of parents to ensure that their children are educated along the lines of parental religious beliefs must show more concern for children's ability to make their own choices if their advocacy is to be regarded as liberal.[28]

Given Galston's claim of Berlinian support it is interesting to note that when White (1999) makes his own case for liberal education, he also claims Berlin as source. White bases his idea of liberal education on Berlin's espousal of self-creation as a good. This commitment to 'negative liberty', to freedom from external constraint, makes Berlin 'the true torchbearer of liberalism' (*ibid*: 198). It has been a feature of this chapter that theorists of education representing both of these 'two faces' of liberalism claim Berlin as source. A central purpose of this book is to examine these different interpretations of Berlin and to assess the implications for education in culturally diverse societies. I will conclude this chapter by saying something about what Berlin himself has to say about education on the relatively few occasions that he makes direct reference to it.

Whether he is writing about scholars working in different academic disciplines or about human beings belonging to different cultural groups one theme that permeates Berlin's writing on education is the need for, and value of, crossing boundaries. In a 1969 paper on the subject of *General Education*[29] and in another entitled *Woodrow Wilson on Education* (2002c)[30] Berlin refers to the danger of specialization and the benefits to be gained from academics and their students coming to understand how their colleagues and peers in very different disciplines operate. When writing about the aims of education more generally Berlin extends this discussion of boundary crossing to understanding other cultures. To know the world as it really is, it is important, says Berlin, to know something of what others have made of it. This liberating potential of cross-cultural understanding is perhaps most clearly stated when he is considering the consequences of prejudice. In his 1981 *Notes on Prejudice* Berlin (2002a)[31] outlines the dangers that arise when members of a community feel a sense of the infallibility of their culture. The idea that one's own culture has the one true answer, says Berlin, leads inexorably to prejudice, stereotyping, and the dark side of nationalism.

For Berlin it is important that children learn to live with doubt, to purposely seek out knowledge of other cultures, so that one's own ideas can be tested and then either confirmed, refined or rejected as appropriate. It is knowledge of other cultures that allows minds to be kept open and civilized and it is certainty that leads to inquisitions and holocausts. It follows that the only cure for prejudice is 'understanding how other societies – in space or time, live: and that it is possible to lead lives different from one's own, and yet be fully human' (Berlin, 2002a: 346). Berlin is very clear that education has purposes that go beyond fitting individuals into a mould determined by the requirements of a particular community: 'I shall assume ... that human beings are in general entitled to have their capacities for thought and feeling developed *even at the cost of not always (or even often) fitting smoothly into some centrally planned social pattern...*' (Berlin, 2000a: 216, emphasis added).

This recognition that education at its best must provide a means for individuals to plough their own furrow is apparent in Berlin's (2002c) discussion of the rather different educational models of Benjamin Jowett, Master of Balliol College, and Mark Pattison, Rector of Lincoln College. Where Jowett saw in university education a distinctly public purpose, the preparation of young men and women for public service, Pattison favoured the more private activity of scholarship for individual satisfaction. In his own commentary on these contrasting pedagogies Berlin finds space for both tendencies; good societies, he says, do depend on the kind of relationships between people that demand some concern with what other people think, but good societies also find space for individuals less bothered about public opinion and less anxious to please. While the values underpinning these two educational paradigms might well prove incompatible, decent societies will always try to combine the best of each tradition.

Berlin's own comments on education ultimately reflect his agreement with John Stuart Mill (Berlin, 1991a: 90) that there is great value in placing individuals in contact with those who are different in lifestyle and beliefs. It is difficult to reconcile this with the support that diversity liberals, such as Galston, claim to get from Berlin's pluralism. Berlin's own views on education appear to be much closer to Zakaras (2003: 516) who concludes that it is cosmopolitan identity and not cultural particularity that Berlin favours: '[For Berlin] the best lives were led in view of the multiplicity and incommensurability of good alternatives'. It is education (for example in the subjects of history, anthropology, literature, art and law) to which Berlin (2002a: 345) turns for the knowledge of these good alternatives that 'opens the windows of the mind (and soul) and makes people wiser, nicer, and more civilized'.

3 Cultural diversity, value pluralism and the curriculum

During the 1990s there was a great deal of discussion in the United Kingdom about the place of values in education and the contribution that schools ought to be making to the spiritual, moral and social development of children. Philosophers of education, not surprisingly, made a significant contribution to discussion about this issue (see, for example, Haydon, 1997). By the end of the decade national curriculum documentation for teachers included a 'Statement of Values' which claimed the warrant of a societal consensus about what values teachers could feel confident in teaching. Commentary on and critique of this approach often focused on the implications of cultural and religious diversity for values education of this kind. Given cultural pluralism, and therefore value pluralism, doubts were advanced about whether there could ever be a genuine consensus about a particular set of values considered appropriate for inclusion in a national curriculum.

I begin this chapter by expanding on the account of Isaiah Berlin's value pluralism that was introduced in Chapter 1. The relationship between Berlin's commitment to value pluralism and his version of liberalism has been the subject of considerable debate in recent years. One perspective from within this debate that is particularly relevant to values education comes from George Crowder who connects Berlinian value pluralism to liberalism through an argument about the requirement of specific liberal virtues among the citizens of a democratic pluralist society. This argument clearly has implications for the kind of values education required for living well in a society characterized by cultural and religious diversity. The final section of the chapter considers these implications in the context of recent debate about accommodating religious perspectives on teaching about homosexuality.

Value pluralism: resisting the utopian pursuit of the ideal

In a footnote to his introduction to *Four Essays on Liberty*, Berlin (2002a: 50 n. 1) identifies value pluralism as fundamental to his thought. So much so that Berlin feels compelled to revise the final passages of his essay *Two Concepts of Liberty* (*ibid*: 216–217) to emphasize that even the negative liberty that is so central to his thought is not to be regarded as completely displacing positive liberty. Such absolute priority of the value of negative liberty would 'constitute precisely the kind of intolerant monism against which the entire argument is directed' (*ibid*: 50). Contemporary value pluralists identify Berlin as the key source for the development since the 1950s of value pluralism as an alternative to relativist and monist approaches to the philosophy of values. Referring to the final section of *Two Concepts of Liberty* William Galston (2002: 4–5) credits Berlin with '[sparking] what may now be regarded as a full-fledged value-pluralist movement in contemporary moral philosophy'.

Chapter 1 made reference to Berlin's essay *The Pursuit of the Ideal* which sets out an outline of the value pluralist thesis and provides some autobiographical detail about the influences which led Berlin to this conclusion. The re-publication of this important essay in Henry Hardy's collection *The Crooked Timber of Humanity* (Berlin, 1991a) is generally credited with stimulating new interest in the 1990s in the value pluralist dimension of Berlin's thought. The essay begins by referring to Berlin's longstanding interest in ethics as a way of understanding the beliefs that humans have had over the ages about what is the proper way to live. This interest Berlin attributes initially to his early reading of what Tolstoy and other Russian writers had had to say about human experience. As an undergraduate at Oxford Berlin found that philosophers through the ages had agreed with these Russian writers that, with the right kind of effort, humans could discover the true answers to the problems they faced. To each problem there was but one true answer and all of these true answers could be combined in harmony; this pervasive philosophy shared what Berlin called 'a Platonic ideal', which he described thus:

> [I]n the first place . . . all genuine questions must have one true answer and one only, all the rest being necessarily errors; in the second place, that there must be a dependable path towards the discovery of these truths; in the third place, that the true answers, when found, must necessarily be compatible with one another and form a single whole, for one truth cannot be incompatible with another.
>
> (*ibid*: 5–6)

It was reading Machiavelli on the incompatibility of the values of the Roman Republic with those of Christianity that shocked Berlin into a recognition of the conceptual impossibility of the monist position described in this quotation. For Berlin this observation by Machiavelli fatally undermined the monist faith that to each problem there was but one true answer and that these answers would be compatible within a system of thought. Berlin goes on to describe how it was Vico's description of a succession of cultures each with its own distinctive set of values and Herder's account of national 'lifestyles' particular to nations and periods that pointed him to the pluralist conclusion that '[t]he values of these cultures are different, and they are not necessarily compatible with each other' (*ibid*: 9).

For Berlin it was always the case that his own thinking, like that of Vico and

Herder, was pluralist rather than relativist. Against relativism Berlin always insisted that, although cultures might be different, even incompatible, each was built by humans in response to shared human problems. This being so, it is always possible to understand what another culture means to its own members. Human beings might differ but not in *every* respect. Berlin believed that values were both objective and plural but not infinitely so. Values cannot be infinite because they must fall within what Berlin regularly referred to as 'the human horizon' (*ibid*: 11). In a discussion of value pluralism that begins from these same Berlinian premises John Kekes (1999) also distinguishes pluralism from relativism by reference to a common ground between cultures that is determined by the minimal requirements for living a good life. These 'primary values' relate to both physiological and social needs shared by humans across cultures and time. Beyond meeting these basic and shared human needs there are many different and legitimate ways to live. In his own recent re-statement of his value pluralism, that he again attributes to the influence of Berlin, Galston (2005) agrees with this when he says that there are some basic goods that any decent society must provide; the deprivation of these goods being an evil that has to be avoided. That said, like Kekes, Galston argues that beyond the provision of basic goods and the avoidance of evils there is a considerable legitimate diversity in the values that humans consider worthy of their choosing.

In discussions of value pluralism there is a tendency to focus on the plurality of *cultures* and their potential incompatibility. Berlin's value pluralism, however, goes further and deeper than this. There is more to value pluralism than the diversity of values that can be attributed to multiculturalism.[1] While Berlin does recognize that value conflict often takes the form of a conflict between cultures, there is also value conflict between groups within a culture, and between individuals within groups. Individuals themselves will also sometimes find that they have values that they hold to be important but between which there are conflicts. Berlin's favourite examples include the clash that often occurs in particular cases when individuals seek to be both just and merciful. Virtue ethicists make much the same point; for example David Carr (2003: 229) notes the conflict between the virtues of honesty and kindness in everyday situations such as, for example, being asked to comment on someone's choice of hat: 'what is gained on the moral swings of this virtue may be lost on the roundabouts of that one'. James Wallace (1999) instances the compassionate teacher who is reluctant to fail a weak student as exemplifying Berlin's observation that justice is not always compatible with compassion. Wallace concludes, however, that the virtues of benevolence and justice can be combined as long as criticism is delivered in such a way as to benefit the welfare of the student. For Wallace this resolution of the problem can be described as a Platonic unity of the virtues, or in other words, harmonization of these apparently conflicting values. No doubt Berlin would agree that the teacher operate much as Wallace recommends though Berlin would see this as a trade-off or compromise decided on the basis of the particular situation and designed to minimize suffering rather than a harmonization of values that must remain in conflict.

The importance of compromise for Berlin is evident in his consideration of the conflict between the values of equality and freedom:

> Equality may demand the restraint of the liberty of those who wish to dominate; liberty ... may have to be curtailed in order to make room for social welfare, to feed the hungry, to clothe the naked, to shelter the homeless, to leave room for the liberty of others, to allow justice or fairness to be exercised.
>
> (Berlin, 1991a: 12–13)[2]

A recent case in the United States illustrates the kind of conflict between equality and freedom that sometimes has to be faced in the context of education. In 1999 the State College Area School District in Pennsylvania introduced a new anti-harassment policy that was designed to create for all its students a safe and nurturing learning environment. Harassment was defined in such a way as to include speech that denigrates individuals on the grounds of personal characteristics such as national origin, religious identity, disability or sexual orientation. David Saxe, a guardian of two students at the school, filed suit against the school district alleging that this policy undermined the constitutionally guaranteed free speech of those religious students with convictions that they took to require them to speak out about the sinfulness of homosexuality. The District Court[3] found in favour of the anti-harassment policy on the grounds that it excluded only behaviour that was already illegal, but this decision was eventually overturned by the Court of Appeals[4] where it was judged that the school district policy prohibited a good deal of speech that would not be actionable under existing anti-discrimination legislation. This court recognized the tension (value conflict) between anti-harassment laws and First Amendment guarantees of free speech but decided against prohibiting students from making negative comments about the 'values' of other students. Put simply the court is arguing that the whole point of free speech protection is to protect speech that some, or indeed many, people find offensive. In 2005 the Woodring Center for Educational Pluralism at Western Washington University cited this case as an example of the kind of educational dilemma thrown up by value pluralism.[5] The case is presented as evidencing the conflict between the values of liberty (the right to express religious views about the sinfulness of homosexuality) and equality (equal opportunity for gay and lesbian students to learn in a non-hostile environment). From a value pluralist perspective there is no way to resolve this case in such a way as to avoid some sacrifice of genuine goods.

Berlin argues for value pluralism on the grounds that this world of conflicts of value *is* the world as we come to know it. In this he is supported by Galston (2002) who draws on his experience as a White House official in the field of domestic policy to argue that the difficult policy decisions were always those that involved choices between competing goods rather than choosing between the good and the bad. For Galston, as for Berlin, this does not rule out the possibility of balancing claims in particular cases. What this does mean, however, is that choices between goods will always involve some sacrifice because '[b]oth personal and political life regularly confront us with situations in which every option entails a sacrifice of genuine good' (Galston, 2005: 16). Joseph Raz (1999: 98) concurs and adds that in multicultural societies this tension between values is inevitable and that 'this involves difficult problems, with sound values pulling in different directions [and] no solution to these problems is possible without sacrifice of the promotion of some sound values'.

So, if we agree with Berlin that, given conflict between competing goods, we cannot have everything, how are we to choose between these goods? Berlin's own conclusion in *The Pursuit of the Ideal* calls for the prioritization of avoiding extreme cruelty and suffering. By always attending to the specifics of any particular situation compromises and trade-offs are to be sought in the interests of preventing these great evils.

In addition to saying that value conflict forms part of human experience, value pluralism of a Berlinian kind also points to the dangers of a belief in the harmonization of all human values and the benefits to be had from retaining a diversity of values. The utopian dream of the compossibility of all that humans value is not only conceptually incoherent but history has also taught that this is a very dangerous belief because belief in such a possibility has persuaded tyrant after tyrant that no price is ever too high to pay in order to achieve such great benefit with the outcome that 'hundreds of thousands may have to perish to make millions happy for all time' (Berlin, 1991a: 15). In a later section of this chapter I consider the implications of this warning for the possibility of ideals in education.

From value pluralism to comprehensive liberalism

Political philosophers have recently debated the contentious relationship between pluralism and liberalism and the effectiveness of Berlin's arguments for a specifically liberal pluralism. Before considering Crowder's development of Berlin in order to re-connect pluralism and liberalism I will briefly review the discussion to which Crowder is responding.

Re-connecting the pluralist–liberal divide

Brian Barry says that 'there is nothing straightforwardly absurd about the idea that there is a single best way for human beings to live' (2001: 262) and that best way is a liberal political system with a central commitment to the value of equality. Rejecting multiculturalist thinking as a kind of twentieth-century version of the Counter-Enlightenment, Barry de-couples the liberal–pluralist connection and opts firmly for liberalism. John Gray (1998) agrees that liberalism and pluralism must, as he puts it, 'part company', but he opts instead for a strong version of pluralism which denies the superiority of any political system so that the best to be hoped for is a politics of peaceful co-existence of several liberal and illiberal ways of life.

Against Barry and Gray there have been several attempts to re-connect liberalism and pluralism in ways that could be seen as attempts to resuscitate the Berlinian project of liberal pluralism. In this section I focus on Crowder's version of liberal pluralism, one that has significant implications for values education, but first I return to Galston's version of liberal pluralism.

Galston's version of liberal pluralism, built on Berlinian value pluralist foundations, argues for a 'diversity state' which finds space for a range of liberal and illiberal communities limited only by the conditions that life be protected and children's capacities be developed in order to equip them for social and economic participation.

The range of legitimate diversity that remains is considerable because of the multiplicity of goods that value pluralism recognizes but it is not unlimited because value pluralists also recognize that there are evils to be avoided. It is in order to protect this legitimate diversity that Galston warns against those 'civic totalists'[6] who argue the legitimacy of interference by the state in the internal workings of illiberal, often faith-based, communities. Galston writes:

> I believe that absent compelling reasons to the contrary, principled liberals must defer to individuals' own sense of what gives life meaning and purpose, and ensure that the intrusion on individual lives is restricted to what is needed to secure the minimum conditions of civic unity and social justice.
>
> (Galston, 2005: 177)

In this most recent exposition of his liberal pluralism Galston seeks to clarify a matter that has been of concern to several of his critics. This concerns an apparent tension between, on the one hand, Galston's critique of autonomy-based education and, on the other, the exit rights that negative liberty is acknowledged by him to require. Galston (2005) now wants to endorse an account of liberalisms that acknowledges the very real tension between these competing liberal goods. In keeping with this somewhat revised position Galston refers to Levy's identification of two streams of liberal thought; pluralist liberals are on the side of the groups and communities they want to protect from overbearing state interference while rationalist liberals are more concerned about local tyrannies that abuse group rights designed to immunize groups from state surveillance and intervention (Levy, 2003: 279). With Levy, Galston now agrees that both streams of thought defend genuine liberal goods and he offers this thought as a correction to an undue and somewhat one-sided emphasis on the pluralist stream in his earlier book *Liberal Pluralism* (2002). Genuine liberals, says Levy, will draw from both streams and he argues against those such as Barry and Gray who would drive a wedge between (rationalist) liberalism and pluralism. In particular Levy (2003: 291 n. 26) criticizes Gray for failing to acknowledge the nuances of Berlin's liberalism, a liberalism that is fully in tune with the proper tension between individual and communal freedoms.

Yet, notwithstanding everything that he now says about rights of exit and autonomy as a genuine liberal good, Galston does not want to see autonomy as a virtue that all must possess. He writes:

> When we incline toward an option, we may do so on the basis of background features of our lives and circumstances that we need not submit to further critical examination [and] while pluralism protects choice, it does not insist that all valid ways of life must reflect choice. From a pluralist point of view, many lives based on habit, tradition, or faith, fall within the wide range of legitimacy.
>
> (Galston, 2005: 190)

Expressive liberty is described not in terms of autonomy but as a form of integrity. Galston accepts that, if individuals are to avoid living a lie, there must be symmetry between the inner and outer life, but he characterizes those lives that enjoy this symmetry as ones of integrity rather than autonomy. Autonomy is but one way to live with integrity.

Crowder's development of Berlin

Crowder (2002: 78–102) examines Berlin's original argument for liberalism from pluralism. Two lines of argument are identified. The first says that the fact of having to choose between competing values causes us to value both the ability and opportunity to choose, and it follows from this that liberalism is to be valued as the political system that is best able to protect opportunities for choosing. Crowder finds this unconvincing because he does not see the necessity of choosing leading to the valuing of choice especially when the necessary choosing is between competing goods and with all that this involves in terms of losses as well as gains. Crowder concludes:

> The basic problem with Berlin's argument from necessity is that it commits a version of the naturalistic fallacy: it tries to derive a value from a fact – the value of choice and the freedom to choose from the fact of having to choose.
>
> (*Ibid*: 82)[7]

It appears to Crowder that, while Berlin has made some kind of link between pluralism and liberalism, he has done so without saying quite what it is.[8] There is, however, a second line of argument in Berlin that Crowder finds more compelling. This is the recognition that politics is about hard choices between incommensurable goods and that this rules out political systems such as Marxism and anarchism which are built on utopian doctrines of the complete harmony of goods. Of the non-utopian political system candidates remaining Crowder opts for liberalism against conservatism and pragmatism. The case for liberalism is made on the grounds that the virtues required for living well in a pluralist society are liberal virtues; in making his case Crowder claims to go beyond but remain within the spirit of Berlin.

Life in culturally diverse societies goes better when citizens possess certain virtues and liberalism is the best political system for encouraging these virtues. In order to reason well in circumstances of value pluralism citizens require the virtue of personal autonomy which is the liberal virtue *par excellence*. It is no surprise therefore that many authors (such as Michael Walzer) have acknowledged an affinity between pluralism, which recognizes a multiplicity of good ways to live, and liberalism, which advocates toleration of these differences. Crowder, however, wants to go further by demonstrating that pluralism *does* require liberalism. What is more, Crowder seeks a justification, not for any kind of liberalism, but for a liberalism of the Enlightenment autonomy-facilitating kind.

Crowder's argument involves identifying four pluralist virtues each with its liberal counterpart. He begins with the pluralist virtue of 'generosity' (2002: 188–190) or 'open-mindedness' (2004: 166) which he describes as an awareness of the great range of values that make up the human experience. The greater the range of values to which an individual is exposed the greater the range of choice available to that individual. The individual possessed of the virtue of generosity has the 'moral imagination' to see the value of ways of life to others even when she would not choose this way for herself. Generosity finds its liberal counterpart in a 'broadmindedness' (2002: 193–194) that is comfortable with peaceful accommodations based on respect for different ways of life that in turn respect others. For Crowder it is this insistence on mutual respect as a limiting condition that makes liberalism both coherent and preferable to a politics of difference that is too accommodating of illiberal cultures. Crowder's second pluralist virtue is that of 'realism' (2002: 190). Choosing one value against another requires the recognition of loss: 'If a good is genuine we must promote it where we can, and where we cannot, we must choose against it with regret' (2004: 166). This realism argues against utopian hopes of a harmony of goods and advocates the liberal virtue of 'moderation' (2002: 194–196) which in turn protects against fanaticism by urging the provisional holding of values. Knowing that our choices might have been otherwise 'is to be discouraged from regarding one's commitments as incontestable absolutes, and so to make it less likely that those commitments will be held fanatically, to the detriment of every other concern and to the concerns of others' (*ibid*: 196). Being 'attentive' to the particulars of a situation is Crowder's third pluralist virtue (*ibid*: 191). Choosing takes place within a context and the needs of particular individuals are what matter here. Crowder recalls here Berlin's frequently expressed objection to versions of positive liberty that relegate individual wishes to abstract notions of what that individual would desire if only their real, as opposed to empirical, self prevailed. For liberals this pluralist virtue is expressed as respect for persons. Finally, Crowder introduces the pluralist virtue of 'flexibility' which evidences in the disposition to apply general rules to particular circumstances. While background commitments remain important their application in concrete situations will allow for revision. The liberal virtue of personal autonomy that parallels flexibility provides Crowder with his strongest link between liberalism and pluralism. With Raz (1986: 369) Crowder defines personal autonomy in terms of deciding on one's own life plan and goes on to link this autonomy with the availability of options that pluralism provides. The availability of options leads to reflection on one's own choices as long as those options are experienced as potential ways of life for oneself.

Crowder goes on to argue that the importance of personal autonomy points to one kind of positive liberty – the capacity for self-direction – that is consistent with pluralism.[9] This recognition of the importance of personal autonomy suggests to Crowder that the kind of liberalism that pluralism points to is not the post-Reformation kind that Galston advocates on the grounds of its tolerating cultural groups but the Enlightenment kind that intervenes in groups that deny personal autonomy to their own members because 'value diversity is not necessarily promoted by cultural diversity if the cultures concerned are internally monolithic or uniform [and] [p]luralist diversity applies within groups as well as among them' (Crowder, 2004: 163).

From liberal pluralism to values education

In this section I consider the implications for values education of Berlinian liberal pluralism. First, I consider the implications of value pluralism for approaches to values education based on some kind of national consensus about what values are to be taught.

What kind of consensus on values?

I began this chapter by making reference to the inclusion within national curriculum documentation for teachers in England of a Statement of Values.[10] This statement appeared towards the end of a decade when discussion about children's spiritual and moral development had been prominent (see School Curriculum and Assessment Authority, 1995, 1996a, 1996b, 1996c). The 1988 Education Reform Act had required that schools pay attention to the moral, spiritual and cultural development of pupils as part of preparation for adult life and since the 1992 Education (Schools) Act school inspectors were required to include the development of children's spiritual, moral, social and cultural awareness in their reporting on schools. In 1993 the National Curriculum Council (NCC) circulated a discussion paper that listed the values that schools should be fostering in their pupils (NCC, 1993: 4) and in a series of speeches Nicholas Tate[11] sought to justify the introduction of the Statement of Values as the outcome of the consensus reached by the National Forum for Values in Education and the Community[12] and found by opinion polls to be broadly supported among the wider public. Tate challenged what he perceived as the widely held view that pluralism in society precluded a consensus on the values to be transmitted in schools and he argued for the need to prioritize values education in order to 'slay the dragon of relativism'.[13] By focusing on cultural differences society was said to have neglected what was in fact a considerable degree of agreement about the fundamental values that teachers could feel confident about teaching (Talbot and Tate, 1997). Tate presents a picture of England as a national community drawing on its predominant Judeo-Christian heritage for a set of shared values and Berlin is cited on several occasions in order to reject cosmopolitanism and to support a view of values as coming from within the shared community. If Berlin is right, says Tate (1997b: para 33):

> Education needs to consider how best to help young people develop a sense of belonging to a common culture [because] [o]nly through recognition of some kind of common culture, however open to outside influence and change, will young people develop a sense of belonging to a real community in which they have a stake.

This optimism about consensus on a values framework based in a common culture is not shared by everyone. It has been argued that any consensus able to do the job that Tate requires of it would need both to involve values thick enough to provide a basis for education yet thin enough to have some chance of appealing to a range of cultural and religious constituencies. Casting doubt on such a possibility Kevin Mott-Thornton (2003) notes that, although many members of society will agree that harming people is to be avoided, they are less likely to agree about what it is that constitutes harm. Where some citizens will regard homosexuality as harmful, he says, others will regard such a view as homophobic and therefore harmful in itself. In a discussion about what consensus might be achieved on issues in sex education Mark Halstead accepts that there might be agreement in favour of advocating responsible sexual behaviour but regards this as 'not very helpful if one person's understanding of responsibility involves wearing a condom and another's includes not being in the same room as a member of the opposite sex without a chaperone' (Halstead, 1997: 327).

Alasdair MacIntyre (1999) doubts whether a version of values thin enough to command agreement in a plural society will have the substance to do the job needed of moral education. Given pluralism, MacIntyre argues, there can be no shared programme of moral education; better that children are educated within their own communities and taught by teachers committed to the same community values. On this view statements of value intended to provide a basis for the education of all children are no more than rhetoric designed to disguise the deep divisions within society.[14]

A further difficulty is recognized by Jasper Ungoed-Thomas (1996) who points out that value pluralism of the kind advocated by Berlin involves the incompatibility of some of the goods often identified in lists of values to be fostered in educational contexts. Citing the kind of value conflicts regularly identified by value pluralists Ungoed-Thomas asks: how does the teacher deal with the values of justice and compassion when circumstances demand choosing between these values?

To some extent Talbot and Tate (1997) acknowledge both these difficulties. In response to the issue of the conflict between values themselves they accept that, 'it is quite clear that there will be situations in which more than one value applies and in which the values, therefore, might suggest two or more incompatible courses of action. The Forum's work has not solved the problems of moral conflict' (*ibid*: 5). Regarding the conflict between communities their response is that agreement on values is quite compatible with deep disagreements about the sources of those values. For example, respect for persons matters more than the reasons that might be given in support of this value. Where one person argues for respect for persons because human beings are all creatures of God another might call for respect on the grounds of universal human rights. Because of this attempt to separate values from their sources Stephen Mulhall (1998) locates this approach to values education within the wider political liberal concern to recognize reasonable disagreement between comprehensive doctrines while seeking consensus on a set of core citizenship values. While Mulhall appears to be less confident about political liberal claims for the possibility of a shared moral education in diverse societies, he does argue that achieving some degree of consensus will involve addressing the differences between comprehensive doctrines rather than seeking to avoid them. As Robert Kunzman (2005: 160) says: 'For many citizens, religious commitment and civic participation are deeply interwoven. To expect these citizens to ignore their moral sources when engaging in civic dialogue threatens to disenfranchise a vital segment of society'.[15]

The pursuit of the ideal

So far I have focused on the difficulties of achieving a consensus around something like a statement of values as a basis for moral education, but should the pursuit of this kind of consensus be seen as such a desirable goal? For Tate it is the common culture that provides the basis for shared ideals in education. Despite his frequent citing of Berlin in support of his own position Tate appears to express the philosophical preference for uniformity and homogeneity that Berlin's pluralism is designed to resist. Nicholas Rescher (1993) warns against the idea that consensus provides the only basis for social order; given that disagreement about issues of fundamental moral importance will not be resolved Rescher advocates 'acquiescence in dissensus' as a more workable solution than consensus. Like Berlin, Rescher fears for a society that insists on consensus where none is likely to be achieved and he cites the expulsion of the Moors from Spain and the massacre of St Bartholomew's night in France as examples of what is likely to happen when consensus remains the objective (*ibid*: 193).

These fears are also reflected in the debate between Frieda Heyting and Doret De Ruyter on the implications of Berlin's warnings about the pursuit of the ideal. Heyting (2004) worries that in making her case for the desirability of ideals in education De Ruyter (2003) pays insufficient attention to Berlin's warnings about the dangers of fanaticism in the pursuit of ideals. Heyting urges a more cautious approach that focuses on attainable goals rather than ideals, one that takes heed of Berlin's warning about the excessive lengths to which idealists have often been tempted in their pursuit of the utopian harmony of human goods. Finally Heyting, again citing Berlin,[16] challenges the implied passivity of children in De Ruyter's account of the offering of ideals to children; if children are to have ideals they should be more actively involved in their creation rather than to have them imposed.

In her most recent treatment of ideals in education De Ruyter (2004a) wants to distinguish her position from that of Berlin whom she sees as overly pessimistic about the dangers of pursuing the ideal. For De Ruyter ideals are important in education and their pursuit need not result in fanaticism; she instances those 'saints, martyrs or peaceful demonstrators' who have pursued their ideals without coercing others. It is not clear, however, that De Ruyter is so far from Berlin in much of what she has to say. Berlin would not have questioned her argument for seeking trade-offs between equality and liberty in order to respond to particular circumstances. In fact his position requires it. Where Berlin differs, perhaps, is in his recognition of the losses involved in such trade-offs against De Ruyter's talk of optimal balances; for the value pluralist there is no optimum balance. In the article to which Heyting is responding De Ruyter does address the dangers of fanaticism, identifying three versions of the fanatic:

> The first fanatic, the excessive believer, is a person who is obsessed with her ideal and cannot think of anything else. The second is the person who is too intensely emotionally tied to her ideals; she takes her ideal so seriously that she overreacts to others' objections or becomes blind to them. The third fanatic overvalues the importance of her ideal at the expense of other ideals or the interests of others. Fanatics are often fanatical in all these ways.
>
> (De Ruyter, 2003: 478–479)

In view of these dangers De Ruyter advocates both that children be taught about how people are committed to their ideals and their actions in pursuit of these ideals. How we become and remain attached to our ideals and what we do in pursuit of these ideals have implications for the interests of others and De Ruyter finds a place for learning about this in her proposed education about values. Notwithstanding her criticisms of Berlin this appears on the face of it to be a very Berlinian approach to teaching about values.

On the need for moral imagination

Berlin has been a source of inspiration for value pluralists such as John Kekes and moral educators such as Michael Pardales (2002) who see in value pluralism the need for education that stimulates the moral imagination. Rejecting monistic systems such as utilitarianism as unable to deal with the complexity and particularity of moral dilemmas Pardales advocates the use of literature to get children to think about the right thing to do in specific situations. With Berlin (1991a: 10)

Pardales argues that knowing when it is right to tell the truth will always depend on the specifics of the situation and knowing rules and principles will never be enough to decide this. Literature enables the teacher to get children to see moral dilemmas from the different perspectives of those involved by inviting the child to consider what it might be like to live the life of another person.[17]

Jack Weinstein (2004) shares this enthusiasm for literature as a vehicle for exposing children to a range of moral perspectives and he stresses that this will not be easy for teachers or for their students who will not experience 'contentment' in a classroom given to this kind of teaching but this is only because '[l]ife is complicated [and our] system of education should reflect this fact' (*ibid*: 246). What children need to learn on this view is that choices have to be made between competing goods and that these choices do not necessarily lead to either a resolution of a moral problem or an easing of the mind of the chooser. Learning to deal with this 'cognitive conflict' is a proper objective for children who will become citizens in pluralist societies; citizens, that is, who have to learn that often there is more than one right answer.[18]

Another important route to the discovery of these different perspectives is provided by ethnographers when they describe the ways of life of their subjects. According to Kekes (1999) ethnographers and novelists can assist teachers in trying to develop the moral imaginations of their pupils. By learning about different ways of life and the values instantiated in those ways of life pupils are encouraged to gain a vantage point from which to evaluate their own tradition. Kekes would have pupils come to appreciate that their own tradition is best seen as 'the currency of inherited wealth, not as shackles fastened by the dead hand of the past' (*ibid*: 181). Because Kekes conceives of what he calls a 'pluralistic moral education' as one which makes clear to children that there are objective differences between some ways of life that are good and some others which are not, children are to be educated to make choices from those that are good and to which they are well suited.

From pluralism to negative liberty

The rejection of monist accounts of value systems requires the rejection of monist accounts of moral education; given the conflict between virtues and between values, Colin Wringe (2000: 663) asserts that 'no single, entirely satisfactory formula for moral education is ultimately to be found'. In words that echo Berlin's pluralism Wringe goes on to deny the possibility of an 'ultimate teleology to which all our actions supposedly contribute or some grand design of God or nature in which the myriads of human actions fit together harmoniously as in some giant multi-dimensional jigsaw puzzle' (*ibid*: 669). Wringe rejects an approach to education in values that begins with a list of prescriptive values; he opts instead for a moral education that begins with the recognition of negative liberty. If the good life is one that is chosen by the individual from the range of worthwhile possibilities then moral education should be about encouraging individuals to use this freedom positively. On this view the virtue to be encouraged is 'moral independence' which means 'taking possession of one's own life' (Wringe, 1998: 235). It is with this view of moral education in mind that I now turn to the vexed issue of values education within a context of cultural and religious diversity.

Value pluralism, cultural minorities and values education

So far I have focused on the conflicts between values themselves and the implications of these conflicts for programmes of values education. Some reference has inevitably been made to value conflicts between cultural groups and it is to this issue that I now turn in greater detail. Andrea Baumeister (2000) argues that Berlin's value pluralism offers greater potential for understanding issues of cultural diversity than those Enlightenment liberalisms that privilege the values of universal reason and individual autonomy.[19] Baumeister focuses on Muslim communities in Britain and uses the example of Islamic critiques of Swann's Rawlsian version of liberal multicultural education to paint a picture of an increasingly multicultural British society made up of incompatible liberal and non-liberal cultures.[20] Given this diversity of values Baumeister concludes that the best that can be hoped for is a *modus vivendi* between incompatible groups of the kind that Gray advocates and which Baumeister takes to be Berlin's position.[21]

On this view the value pluralist emphasis on incompatible traditions highlights the importance of politics which must take the form of negotiation and the weighing of claims and counter-claims; this is a search not for truth, but for peaceful accommodations between competing perspectives. Value pluralists recognize that while conflict might, and should, be managed, it can never be transcended.

The debate in Chapter 2 focused on discussion about the kinds of accommodations that might be made in resolving the claims of North American non-liberal groups such as the Amish who are both relatively small in population and territorially concentrated. Baumeister acknowledges that accommodations with larger and more territorially dispersed groups such as British Muslims will not be easily resolved by the liberal state. The problem is compounded when the respect that pluralist liberals show for non-liberal minorities is not always reciprocated by these groups who may well see negotiation and compromise not as goods to be valued but as evils to be tolerated by a minority, and therefore relatively powerless, community (*ibid*: 191). In the remaining part of this chapter I turn to some of the issues that have dominated discussion about the kinds of accommodations that non-liberal religious minorities seek in the area of values education.

Mark Halstead's proposals for accommodating non-liberal religious citizens[22]

In his most recent version of Berlinian value pluralism Galston (2005: 35) appears to agree with Baumeister when he says that 'a policy of living peacefully with continuing differences may often be the best that we can do'. Claiming moral accommodation as an essential virtue in this kind of context Galston resists the 'civic totalist' importation of democratic politics into what must remain the properly private realm of families and voluntary associations. Civic purposes must not, therefore, always be allowed to trump the wishes of non-liberal individuals and groups. Galston's pluralist politics works by dividing human life into a series of spheres each enjoying a considerable degree of autonomy; this is what Galston in his earlier work called 'maximum feasible accommodation'. It is this sphere autonomy that allows individuals and groups the necessary degree of 'expressive liberty' to live according to their own views of what gives life its greatest meaning. While there is potential for the kind of group tyranny that liberals fear this can be protected against by the insistence on exit rights for dissenting individuals.[23]

In what remains of this chapter I propose to examine one example of the kinds of accommodations that value pluralism has been taken to require of the liberal state. It concerns the accommodation that has been argued for as necessary if Muslims in Britain are to enjoy the kind of 'expressive liberty' that Galston defends. I will go on to discuss these proposed accommodations in terms of the kinds of values that Berlin's liberal pluralism identifies as necessary for multicultural societies.

Contrary to Baumeister's view that Berlin's version of liberal pluralism offers considerable potential for accommodating non-liberal religious minorities such as British Muslims, Halstead (1996a) focuses on the problems that these Muslims encounter in mainstream schooling which he characterizes as being based on Berlinian liberal values such as individual autonomy and designed with the intention of taking pupils 'beyond the present and particular'.[24] In marked contrast to this liberal model of schooling Halstead describes an Islamic education that aims 'to nurture children in the faith, to make them good Muslims [who are not expected] to question the fundamentals of their faith but are expected to accept them on the authority of their elders' (*ibid*: 28).[25] While Halstead (1996b) accepts that any society must have some shared values, in a multicultural society these values will have to be of the most minimal kind because even democratic procedural values will present a threat to some traditional communities.

Aiming to base schooling for Muslim children on very 'thin' societal shared values and a 'thicker' set of Islamic community values Halstead (1995) proposes culturally differentiated schooling made up of three distinct but complementary parts. First, from political liberalism Halstead adopts a common citizenship education designed to encourage political participation in society. This is to be political rather than cultural citizenship education in order to avoid the kind of spill-over from political into cultural liberalism that political liberals such as the later Rawls acknowledge to be likely even if unintended. Second, drawing on communitarian critiques of liberalism Halstead identifies the need for education for cultural attachment. Where children come from liberal communities this will take the form of an education firmly based on cultural liberalism and an educational aim of individual autonomy but for Muslim children education for cultural attachment will be defined by Islamic ideals. Third, and in recognition that there is some danger that this second element of schooling might produce inward-looking individuals, Halstead advocates an education for cross-cultural under-standing but this, he says, will take different forms in different communities.

In a recent re-statement of this argument for differentiated curricula Halstead (2003) seems to have been persuaded by Gray that Berlinian liberalism *is* in fact consistent with an education system that accommodates non-liberal minorities. Here Halstead argues that his proposal for differentiated schooling operates on a middle ground between liberal assimilation and radical separatism. In exemplifi-cation of what this model would mean in practice Halstead suggests the follow-ing programme from which Muslim pupils would learn about homosexuality: in education for citizenship children would learn that homophobic bullying is wrong; in education for cultural attachment these same children would learn what Islam teaches about homosexuality; and in education for cross-cultural understanding Muslim children would learn that not all cultural groups view homosexuality as Muslims do. This proposal comes in the context of expressed disapproval by some Muslims about sex education in schools and in particular concerns about teaching about homosexuality. Schools are criticized for teach-ing that homosexuality is a 'natural' form of sexual orientation whereas Muslims regard homosexuality as both physically and spiritually harmful (Ashraf, Mabud and Mitchell, 1991; Sanjakdar, 2004).[26] In 1994 the Muslim Parliament of Great Britain advised Muslim parents to implement their right to withdraw their children from sex education lessons. Ten years later Baroness Uddin launched a report *Muslims on Education* which continued to protest about the lack of attention in the mainstream curriculum to Islamic perspectives on issues such as homosexuality (Forum on Islamophobia and Racism, 2004).

In a series of articles Halstead (1997, 1998[27], 1999a, 1999b) expands upon the kind of accommodations he believes should be made with regard to the edu-cation of Muslim children about homosexuality. In the context of sex education generally Halstead wants Muslim children to learn that it is proper to 'tolerate' sexual behaviour that is, from an Islamic perspective, unacceptable. 'Tolerate' is being used here in the sense of 'not interfering with that which is considered unacceptable' and Halstead is clear that toleration in this sense falls well short of being able to 'celebrate' or welcome diversity in sexual values.

It is in order to remove any tension between the citizenship requirement that education must challenge homophobic attitudes and actions and Islamic educa-tion for cultural attachment that teaches that homosexuality is an abomination that Halstead and Lewicka (1998) build their argument on the basis that Islam simply does not recognize homosexuality as a 'lifestyle'.[28] Despite a title that refers to 'a Muslim perspective' Halstead and Lewicka go on to talk about 'the Muslim perspective' as one that perceives homosexuality as behaviour rather than orientation (*ibid*: 57). Individuals on this view are no more created homo-sexual than they are created adulterous and homosexuality is to be seen as a kind of sinful behaviour that individuals should resist. Halstead and Lewicka deny that these Islamic beliefs about homosexuality are to be categorized as homophobic because homophobia is defined as a reaction to fear of homosexuality and Muslims do not fear homosexuality.

Given these 'incommensurable perspectives' between Muslims and what Halstead and Lewicka regularly call the 'gay and lesbian agenda' how are Muslim children to be educated about homosexuality? The approach that is recommended is one that Halstead (1999b) also favours for educating Muslim children about family values generally. This involves applying the three-part curriculum of citizenship, cultural attachment and cross-cultural understanding variously according to the age of the children. In the early stages of schooling children are to be taught in a way that is congruent with the values and teaching of their own families and community. Young Muslim children will be taught the Qur'anic version of the story of Lot as the basis for Islamic teaching on homosexuality.[29] In later secondary education Muslim children will learn that other communities take different views on what Halstead argues should be presented as a 'controversial' subject. The subject is described as necessarily controversial because Halstead (1999a) rejects any legitimate grounds for teaching that homosexuality is morally acceptable because to do so would be to deny respect to any religious community that denies this. Echoing Gray and Baumeister, Halstead adds: 'The most one can expect is an enlightened live-and-let-live' (*ibid*: 132) and he goes on to claim that pluralism requires of schools that they resist articulating the non-neutral view of sexuality as a matter of personal autonomy. Here then is the dilemma: how can value pluralists reconcile a commitment to equal opportunities for individuals irrespective of sexual orientation with the equally valued commitment to respect the moral perspectives of religious citizens who refuse to recognize same-sex orientations as part of legitimate human diversity?

Liberal pluralist virtues and accommodating orthodox religious views on homosexuality

Following Berlin, Crowder identified the pluralist virtue of awareness of diversity and its liberal counterpart, broad-mindedness, as crucial to living successfully in a multicultural society. Citizens do best when they have the moral imagination to see the value of, and have respect for, ways of life that they do not, and have no wish to, share. Liberals also link the capacity for self-direction with a willingness to hold views in a way that is sufficiently provisional to allow for revision of background commitments; this is something Crowder called flexibility, and saw as fundamental to personal autonomy. Liberal pluralists accept that choosing values involves loss as well as gains, a recognition that urges moderation and drawing back from holding values as absolutes. Finally, liberal pluralist respect for persons requires attention to the particulars of a situation and especially what individuals themselves express as their own wishes; this stands in marked opposition to the notion that individuals sometimes have to be made to see what is in the interests of their 'real' as opposed to 'empirical' selves.

Will Kymlicka (1996b) usefully identifies two models of pluralism and tolerance. The first of these models of pluralism is based on the tolerance of individual differences and Crowder's Berlinian liberal pluralist virtues are clearly consistent with this model of pluralism as respect for the right of individuals to direct their own lives. Kymlicka's second model of pluralism and tolerance is group-based and usually characterized as the form of toleration practised within the Ottoman Empire. This 'millet' system, as it is known, afforded considerable autonomy to religious groups. What it did not do was to protect the individual autonomy of dissenting members within the constituent communities.[30] It is this second group-based model of tolerance that is favoured by Halstead (1996c) who suggests that liberals have much to learn from this approach to tolerance.

These two models of pluralism and tolerance suggest quite different approaches to teaching about homosexuality in a diverse society. Halstead, we have seen, adopts the group-based version of tolerance to urge that education about homosexuality be culturally congruent with particular communities. John Beck (1999) responds by arguing that tolerance requires that schools teach that homosexuality is an acceptable way of life and one that individual pupils may eventually make their own. Pointing out that some Muslims are homosexual Beck denies that Islam and homosexuality are incommensurable in the way that Halstead's case requires. There is empirical evidence which supports the argument that Halstead is insufficiently attentive to diversity within the Muslim community in terms of sexual orientation and attitudes to sexual orientation (Merry, 2005a: 34 n. 8)[31] and which demonstrates the damage done to gay and lesbian students when same-sex orientation is either neglected or disparaged in the classroom (Ellis and High, 2004; Illingworth and Murphy, 2004).[32]

The approach that Halstead takes denies individual gay and lesbian Muslims the opportunity to live a life of sexual intimacy without guilt while remaining as members of their own community in good faith. Jacob Levy (2005) suggests that, given the existence of religious communities hostile to homosexuality and acknowledging the restraint that liberalism properly shows in not interfering with religious communities, this conflict between primary goods is probably inevitable. Citing Berlin, Levy considers it 'wishful thinking' to '[imagine] that eventually all good things will go together' (*ibid*: 174). On this view exit remains an important option for dissenting community members and liberals are limited to ensuring that dissenters have a safe and just space to exit to. Creating and maintaining a social space that is safe and just for all citizens irrespective of sexual orientation will require, says Levy, that civil codes are uninfluenced by religious heritage. Same-sex marriages must, for example, be sanctioned; there must be no restrictions on gay and lesbian citizens serving in the military. There will also be implications for public sector schools and universities.

I have already referred to the Saxe case where orthodox Christians claimed the right to speak out against homosexuality on grounds of free exercise of religion. Berlin's value pluralism clearly recognizes conflicts of just this kind when he argues that the freedoms of some will sometimes have to be curtailed in order to protect the freedoms of others. Berlin (1991a: 12) famously noted that 'total liberty for the wolves is death to the lambs, total liberty of the powerful, the gifted, is not compatible with the rights to a decent existence of the weak and the less gifted'. Barbara Applebaum (2003) and John Petrovic (1999) both adopt this argument of Berlin's when addressing how teachers ought to deal with homosexuality as a pedagogic issue. According to Petrovic, Berlin's argument supports his own demand that teachers refrain from expressing negative views of homosexuality.[33] Applebaum draws on Berlin's argument for limiting the freedom of some to protect the freedom of others when she addresses the views of religious students who speak out against homosexuality. For Applebaum public expression of what she calls 'assaultive speech' both wounds and silences marginalized voices in the classroom. Drawing on one of her own classroom experiences Applebaum refers to a religious student who expresses negative opinions to a gay male student who feels unable to respond publicly. Commenting on this incident Applebaum (2003: 156) argues that '[h]er freedom of expression constrains his; her freedom to speak silences him and perhaps, others like him. Her integrity compels him to waive his'. Until gay students experience equality Applebaum feels justified in adopting what she calls an 'affirmative classroom pedagogy' that silences this type of 'wounding' speech.

Conclusion: towards compromise?

Value pluralists who recognize both the rights of orthodox illiberal religious groups and the individual rights of all citizens irrespective of sexual orientation appear to face a real dilemma here. Berlin is always clear that harmonious solutions to dilemmas of this kind cannot always be found and compromise must be sought. There have been a number of attempts to resolve this dilemma and I will conclude by considering the possibilities for the kind of compromise that Berlin urges.

Jan Steutel and Ben Spiecker (2004) consider the way that Islamic leaders in The Netherlands have recently been criticized by liberal Dutch politicians for speaking out against homosexuality. These Dutch liberal politicians have feared for their liberal institutions and urged Muslims to reconsider their position.[34] Steutel and Spiecker seek reconciliation of Islamic and liberal perspectives by distinguishing a shared public morality which says that homosexuals have the right to act as they do without interference from what must remain private moralities that address the moral acceptability of homosexuality. Tolerance of homosexuality among consenting adults in the sense of non-interference provides the basis for a public morality and a sex education policy suitable for schools. All citizens, including orthodox religious citizens who disapprove of homosexuality, can be expected to sign up to this. Acceptance or non-acceptance of homosexuality is regarded as belonging within a private morality and provides no basis for public policy on sexuality including school sex education. As long as Islamic leaders acknowledge that homosexuals have the right to live their lives without interference they should be free to deny that homosexual behaviour is morally acceptable without incurring liberal criticism. Equally liberals must accept that their view of homosexuality as morally acceptable is a private morality and not one, therefore, that provides the basis for public sex education.

Stephen Macedo (2003) also examines the pluralist tension between the value of free association in illiberal groups and the individual freedoms of group members. Macedo's example comes from the American university campus where orthodox Christian student groups have sought to debar gay members from seeking office within Christian campus associations. These student groups are officially recognized on campus and therefore subject to anti-discrimination rules. Macedo argues for the right of such groups to speak out against what they see as the sinfulness of homosexuality as long as they do not exclude dissenters from seeking office and thereby seeking to change the group's view of this issue: 'Building the freedom to contest and revise opinions into expressive student groups seems to me altogether consistent with the mission of a liberal arts university' (*ibid*: 429). Turning to schools Macedo argues that it would be draconian to close religious schools that teach the sinfulness of homosexuality; to some extent Macedo draws on the lack of a social consensus on this issue to justify the right of religious schools to teach a view that many Americans share. Subject to the conditions that schools do not teach 'hatefulness' towards homosexuals and that hiring policies are non-discriminatory Macedo is content to allow religious schools to teach their intolerant views.

Not all liberals have been satisfied with this outcome. John Horton (1996) offers some reason to question the adequacy of this kind of compromise when reminding us that tolerance involves both reasons to show restraint towards that which is considered objectionable and reasons for regarding some particular practice as objectionable. If I am the kind of person who finds many practices of my fellow citizens objectionable but do nothing to interfere with them am I a tolerant person or a 'narrow-minded bigot who shows restraint'? (*ibid*: 38). While bigots who show restraint are to be preferred to those who do not, must liberals accept that this is the most that can reasonably be hoped for? Baumeister and Gray clearly thought so and they cited Berlin as authority for this view, but Berlin also worried about what freedom for the powerful can mean for the powerless. While Halstead likes to present what he calls the 'gay and lesbian agenda' as all-powerful in shaping sex education practice in schools it is worth noting that he also refers to the widespread opposition in society to homosexuality. This lack of public approval for homosexuality and continuing widespread discrimination on grounds of sexual orientation shapes the context in which gay and lesbian individuals live their lives. Harry Brighouse (1998), for example, notes that in America gay teenagers commit suicide at a rate far higher than their heterosexual peers; he attributes this clear and extreme case of unequal opportunity to the feeling these young people have that 'the world lacks a place for them' (*ibid*: 732). This situation, Brighouse argues, urges an education that recognizes homosexuality as 'a morally permissible choice within many ways of life' (*ibid*). This suggests that advocating that religious citizens 'tolerate' homosexuality is an inadequate response because there are no legitimate reasons for objecting in the first place. As Horton says, where there is no valid reason to object, there are no grounds to require tolerance. What *is* needed is not more bigots who show restraint but fewer objections to that which is unobjectionable. Bernard Williams (1996) notes that the development of more tolerant attitudes is often the outcome of a change in attitude towards that which was previously found objectionable but when, as in the case of homosexuality, there are no grounds for objections past or present, Williams prefers to call the appropriate attitude one of 'indifference' rather than toleration.

The kind of compromise that is needed here will require that religious citizens be prepared to reconsider and perhaps even sacrifice some aspect of their identity. This is the view of Stephen Gilliatt (2002) who worries that passionate commitments to identity groups make peaceful shared living impossible. Although Gilliatt is primarily concerned with ethnic conflicts such as that which divide Northern Ireland and Israel he does address religion and homosexuality:

> Jews, Muslims or Roman Catholics believe homosexuality is inherently wrong. They do not just claim to have an alternative publicly justifiable view. They claim to have a superior one that, however badly it does in debate with its opponents, remains true and unmodified because its truth is guaranteed by a sovereign law regarded as superior to the results of any democratic discussion.
>
> (*Ibid*: 28)

If Gilliatt is right when he says that '[t]he integrity of one group . . . exists only at the expense of the other' (*ibid*: 26) then values education will have to look beyond group-based values, and recognize internal group heterogeneity. This kind of values education would be more in keeping with Berlin's own reflections when he said:

> Happy are those who live under a discipline which they accept without question, who freely obey the orders of leaders, spiritual or temporal, whose word is fully accepted as unbreakable law; or those who have by their own methods, arrived at clear and unshakeable convictions about what to do and what to be that brook no possible doubt. I can only say that those who rest on such comfortable beds of dogma are victims of forms of self-induced myopia, blinkers that may make for commitment, but not for understanding of what it is to be human.
>
> (Berlin, 1991a: 13–14)

4 Faith-based and cultural identity schools

A liberal defence?

Context: recent events and support for faith-based schools

Religion and the 'School Question' in the United States of America[1]

It has been argued recently that disestablishment can work for American public schools in much the same way and for the same reasons that it has worked for religion (McConnell, 2002). According to this argument, the 'liberal-progressive hegemony' in public education denies religious citizens schooling at public expense and restricts religious schooling to those families with the necessary financial resources. For Michael McConnell disestablishing the education system, by using vouchers to end the state monopoly of providing public schooling, so that communities, including religious communities, can use public money to support their own schools, would have several benefits. It would improve schools through competition, resolve the 'culture wars' around specific curriculum areas, and educate children for democratic citizenship at least as successfully as the common school.

McConnell is arguing for a pluralistic education which he believes is more compatible with liberalism than the current American state monopoly provision of public schooling. Following John Rawls's political liberalism McConnell builds his case on the reality of an American society increasingly characterized by cultural and religious worldviews that are different and reasonable, but irreconcilable. The founders of the American state took a risk, says McConnell, in leaving religion to the private sphere but this was an essentially liberal response to pluralism. While each religious group would have liked to form the established church, none could be sure that in the event of establishment it would be their own church that would emerge dominant. In these circumstances it made sense to choose the next best option – disestablishment.[2]

The McConnell argument proceeds by claiming that an establishment approach to schooling has differed from the disestablishment doctrine that has prevailed in other areas of American policy on opinion formation. Although initially provided by religious groups, American schools came more and more to be provided by public bodies and it came to be accepted by the majority that those parents choosing a religious education for their children would have to pay for this. This process, says McConnell, has severely disadvantaged those families who understand education as needing to be closely tied up with (their own) religious belief. But if the argument is for schools that can reproduce society then a pluralist American society requires a pluralist education system, one that will 'allow subgroups to pursue their own understanding of educational aims, within bounds of reasonableness' (*ibid*: 101). Much of this chapter is concerned with what might be meant by these 'bounds of reasonableness'.

It is because he accepts that schooling can never be neutral that McConnell fears that a left-progressive 'lowest common denominator' approach to the curriculum, while too 'thin' to provide the cultural coherence necessary to underpin moral values in school, will be 'thick' enough to be as assimilative of contemporary religious citizens as the nineteenth-century Common School Movement was of Catholic children. Just as it was in the nativist era of the 1920s when Catholic citizens were suspected of lack of loyalty there is distrust of the democratic potential of religious citizens today. For McConnell, 'the Protestant hegemony of the past' has shifted to become 'the secular progressive hegemony of the present' (*ibid*: 117–118) and religious citizens are left with only the right of exit from public education that they gained through *Pierce* back in 1925.[3]

McConnell concludes that public funding of faith-based schools will allow schools to provide moral teaching based in the particularistic curriculum of a coherent cultural context. All that citizens need agree about are the political principles of a society of free and equal individuals with each group free to ground these principles in its own comprehensive tradition. Faith schools would, says McConnell, be no less segregated than existing public schools and no less committed to democratic values and so he concludes that America has as much to gain from educational disestablishment as it has from the same approach to religion.

There is little in McConnell's account that suggests what he might mean by 'reasonable limits'. His survey of American religious groups reveals no worries about democratic compatibility other than the Anabaptist reluctance to vote. Even the Bob Jones University[4] appears to McConnell to be acceptable in terms of its racial teachings. Neither is there any reference to the kind of gender issues that have concerned liberal critics of fundamentalist religious education.[5] There is only some suggestion that if religious groups were to be so authoritarian to provide children with 'little choice but to conform to religious dictates imposed by their families' (*ibid*: 133) this would constitute a problem for liberalism but it is 'materialist hedonism' that strikes McConnell as the greater threat to youthful independence. In response to McConnell's pluralism, Amy Gutmann (2002) denies that a diversity of schools is a good in itself. Schools, she argues, should be valued for what and how they teach rather than simply because they are chosen by parents. Greater diversity of schools would be achieved by lifting restrictions on discrimination but this is not something that liberals should favour. What this debate between McConnell and Gutmann reveals is the centrality to the faith schools debate of what conditions, if any, ought to determine liberal support for faith-based schooling.

Faith-based schooling in England

For almost two centuries the British government has been involved in funding faith-based schooling of one kind or another. First to receive the benefits of state funding were the Church of England and the Non-Conformist churches followed by the Catholic and to a lesser extent the Jewish faith communities. Since 1998 Muslim, Sikh, Seventh Day Adventist and Greek Orthodox schools have extended the diversity of state-funded schools founded on a religious identity. In his historical account of the development of faith-based schools George Skinner (2002) shows how the dual system of secular and religious schools was intended to provide the basis for state support of religious schools while retaining a degree of commonality through the curriculum and its inspection. Although this long-established dual system of religious and secular schools provided a framework for extending funding to religious communities more recently established in the United Kingdom, this has not taken place without some considerable debate and the principle of funding for a range of faith communities that fall outside the more liberal wings of the Judeo-Christian tradition is by no means uncontested. This chapter will be concerned with several attempts to provide a liberal defence of faith-based schooling in the face of arguments that faith schools undermine social cohesion and seriously inhibit the development of children's individual autonomy.

Since the 1980s faith-based schooling has enjoyed something of a resurgence attracting growing numbers of children from the Islamic and Jewish communities in particular. Catholic schools have enjoyed growing recognition of their particular qualities and the Church of England has been responding by making the case both for increasing the number of church schools and making clear their particularity.[6] Helena Miller (2001) reports a doubling of the number of children in full-time Jewish education during the last quarter of the twentieth century. She puts this increase in demand for Jewish schooling into the context of calls by senior members of the community for education that supports Jewish identity and continuity (see for example Sacks, 1994). Whereas private and public schooling both provided opportunities for Jewish parents to choose a faith-based education for their children, Muslim parents wanting a similar educational experience for their children prior to 1998 were forced into private provision by the absence of state-funded Islamic schools. The history of the Islamia School in Brent, London, provides the best-known example of the unsuccessful campaigning for public Islamic education that featured regularly in the educational press and in academic journals through the 1970s and 1980s (see for example Iqbal, 1974, 1977). Islamia was established as a private Islamic school in 1982 and its early applications to join the dual state system through voluntary-aided status were rejected first on grounds of inadequate buildings and then because of the availability of surplus school places in the district of the school. Outside London the story was much the same. In 1983 the local education authority in Bradford turned down applications from the Muslim Parents' Association in that city to turn five schools with a majority Muslim population into Islamic voluntary-aided schools and in 1989 the neighbouring authority Kirklees Local Education Authority rejected an application for the same status for Zakaria Muslim Girls' School.

Muslim campaigners protested at the apparent inequity in refusing state funding to Muslim schools when most Christian and some Jewish parents enjoyed this facility relatively unproblematically. Local and central government appeared to be unmoved by this argument and a majority of the members of the Swann Committee Inquiry into the Education of Ethnic Minority Children (Great Britain: Department of Education and Science, 1985) supported a stance that rejected extending funding to Muslim schools on the grounds that religious, and the consequent ethnic, segregation would not be helpful either to race relations or to the educational performance of minority culture children.[7] Supporters of the Islamia campaign pointed to the ethnic diversity of this mono-faith school and contrasted this with the ethnic homogeneity of the pupil population of many secular schools.

New legislation in 1988 and 1993 appeared to offer the possibility of state funding for Islamic and other kinds of faith-based school (Walford, 2000). Some campaigners encouraged Muslim parents to use the arrangements introduced by the 1988 Education Act that allowed parents to vote to take their schools out of local authority control and to take their funding directly from government; schools 'opting out' in this way were to become what were known as grant-maintained schools. Where a school had a majority of Muslim students this seemed to offer the opportunity to secure grant-maintained status and eventually change the nature of the school to one of a faith basis (Cumper, 1990). Then in 1993 the Education Act offered the option of organizations, including faith groups, applying to sponsor a grant-maintained school. Despite the rhetoric of parental choice that was said to underpin these two Conservative strategies for diversifying the nature of schools available to parents, neither led to the creation of any faith-based schools outside the existing Christian and Jewish traditions. This came about partly as a result of rejection of applications received and partly as a result of religious communities rejecting the conditions of curriculum control that would have accompanied state funding (Walford, 2003).

It was not until the election of the Labour Government in 1997 that funding was finally granted to faith schools that stood outside the existing pattern of mainly Christian schools along with a small number of Jewish state-funded religious schools. Having given early notice of its intention to honour its manifesto pledge to look seriously at the question of extending funding to a range of faith-based schools previously denied this kind of support the new government admitted two Muslim schools, one being Islamia School, to the state-funded sector. These Islamic schools were soon joined by a small number of other faith-based schools.[8]

In 2001 the government announced its intention to continue this policy of increasing the number and types of faith-based school when it published the Green Paper *Schools: Building on Success* (Great Britain: Department for Education and Employment, 2001: para 4. 19). This underlined the government's

intention to support a major expansion of faith-based schooling as part of its programme of favouring diversity and choice in education. Faith schools were seen as
deriving both academic and social benefit from their distinctive mission and ethos;
something that set them apart from 'ordinary' schools. Almost immediately,
however, circumstances conspired to cast doubt on the wisdom of this policy.
During the summer of 2001 there were conflicts between ethno-religious groups
that led to rioting in several northern towns (Bradford, Oldham, Burnley) and this
situation brought about some reconsideration of what faith schools had to offer so
that, when a decision was taken to extend state funding to a Muslim girls' school in
Bradford (Feversham College), opposition grew.[9] In the wake of these disturbances
and uncertainties the Cantle Report, *Community Cohesion* (Great Britain: Home
Office, 2001) questioned the contribution of faith schools to a cohesive society and
argued for a more inclusive approach to school admissions in order to give pupils a
more direct experience of a range of communities. By the time of the publication of
its White Paper, *Schools: Achieving Success*, in September of 2001, the Department
for Education and Skills had shifted position somewhat to emphasize the desirability of faith schools that were more inclusive in their pupil population (Great Britain:
Department for Education and Skills, 2001). The terrorist attacks in the United
States in September 2001 and the resulting inter-community tensions in the United
Kingdom reinforced fears about segregation so that, by Spring 2002, teachers
attending their annual conferences were expressing major concerns about faith
schools.[10] These teacher union fears about the proliferation of single faith schools
resurfaced in 2004 in response to a report *Muslims on Education* produced by the
Association of Muslim Social Scientists which called for more Islamic schools
(Forum on Islamophobia and Racism, 2004). Both the National Union of Teachers
and the Secondary Headteachers Association expressed concern about what they
perceived as the ghettoization of schools.[11] These concerns of teachers have also
been reflected in the views of members of the Office of the Deputy Prime Minister's Select Committee in 2004 and in the results of opinion polls suggesting public
concern about faith schools in the wake of the terrorist attacks in London in July
2005. Despite these expressions of concern the government is, at the time of
writing, pressing on with plans to find ways to integrate some of the existing
independent faith schools into the state sector.[12]

The faith schools question can be seen as part of the much wider debate about
liberal responses to cultural groups. It is also important to note that liberal criticism of the threat to individual freedom that these groups can present has come
from within as well as from outside minority cultural groups. Black and Asian
women's groups have complained that the state fails to protect the individual
interests of minority women because of its uncertainty and lack of confidence in
responding to discriminatory practices when these are seen as culturally based.
For example, in a letter to the *Independent* newspaper in June 1999 Hannana
Siddiqui and Shamshad Hussain complain about state agencies such as the
police failing to treat the domestic abuse of Asian women seriously, 'often
adopting a mediatory and conciliatory approach, appeasing men for the sake of
good community relations'.[13]

These arguments are well known to philosophers of education who have often debated the compatibility of religious upbringing and schooling with liberal educational aims designed to foster children's personal autonomy (for example: Groothius, 2004; Hand, 2002, 2003, 2004; Short, 2003; Siegal, 2004). In what follows I initially identify two versions of the liberal defence of faith schools. The first of these defences questions the belief that faith schools are necessarily socially divisive (Short, 2002). The second defence disputes the claim that faith schools are insufficiently supportive of individual autonomy; in fact, given particular institutional circumstances, faith schools, on this account, are supportive of an individual autonomy that benefits from early education in an institutional context that is culturally congruent with the family and community (De Jong and Snik, 2002; Williams, 1998). I then develop my own argument (Burtonwood, 2003b) that these defences rely on a division of faith schools into 'strong' and 'moderate' types with the defence applying only to those of the moderate kind. Many faith communities aspire, I argue, to faith schools of the strong variety and cannot be accommodated by these conditional liberal defences. Alan Dagovitz (2004) acknowledges these circumstances and seeks an alternative liberal defence based on political liberalism. After arguing against this third attempt to find a liberal defence of faith schools I conclude with a consideration of what a Berlinian liberal pluralism would contribute to the debate about the place of faith-based schooling in culturally diverse societies.

Liberal defences of the faith-based school

Liberals who oppose faith-based schooling have been accused of 'neo-colonialist' oppression of minority religious groups (Wright, 2003) and of 'intellectual prejudice' bordering on ethnic prejudice (Grace, 2003). Specific criticisms of Islamic schools have been described as 'Islamophobic' (Donohoue Clyne, 2004). Not surprisingly, then, Dagovitz (2004) regards the issue of faith schooling as crucial if the tension between religion and liberalism is to be resolved. This tension is apparent within and between liberal documents such as the Universal Declaration of Human Rights which establishes parental rights in decisions about the schooling of their children (Article 26/3) and the Convention on the Rights of the Child (Article 29) which establishes children's rights to freedom of opinion and expression. Similar tensions have arisen in the United States where government has recently given some grounds for optimism to those religious groups campaigning for state support for religious activity. Laura Underkuffler (2001) notes that those Americans supporting greater government funding of religious groups restrict that support to well-known and long-established religious communities who are seen to be consistent with mainstream values and she concludes that, given the 'deep, divisive, and volatile' nature of religion in a plural society, government is well advised to avoid constitutional difficulties by remaining out of the faith schools picture.

The argument from social cohesion

In response to liberal concerns about the role of faith-based schools in culturally diverse societies there have been two major replies. The first argues that faith-based schools present no threat to social cohesion; the second claims that concerns that faith-based schools interfere with the development of the individual autonomy of pupils are ill-founded. I will start with the argument from social cohesion. Geoffrey Short (2002) draws on his empirical work on Jewish schools to argue that, given an appropriate curriculum, faith schools need not be socially divisive.[14] Teaching about other cultures is, he says, sufficient to compensate for the religious homogeneity of the faith school. Short divides his sample of Jewish schools broadly into two categories. First there are the (mainly progressive) schools where teachers are keen to teach about other cultures and religions, and seek to give their pupils opportunities for inter-cultural contact wherever possible. These schools could be described as 'moderate' in the sense that Kevin McDonough (1998) uses this term to describe a type of cultural identity school in the United States. Moderate cultural identity schools seek to provide children with an initial conception of the good but one that is revisable by pupils as they mature. On this moderate view children are expected eventually to subject their own traditions to critical review. In marked contrast the orthodox schools referred to by Short approximate more closely to what McDonough called 'strong cultural identity schools'. I will begin with an account of this type of school.[15]

The strong cultural identity school

The case of the Torah Maczikei Hadass School in London in 1985 provides some insight into the strong version of cultural identity school. On being criticized by inspectors for failing to prepare pupils for life in the wider society the governors of this independent Orthodox Jewish school declared no interest in this particular educational purpose. Their community, they said, was unimpressed by the wider society and was concerned only to prepare their children for life within their own limited cultural context.[16] In her historical account of the development of the Jewish school in the United Kingdom, Miller (2001) refers to this type of school as a 'thickening agent' designed to resist secularization and assimilation in the interests of intergenerational cultural and religious continuity – a gain that is achieved, she acknowledges, at the price of considerable insularity.

Some advocates of the Islamic school for Muslim children build their case on the need for an education of this strong identity kind. Religion, on this view, must underpin the whole educational experience within an all-embracing and comprehensive culture (Ashraf, 1993). A similar defence of Islamic schooling (Bleher, 1996: 64) asserts the extensiveness and durability of this education in stating that '[t]he main aim ought to be to install certain essential concepts within the personality of the child such that they become an integral part of his or her being'. This comprehensiveness challenges the public–private distinction favoured by political liberals by arguing instead that Islam provides a code of conduct for the whole of life (Siddiqui, 1997); where the National Curriculum conflicts with community educational values, state funding has to be rejected (Hewitt, 1996).[17] The comprehensiveness of the strong identity model is again reflected in Shaik Mabud's (1992) account of an Islamic science curriculum. Here science is based on faith and the curriculum is developed in such a way as to include the 'Divine origin' of all creation. On this account science must not be allowed to conflict with religious teaching and scientific values such as precision and accuracy are less important than religious values such as compassion and mercy. Knowledge based on rational investigation is less valued than that which comes from God. Chris Hewer (2001: 522) agrees with Mabud that in such schools the pedagogy is properly based on the authority of the teacher who is expected to expound what is regarded as ultimate truth. Evidence of this pedagogy can also be found in Doret De Ruyter's account of schools belonging to the Dutch Reformed Church; here critical thinking is frowned upon and children are encouraged to think of their futures in terms of gender-specific roles. There is no attempt to demonstrate respect for members of other faiths (De Ruyter, 1999; De Ruyter and Miedema, 2000).

Clearly schools that reflect the strong cultural identity model will have difficulties in accepting the kind of conditions that are attached to state funding in the United Kingdom. Geoffrey Walford (2001, 2002) demonstrates the lack of interest in state funding shown by some evangelical Christian schools when he quotes the headteacher of one such school: 'I believe most Christian schools are set up to be independent . . . any compromise on this idealism (such as teaching evolution as fact, deviant sex education, acceptance of other faiths as alternatives) would soon weaken their stand and nullify their reason for existence' (Walford, 2001: 372–373). These schools use science materials that acknowledge Biblical infallibility; teach history as 'the record of how God is working out his purpose'; and offer mathematics as evidence of 'the amazing order and patterns that God has provided' (Walford, 2002: 411).

The orthodox schools in Short's investigations are of this strong cultural identity kind. In these schools multiculturalism is 'a taboo subject' and one that is 'not in the ethos of the school' (Short, 2002: 48). Parents are described by teachers as uninterested in multicultural education, perhaps even attracted by the 'all-white' nature of the Jewish school. Books and resources to be used in the school are vetted for inappropriate images to ensure that schooling is consistent with the values of the home. These schools clearly approximate to what McDonough calls 'strong' cultural identity schools which 'seek to foster a separate education of extensive scope and duration that is meant to ensure that children adhere to a distinct ancestral identity throughout their lives' (McDonough, 1998: 464). They are the kind of schools favoured by communities that Michael Walzer (2003: 126) refers to as 'totalizing', in that they claim 'a right to reproduce themselves – that is, to do whatever they think necessary to pass on their way of life to their children'.

The moderate cultural identity school

In contrast to the strong identity version McDonough (1998: 464) describes the moderate cultural identity schools as providing 'an education of more limited scope and duration', one that 'is meant to offer young children an initial, stable conception of the good'. This type of school is more cosmopolitan in its openness to a range of cultures while retaining the value of an education particular to a cultural context. Children learn to appreciate their ancestral traditions but in a way that allows them to eventually examine these traditions in the light of alternatives. There is empirical evidence to support the view that children educated in moderate faith-based schools take a positive view of diversity while retaining a sense of their own identity. For example a small-scale study of teenage children in Catholic and Jewish schools reported that '[w]ithin both schools there is a recognition, even a positive valuation, of diversity which goes alongside quite a strong sense of identity' (Scholefield, 2001: 52). De Ruyter (1999) notes how liberal Christian schools in the Netherlands (in contrast to those of the Dutch Reformed Church) seek to incorporate criticality into the curriculum by recognizing criticality as a Christian tradition. These schools perceive no conflict between their religious and civic purposes. There are Islamic schools that also have the characteristics of the moderate school. Walford (2002) refers to some Islamic schools that employ non-Muslim teachers and where there is only a very limited attempt to integrate Islam throughout the curriculum. In another small-scale study of Church of England aided secondary schools headteachers are reported to prefer to think of their schools contributing to the whole diverse community rather than providing a specifically religious education for one part of that community; as one of these headteachers put it: 'We don't try to be a Church. Their Churches are at home' (Colson, 2004: 80).

In response to critics of faith-based schooling Gerald Grace and Geoffrey Short both argue that there is no evidence to support the view that faith schools undermine social cohesion. Grace (2003) is particularly concerned with Catholic schools and he describes the post-Vatican II version of the Catholic school as perfectly in tune with liberal society and the claims of social justice. Short's account of his sample of Jewish faith schools approximates closely to the moderate version of cultural identity school. He refers to the way that these schools adopt multicultural curricula, employ non-Jewish teachers and seek every opportunity to put their children into contact with members of other faith groups. These characteristics of the moderate school are central to Short's argument that these schools present no threat to social cohesion. The argument proceeds in five parts. First, there is a challenge to the contact hypothesis on which much criticism of faith schools is said to rest. According to the contact hypothesis social cohesion requires that children gain experience of members of other cultural groups through direct contact; the common school provides the obvious opportunity for this kind of inter-cultural experience. Put simply, we learn to get on with others by getting to know them and, in so doing, we break through the usual stereotypes that hinder cross-cultural understanding.[18] The contact hypothesis has been subjected to several challenges. Interpersonal contact may not lead to positive evaluations of out-group members, it has been argued, unless certain conditions are met. These conditions relate to such things as the nature of the collaborative tasks undertaken and the status and skills of the individuals taking part.

Even where supportive conditions are present and the contact is successful, there is no guarantee that positive evaluations are extended beyond the particular individuals with whom the contact has been experienced. Although in earlier work Short (1993) appeared to be persuaded that, given appropriate conditions and suitable warnings about the dangers of generalizing from limited experience, educational benefit could be gained from contact between members of different cultural groups, he is now much more dismissive of these benefits. Short (2002) doubts that the necessary conditions for successful inter-cultural contact are likely to be present and he argues that it is the curriculum that is important rather than opportunities for direct experience of peers from other cultural groups.

Short develops the second part of his case for the faith school on his evidence that the moderate schools within his sample adopted a curriculum that included teaching about other cultures. In his earlier work on Holocaust education Short (1994) is very specific about the importance of this kind of multicultural education when he argues for educating all children about Judaism and Jewish culture; this is necessary, he says, to counter existing misconceptions and stereotypes. It is therefore somewhat surprising that although he recognizes that strong identity schools resist this type of teaching, preferring to rely on a generalized respect for human beings as a basis for living in a culturally diverse society, Short refuses to rule out the possibility that the generalized respect for human beings taught in the orthodox schools might be sufficient to achieve social cohesion. In order to support this conclusion Short turns to his evidence of pupils in the orthodox schools complaining that their schools fail to address multiculturalism in their teaching. What this pupil complaint shows, says Short, is that regardless of their neglect of cultural diversity, these schools have managed to produce individuals whose social awareness is sufficient to see what is lacking in their own education.

Third, Short turns to the claim that faith schools achieve better academic results. He attributes this to the identity-enhancement and high levels of self-esteem that in turn are said to improve employability, tolerance and ultimately social cohesion. Fourth, Short denies any necessary link between ignorance and negativity towards other groups. Nothing, he argues, follows logically from ignorance; the most he will allow is that ignorance may leave individuals susceptible to prejudice. Finally, Short makes much of the willingness of the schools he investigated to employ teachers from outside the Jewish community; these teachers, he notes, are often used in the moderate schools to teach children about the different cultures that they represent.[19] In summary, Short argues that faith schools of the moderate type contribute to social cohesion despite not being inclusive in their pupil population. The more orthodox schools present more of a difficulty, but even here Short does not rule out the possibility that, with some reform of their curriculum practice, such schools can operate as a force for social cohesion.

Critics of faith schooling, such as Susan Moller Okin and Rob Reich (1999), would challenge those teachers in Short's sample of schools who appear to see their role as necessarily restricted by the prejudices of parents. The school has a civic responsibility to go beyond these limits by providing an environment where pupils can 'come into dialogue with and negotiate issues of moral and cultural difference' (*ibid*: 293). Recent work in the field of religious education demonstrates the value of this kind of dialogue across religious traditions both in culturally diverse settings (see, for example, Weisse, 2003) and in situations where demographic patterns demand more creative solutions to bringing pupils into contact (Ipgrave, 2003).[20] Short himself does sometimes appear to be more open to the benefits of contact for reducing stereotypes; when regretting, for example, the way that the use of Saturday for inter-school sports events reduces opportunities for Jewish children to get involved with their peers from other communities (Short and Lenga, 2002: 344).

It has been demonstrated by Sally Schagen *et al.* (2002) that arguments for faith schools that suggest causal links between academic achievement, enhanced self-esteem and greater tolerance toward out-groups rely on empirical evidence that is less than convincing and it is therefore generally conceded by supporters of faith-based schooling that the argument from academic achievement is the weakest part of the pro-faith school case (Jackson, 2003).[21] It is also true to say that academic achievement is not necessarily a major motivation for many supporters of strong identity faith schools.

Short claims much for the willingness of Jewish schools to employ non-Jewish teachers and for the role that these teachers play in providing a window through which Jewish children might view other cultural backgrounds. For a view on the employment of teachers in the strong identity version of faith schools it is pertinent to turn to Chris Hewer's (2001) defence of Muslim schools. Hewer makes a case for the funding of Islamic schools, not on the basis of their moderate qualities, but because of Muslim requirements for the strong version of cultural identity school where the curriculum and pedagogy reflects an epistemology of divine revelation. Teachers in such schools, he says, must model the Islamic moral code and in all aspects of their lives. Following this line of reasoning, Hewer suggests the need to allow teacher contracts in these schools that would enable governors to remove staff who do not meet these requirements. Specifically Hewer is concerned that equal opportunities legislation would preclude an Islamic school from removing a teacher on grounds of sexual orientation. This, as we have already seen, is the kind of case made by William Galston (1995) for allowing a fundamentalist Christian school to remove a married woman teacher who wanted to return to work soon after the birth of her child. Galston recognized the harm done to the individual rights of this woman but decided in favour of a religious community to assert its view that mothers of young children belong at home.

Faith schools of the strong identity kind resist the kind of conditions that

Short requires if he is make the case for the socially cohesive potential of faith schools. Schools of the moderate kind might well have a part to play in a culturally diverse but socially cohesive society but these are not the schools that, at least some, religious communities actually want. There may be a case for supporting strong faith schools but that case needs to recognize these schools for what they are and to accept that at least in some instances that case is not to be made on grounds of social cohesion.

The argument from cultural coherence and individual autonomy

A second line of argument for the faith-based school rejects the claim that these schools interfere with the development of children's individual autonomy. In an early statement of this position Elmer Thiessen (1987) rejects liberal criticisms of faith-based schooling that draw upon a contrast between education as transmission and education as the development of rationality. For Thiessen these are not different models of how children should be educated but different phases of an education for rational autonomy; an early transmissionist phase provides the context against which children can eventually develop critical rationality. On this view the faith school provides an ideal institutional context for managing the gradual transition between these two equally important phases.

This argument has recently been developed by Johan De Jong and Ger Snik (2002)[22] who base their liberal defence of the faith-based school on Kymlicka's account of the relationship between liberalism, cultural context and individual autonomy. Will Kymlicka (2001) argues that liberals committed to the value of individual autonomy must support minority rights to public institutions that foster cultural identity because it is within this cultural context that individuals actually practise autonomy, that is by making choices about their life plans and projects. In valuing choice, liberals must value the cultural contexts within which individuals make those choices. For De Jong and Snik this translates into a defence of the faith school as providing support for this kind of cultural context.[23]

This is, however, far from being an unqualified defence of the faith school. Cultural contexts, and therefore faith schools, are to be supported only insofar as they contribute to the ultimate achievement of individual autonomy. Like Thiessen, De Jong and Snik adopt a phased approach to the schooling of the children of religious communities by restricting faith-based schooling to what they call the 'formative education' characteristic of the primary phase of schooling. This is to be balanced by an education beyond the primary phase that will privilege individual autonomy. In a similar defence of faith schooling Kevin Williams (1998) refers to this as what he calls the 'educational condition' which requires that teaching is conducted in such a way as to foster individual autonomy because although:

> [l]iberal democrats aspire to respect, within the limits of potential harm to others, the right of groups or communities to live the kinds of lives they

choose for themselves ... the right of these communities is qualified by the rights of individuals to make choices for themselves about their beliefs, commitments and lifestyles and to be enabled through education to make these choices.

(*Ibid*: 36)[24]

Faith schools are also expected to contribute to civic culture by providing an education that enables children to develop as citizens of a liberal democracy and this constitutes Williams's second (civic) condition for supporting faith schools. De Jong and Snik agree that faith schools must cultivate values consistent with liberal democracy and they specify that faith schools, including those in the primary phase, must be open to diversity, and so 'the primary culture to be cultivated in denominational schools should be liberal' (De Jong and Snik, 2002: 584). In effect this means that the liberal defence of faith schools that calls upon arguments to do with individual autonomy is restricted to moderate cultural identity schools in just the same way as the defence based on social cohesion.

It is far from clear that all religious communities would be prepared to accept any proposal to restrict 'formative education' to the early years.[25] As indicated earlier, what distinguishes strong cultural identity schools is a concern to retain this kind of education throughout children's schooling. Individual autonomy as defined by some liberal educators (for example, Steutel and Spiecker, 1999) requires that individuals have the ability and disposition not only to assert a particular view of the good life but to step back from that view and subject it to critical analysis. I have already noted that for De Jong and Snik this kind of review is both important and best facilitated by children being made aware of alternative religious beliefs and traditions. But as Nomi Stolzenberg (1993) showed in connection with the *Mozert* case, this is a view of education emphatically rejected by the Christian fundamentalist Mozerts who regarded the exposure of their children to alternative religious perspectives as enough to risk their own salvation and that of their children. On this view even where children reject alternatives and remain true to their own heritage this would still involve what is essentially a loss of innocence.

Consider how the condition of eventual autonomy facilitated by exposure to alternative religious beliefs must appear to advocates of integrated Islamic schooling. Hewer's view has already been cited in connection with teachers as models of community values. Hewer (2001: 52) also argues that, because there are no secular subjects in the Islamic worldview, '[e]very aspect of study should be permeated by Islamic values and the divinely ordained harmony should be brought out by the educational process'. On this view ultimate truth is given and immutable and the role of the school is to transmit that truth. Reference has been made to a model of Islamic science (Mabud, 1992) that operates exclusively within the sphere of religious faith and this supports Halstead's (1996a) argument that the schooling favoured by some religious communities is one that is at odds with liberalism. A distinguishing feature of the strong version of faith schooling exemplified by Mabud is the denial of the possibility of compartmentalizing knowledge. This denial is in marked contrast to those liberal defences of moderate faith schools that rely on the compartmentalization of knowledge. Graham Haydon (1994), for example, invites us to think about a Christian teacher of science who thinks about science in a way that is 'qualitatively indistinguishable' from an atheist. Insofar as this is true, then according to Haydon, any school that teaches science cannot fail to expose its pupils to the secular world and secular ways of thinking. But it is this compartmentalization between the sacred and the secular that Mabud, and at least some faith schools, would resist.

It has been argued by Michael Hand (2003) that faith schools are indoctrinatory in a way that parents, who set out to initiate their children into their own religious tradition, are not. Short (2003) responds by arguing that faith schools (i) do not set out to indoctrinate and (ii) would likely prove unable to do so successfully even should they try because of pupils' exposure to other traditions in a diverse society. Short offers evidence for this defence by providing Anglican and Catholic school curriculum documentation favouring non-indoctrinatory pedagogy together with statements from those Jewish schools (Short, 2002) where headteachers report a commitment to multi-faith religious teaching. To Hand's argument that parents are absolved of indoctrination because it is rational for children to believe what their parents, as perceived authority figures about religion, tell them while teachers cannot be so absolved because they are not perceived by pupils to be authorities on religion, Short replies that there is no evidence for this suggestion and every reason to suppose that some teachers at least are likely to be perceived as religious authorities. The main thrust of Short's argument for excluding faith schools from the charge of indoctrination, however, relies on faith schools adopting particular pedagogic approaches and we have already seen that these approaches are acceptable to some but not all faith schools. Short's version of the defence against the liberal criticism of indoctrination by faith schools is therefore conditional on type of faith school and restricted to those of the moderate kind.

While some liberal defenders of the faith school such as De Jong and Snik, and Short, rely on the part that awareness of other traditions plays in facilitating individual autonomy, other supporters of a phased initiation into autonomy seem to believe that this can be achieved without going beyond children's own religious tradition. Ian MacMullen follows Thiessen in arguing for a two-stage education towards autonomy, one that includes an elementary schooling that provides a 'relatively secure *provisional* ethical identity' (MacMullen, 2004: 602, original emphasis). Here the ethical messages transmitted in school must be in harmony with those of the home so as to provide a secure and stable starting point but one that is not 'so firmly rooted as to be immune from future reflection and revision' (*ibid*: 603). According to MacMullen, De Jong and Snik are wrong to require exposure to alternative traditions during the elementary phase of schooling because the 'reasoning capacities and inclinations that are the first step on the road to ethical autonomy' (*ibid*: 613) can be developed by alerting children to the difficulties in interpreting religious authorities within their own tradition and thereby gaining their acceptance of reasonable disagreement. In this way the foundations of future autonomy are laid because children are initiated into their own religious tradition in a way that does not by-pass their reason. This appears to be the kind of balance between 'rootedness' and 'openness' that Terence McLaughlin has often sought in arguing for the compatibility of a religious upbringing with liberal principles (McLaughlin, 1984, 1990). In a recent defence of a type of religious education based within a religious tradition Alexander and McLaughlin (2003) start from 'rootedness' in the tradition but this is then developed in a way that excludes the possibility of indoctrination. This is said to be perfectly compatible with those religious traditions that have 'embraced the challenges of the Enlightenment' (*ibid:* 369) and, although McLaughlin's defence of faith schooling has mostly been couched in the context of liberal Catholic schools (for example, McLaughlin, 1996), Alexander and McLaughlin call for sensitivity before ascribing any 'uncritical confessionalism' to other religious traditions that rely for their criticality on internal debate rather than reflection stimulated by an awareness of different perspectives.[26]

Even with these sensitivities in mind it does appear that liberal defences of the faith school are hedged with conditions, both civic and educational, that limit this line of defence to what has been referred to here as the moderate cultural identity school. Some members of religious communities argue the case for separate schooling in terms much more closely related to the strong version of faith schooling. How to react to this strong version of faith schooling that denies a division between the sacred and the secular and bases its pedagogy on a cultural transmission model of knowledge transfer is the real challenge facing liberals. It is not only the moderate faith school but the strong cultural identity version that demands a response from liberals.

The argument from political liberalism

Dagovitz (2004: 165) puts the issue of faith schooling at the centre of the debate about tensions between liberalism and religion and he warns that, '[i]f faith schools are necessarily incompatible with liberal values, then liberals will have to admit that publicly funded denominational schools are an impossibility, or at least a liability, in a state that seeks to prepare students to be good liberal citizens'. Dagovitz refers to attempts to reconcile faith schooling with liberal values but he agrees that the condition of individual autonomy required by those who seek this reconciliation ultimately proves unacceptable to, at least some, religious communities that seek their own publicly funded faith schools. Nevertheless Dagovitz believes that a liberal defence of faith schooling remains possible as long as the liberalism is of the political, rather than comprehensive type.[27] Political liberalism, says Dagovitz, is not tied to individual choice in the area of religion in the way that comprehensive liberals require. All that political liberalism requires is that individuals are able to form and revise a conception of the good in the way that Rawls (1993: 19; 1999: 146) requires, and Rawls says nothing about choosing one's religion because many religious citizens will reject a notion of individual autonomy that extends beyond the political realm to include moral issues. Political liberalism, then, allows a notion of autonomy that excludes choice between religions. It follows that faith schools that limit their pupils' ability to choose between religions are compatible with political liberalism.

Dagovitz distinguishes 'conception of the good' from 'comprehensive doctrine' in Rawlsian political liberalism in the following way. A conception of the good is a collection of values, such as 'treating people kindly, being industrious and respecting my family' (*ibid*: 171); it is the *justification* of such values that depends on an individual's comprehensive doctrine which might very well be a religion. As examples Dagovitz cites the Christian who offers a Biblical justification for treating people as free and equal persons and the Kantian who justifies the same value in terms of recognizing people as ends in themselves rather than means. Equally two Christians might have different conceptions of the good, one may be liberal and the other conservative, yet they 'share an epistemological stance: they believe that the doctrine of Christianity is the source of justification for moral beliefs' (*ibid*: 171). These liberal and conservative Christians may have very different views on homosexuality (different conceptions of the good) and political liberalism requires that they be able to reflect on these views critically. What political liberalism does not require is that they reflect critically on religion as though this was also a matter of choice.

Dagovitz goes on to develop this line of argument by defending the faith school in terms of compatibility with political (but not comprehensive) liberalism. Unlike Gutmann (1995) Dagovitz believes that the civic education demanded by political liberalism differs from what comprehensive liberals require. While political liberals require citizens to show respect for members of different communities they do not assume that only individuals capable of standing back critically from their own way of life are capable of such respect: 'In the end, there is no logical connection between unswerving religious faith and illiberal values in the political sense' (*ibid*: 176). Liberal philosophers (Dagovitz cites Burtonwood, 2003b and Gutmann, 1995) are said to make this connection by focusing on extreme religious groups such as the Mozerts and, to a lesser extent, the Amish, who make claims that are atypical of religious groups generally. For the most part, says Dagovitz, the claims of faith school advocates, including those who favour the strong cultural identity version (though not the Mozerts and maybe not the Amish: see *ibid*: 176–178), are compatible with political liberalism as long as they teach liberal values such as anti-racism, anti-sexism, mutual respect between faith groups, and recognition of society as an association of free and equal persons.

It is not clear to me that Dagovitz achieves the reconciliation he seeks. He sets out to show that once the claims of political liberalism are accepted as less demanding than those of comprehensive liberals – and specifically exclude the comprehensive liberal requirement that individuals choose their religious commitments – then liberalism becomes compatible with faith schools of both moderate and strong types. In fact he seeks to make the moderate/strong distinction irrelevant to arguments for faith schooling. But by admitting that many of the Mozert and Amish claims are incompatible with political as well as comprehensive liberalism he re-admits the significance of this distinction and opens the door to arguments that the category of faith schools incompatible with both forms of liberalism goes beyond the Mozerts and the Amish. For example, Dagovitz cites Meira Levinson (1997) for evidence that British Muslim advocates of faith schooling accept a national curriculum that emphasizes liberal values. While this is true of some Muslims it is clearly challenged by others who specifically make their case for faith schooling on the grounds of the inappropriateness of a liberal curriculum for Muslim pupils. In the end Dagovitz uses the less demanding claims of political liberalism to broaden the category of moderate faith schools compatible with liberalism but there remain those strong identity schools that even political liberals must reject.[28] Defending these schools requires a different kind of liberal argument and it is to this that I now turn.

Berlin and an alternative approach to faith-based schooling

Eamonn Callan (1988: 183)) asks whether the examined life can be made compatible with a life of faith and, if so, how any residual tensions are to be managed in terms of faith-based schooling. Identifying the tension between religious faith that requires belief in God and a liberal rational-critical principle that is bound to expose such belief to doubts, Callan worries that such commitments render the choice of a life of faith ineligible for liberals. In order not to exclude this kind of option Callan seeks some rapprochement between liberalism and the faith school. Children will only come to understand the nature of the religious life by gaining some experience of it from an insider perspective and this will require setting aside the kind of doubts that rational criticism is likely to inspire. To reject the life of faith without this experience, says Callan, would be to act with as little freedom as any religious zealot. On this view liberals ought to be more hospitable to religion than they have often been, while at the same time keeping before children the tensions between faith and the examined life. Therein lies a challenge for educators but for Callan (*ibid*: 193) the prize is considerable because '[t]hose whose faith can survive the experience [of this tension] will not be entirely at home in either Athens or Jerusalem, but if there is a faith worth having, they are the ones who have it'.

Faced with the dilemma of accommodating faith-based schooling within liberal and culturally diverse societies, liberals have generally responded by seeking to reconcile their concern for social cohesion and individual autonomy by making conditions which in effect restrict liberal support to the moderate version of faith school. Williams, we have seen, argues for a civic condition which calls for inter-community contact and an educational condition of curriculum and pedagogy consistent with pupils attaining individual autonomy. Short's argument for the compatibility of moderate faith schools with social cohesion and De Jong and Snik's account of faith schooling as an alternative starting point for acquiring individual autonomy represent the most recent versions of liberal support for faith schooling subject to these civic and educational conditions. I have suggested that by focusing so much on the moderate version of faith schooling these liberal defences ultimately prove irrelevant to the kind of faith schooling that many faith groups actually want. Some of these citizens of faith argue their case for their own schools on grounds of the need for a holistic religion-based curriculum and a cultural transmissionist pedagogy; in doing so they make claims that approximate much more to what has been referred to here as the strong version of faith schooling that is much less concerned with social cohesion and individual autonomy. This version of faith schooling is evident in those Christian and Islamic schools that Walford identified as rejecting of any state funding that comes with conditions that proscribe the strong version of schooling they favour. De Ruyter (1999) accepts that there are Christian schools in The Netherlands belonging to the Dutch Reformed tradition that reject the moderate version of schooling and she excludes these schools from liberal support. It is clear that advocates of the strong identity school do not wish to see their version of education restricted to the early years of schooling along the lines of the model that liberals such as De Jong and Snik, and Thiessen defend. Reviewing his own sample of Jewish schools Short had to accept that the more orthodox schools had little time for multicultural education.

While Dagovitz has accepted that the liberal defences identified so far fail to acknowledge the type of schooling that many citizens of faith actually want for their children, he attempts to rescue this type of liberal defence by replacing these comprehensive liberal concerns with autonomy with a political liberal position that restricts autonomy to conceptions of the good and leaves religious identity as something that is given rather than chosen. In this way Dagovitz hopes to reconcile faith schooling with (political) liberalism. But Dagovitz eventually re-introduces the moderate–strong distinction between faith schools when he warns against focusing on the more extreme claims of some religious groups such as the Mozerts and the Amish. The effect of this line of argument might be to make the moderate category of schools more inclusive by restricting the claims that liberalism makes but even Dagovitz has to accept that this still leaves some forms of religious schooling outside the liberal fold.

The issue that remains is how liberalism responds to claims that derive not from the centrality of choice (whether political or comprehensive) but from other human goods. It is in this context that Berlin's liberal pluralism appears to be more accommodating. Liberals such as De Jong and Snik defend the faith school because it supports cultural contexts that in turn provide the context for choice. But this is not the reason that many traditional community members value their cultures. Monique Deveaux (2000: 132) makes this point when she shows how cultural groups provide a 'sense of place and belonging' not by offering a context of choice but often by *restricting choice*. The human goods that Deveaux recognizes in cultural groups are those that Kenneth Strike (1999, 2000) calls the non-cognitive benefits of cultural membership – a sense of narrative, solidarity and identity. There is a clear connection between these qualities and McDonough's characterization of the strong cultural identity school.

Zygmunt Bauman (2001) covers much the same ground when he talks about the search for security in an unsafe world, and he is very clear that, while security is a human good, it comes at a price, one that is paid, he says, 'in the currency of freedom' (*ibid*: 4). The point I want to make from Bauman here is the realization that security and freedom are values that cannot be fully reconciled. Although Bauman himself does not cite Berlin, the following words could so easily have come from Berlin himself: 'These two qualities (security and freedom) are, simultaneously, complementary and incompatible ... Though many forms of human togetherness have been tried in the course of history, none has succeeded in finding a flawless solution to this truly "squaring the circle" kind of task' (*ibid*: 19). Berlin recognized that human goods are many, and often incompatible. The outcome is that we are forced to choose between these goods; in Bauman's words again: 'Whatever you choose, you gain some and you lose some' (*ibid*: 4).

And so it is with the faith schools argument. Faith schools can be defended in terms of the contribution they make to the sense of belonging and security that human beings rightly value. But these qualities are achieved at a price, the loss of some individual autonomy. This tension is perhaps best revealed in an exchange between Berlin himself and Charles Taylor (Berlin, 1994b; Taylor, 1994b). Although Berlin resists what he suspects as cultural determinism in Taylor's enthusiasm for Herder both agree the human value to be got from cultural belonging that is such a feature of Herder's philosophy. In turn Taylor acknowledges the reality of the cultural pluralism for which Berlin is best known and he concludes that with respect to the values of liberty and security: 'We can only make difficult judgements in which these demands are balanced against each other, at some sacrifice to one or the other' (Taylor, 1994b: 214).

Faith schools present us with choices, ones that cannot be avoided by making conditions that undermine the very qualities that traditional religious communities seek in their faith schools. Rather than trying to reconcile what cannot be reconciled, liberals must accept what Berlin recognizes as the tragedy of choosing between rival goods. In choosing to support faith schools for the qualities of community that they bring to their pupils, liberals must acknowledge the price that is paid by individuals in terms of some loss of autonomy and by society in terms of some loss of cohesion. Walzer (2003) has recently put the dilemma as follows: parents have a right to try to sustain their way of life and this includes parents who are members of so-called 'totalizing or all-embracing communities'; equally, liberal states have a right to try to educate children because they will grow into citizens. These rights will sometimes conflict and there will have to be trade-offs and compromises. This is so, says Walzer, because liberals and members of traditional religious communities are basically unhappy with each other – yet they must find a way to live together.

So it is with faith schools. Liberals will find no resolution of this dilemma by characterizing all faith schools as compatible with liberal values. While some may well be, others most certainly will not. Many of those who call for faith schools would neither recognize nor value the moderate version of faith schooling that is being claimed as the basis for reconciliation. The real challenge for liberals lies in dealing with the strong version of cultural identity schooling. Support for such schools will bring both gains and losses and, as Galston (2002) observed in his own account of liberal pluralism, what has always proved difficult is not choosing between what is good and bad for human beings, but the choices that often have to be made between rival goods.

While I have argued here that Berlin's recognition of belonging as a legitimate part of the diversity of human goods suggests some degree of accommodation with strong as well as the less problematic (from a liberal perspective) moderate faith-based schools, I hope that enough has been said up to this point to indicate that Berlin's liberal pluralism does set some limits to the kind of faith schooling that a liberal state is able to accept. These limits are perhaps best considered in the context of the debate about the protection of the educational interests of the individual members of cultural groups and it is to this subject that I turn in the next chapter.

5 Cultural communities, education and right of exit

Cultural communities and rights of exit: the problem identified

In his widely cited account of the vulnerability of internal minorities Leslie Green (1995: 268) says this: 'Minorities are badly off, but internal ones are often worse off. They suffer from being members of minority groups who need to defend themselves not only from the majority but also from other members of their own minority'. Whether it is gay members of the Mennonite religious community or English speakers in Quebec, internal minorities, says Green, find themselves in this kind of position; a situation that has recently been referred to as the problem of 'minorities within minorities' (Eisenberg and Spinner-Halev, 2005). Green is both surprised and worried that liberals have appeared relatively unconcerned about the citizenship rights of individuals disadvantaged or maltreated within their own communities. A liberal society that fails in this way, he says, runs the risk of becoming a 'mosaic of tyrannies' (Green, 1995: 268).

The right of vulnerable and maltreated members to exit their own community (along with a realistic opportunity to implement this right) has played a fundamental role in the kinds of discussion that political philosophers have had about how liberal democrats ought to respond to their obligation to protect the citizenship rights of minorities within minorities. For several liberal philosophers it is the fact that dissenting individuals have a right of exit from their communities that is taken to justify liberal abstention from intervening in the internal norms and practices of illiberal communities. For example, we have already seen how Jacob Levy (2005) argues that the liberal state can only justify non-interference in the way that illiberal religious groups discriminate against their gay and lesbian members on condition that the wider liberal society sanctions same-sex marriage and allows these vulnerable citizens an exit opportunity from their community that offers full citizenship rights and equal participation within the wider society. He writes:

> [A]s long as there are religions that proscribe homosexuality, exit will continue to be what similarly situated gays and lesbians do. Abolishing or even deliberately radically transforming the religions is not an option for the

liberal state. We outsiders are limited to providing a safe, free and just place for [gays and lesbians] to exit *to*.

(ibid: 177, original emphasis)

Other liberal philosophers whose views will be considered in what follows argue that reliance on the exit option is dangerous in at least two ways. First, it suggests an option to leave that is neither wished for, nor experienced as a real possibility by, many dissenting and maltreated members of minority groups. What has often been referred to in the literature as a choice between 'your culture or your rights' does not appear to be a real choice and certainly not one which any individual should be expected to face. Much of the recent discussion of exit rights relates to Ayelet Shachar's observation that it is those individuals who are most disadvantaged within communities – often women and children – who are least able to access the exit option. Women, according to Shachar (2001: 69), often lack the education, economic power, connections, and 'know-how' to make exit a real possibility, let alone a success. More to the point many of these women, despite suffering disadvantage at the hands of their male co-members, do not want to be forced into a choice between their valued cultural membership and their citizenship rights.[1]

Children constitute another group of vulnerable individuals who neither chose to be members of a particular community nor, for the most part, enjoy any real opportunity to leave. Both James Dwyer (1998) and Rob Reich (2002) draw particular attention to the situation of children. As persons who are 'involuntary and unwitting participants' (Dwyer, 1998: 106) children should be protected in law from the practices of their own community in the same way as outsiders ordinarily are.

The second danger lies in the possibility that the exit option will be enough to persuade the liberal state to abstain from taking the kind of steps necessary to protect the interests of vulnerable members of illiberal communities. Oonagh Reitman (2005) identifies three roles attributed to exit rights in multiculturalism theory. First, there is the basic and passive role of exit as the option to leave one's cultural community and join the wider society. Liberal democratic societies must, says Reitman, offer this possibility to all their citizens. Second, multiculturalists defend exit rights as having a protective role in shielding individuals from oppression by their fellow members. Third, exit serves a transformative role as a catalyst for cultural changes that benefit vulnerable members.

These protective and transformative roles are often argued for on the grounds that community leaders, fearing loss of members, will desist from oppression and reform their practices in order not to lose members through the exit option. Reitman is unconvinced by this and responds that the opposite effect might well prevail. Faced with this kind of reforming challenge patriarchal leaders of illiberal religious groups are more likely, she argues, to protect the existing culture by allowing dissenters to leave thus keeping the original culture pure for those orthodox members who remain. Survival in this sense is not about numbers but about retaining orthodoxy and 'by counting upon exit as the catalyst for change, one runs the risk of aggravating precisely those forces which stand in the way of change' (*ibid*: 207). While Reitman acknowledges that there are risks in intervention, she argues that reliance on exit rights is usually an indication that the liberal state has given up too easily when it comes to intervening to protect the interests of vulnerable members.

The reticence to intervene in the internal workings of illiberal groups that worries Reitman is very evident in discussion about education and exit. Defenders of exit rights tend to disagree about how far the liberal state is entitled or required to go in seeking to make exit rights meaningful in terms of the kinds of support that might be offered to exiting or potentially exiting individuals. Education has been central to this debate and in what follows I will be considering the various positions taken by defenders of exit rights on the kind of education necessary for individuals to make exit a meaningful option.

Freedom of association has been an important constituent of the package of rights that liberals see as contributing to the kind of society within which individuals flourish. This concept of freedom of association has been developed largely in the context of the kind of voluntary associations that individuals can join and leave with some ease; that is to say, members are able to leave voluntary associations without having to bear too much in the way of costs and burdens. In recent debate about how liberals might be expected to respond to claims by illiberal groups to be left free from liberal interventions in the internal workings of their communities the emphasis has shifted away from these genuinely *voluntary* associations to ascriptive groups where membership is not chosen and where exit comes at a heavy price. Membership of communities based on religion or culture is, for the most part, the outcome of birth and exit from such a community is of a different order from resigning membership of the local golf or tennis club.[2] In an important sense every aspect of living as part of a cultural group represents a barrier to exit and this leads Levy (2000) to describe how exit from a culture must always involve costs. Often an exiting member will need to learn another language and will need to come to terms with a new set of cultural norms and practices. Giving up the familiar is in itself, says Levy, a cost to be borne. Some of these barriers are simply the outcome of being a member of a group; others are deliberately put there to make exit problematic. Groups that fear loss of members by assimilation will be tempted to raise the barriers and, although it is these groups that will often be the ones that are criticized for prejudicing the voluntariness of remaining in a group, Levy (2000: 114) points out that, '[if] the existence of exit barriers is enough to make us see communal membership as unfree and illiberal, then there is no membership which is not illiberal'.

Accepting with Levy that exit from any group presents difficulties and exacts costs it will still be useful in what follows to consider in some detail the differences between groups and the impact of these differences on rights of exit. When discussing the conditional liberal defence of faith-based schools (Chapter 4) I argued that the kind of conditions that liberals wanted to require of faith schools were often most burdensome to the communities that were most keen to have their own schools. Moderate identity schools presented no problem to liberals because liberal conditions were happily met; strong identity schools on the other hand existed specifically to avoid the kind of schooling required by liberal conditions. Much the same situation appears to hold with regard to exit rights. It is the strong identity communities that, from a liberal perspective, often generate the greatest need for the protection of exit rights but from which exit proves to be most problematic.

I will begin by outlining in brief the role that exit rights play in several liberal accounts of the relationship between the liberal state and illiberal groups. We have already seen that in William Galston's version of liberal pluralism exit rights play a key role. While it is Isaiah Berlin's value pluralism that inspires much of Galston's brand of diversity liberalism, it is Berlin's account of negative liberty as the absence of coercion that underpins Galston's defence of exit rights:

> The surest sign of unfreedom occurs when individuals are coerced to remain in ways of life they wish to leave. The politics of negative liberty seeks, first and foremost, to protect the ability to leave – although not necessarily to cultivate the awareness and reflective powers that may stimulate the desire to leave.
>
> (Galston, 2002: 51)

Galston's acknowledgement of the significance of negative liberty to Berlin is in line with Daniel Weinstock's (1997) argument against John Gray that Berlin's pluralism is of a restricted kind, restricted in the sense that, while admitting of a wide range of ways of life, negative liberty is to be included as a necessary element in any legitimate way of life. For Galston negative liberty features within the diversity state at least in the minimal sense that members have the right to leave a community to which they no longer wish to belong: '[The value pluralist liberal state] will vigorously defend the ability of individuals to exit from ways of life with which they have ceased to identify' (Galston, 2002: 62). In his most recent account of liberal value pluralism Galston (2005: 191) reaffirms his view that 'illiberal associations *with full exit rights* are consistent with value pluralism' (emphasis added).

I showed in Chapter 2 how Brian Barry's liberal egalitarianism attempts to steer a course that seeks to protect individuals from maltreatment at the hands of fellow group members while avoiding interfering with the internal practices of illiberal groups. The right of exit plays an important role in his account. Barry (2001) acknowledges that liberalism does not require forcing liberal principles on groups made up of individuals who have chosen to associate together. Adults who make a choice to associate are free to act as they wish as long as no harm comes to outsiders and members enjoy a right of exit.

For Barry it is the freedom to disassociate that enables liberals to abstain from interference. That said, Barry agrees with Levy that there are bound to be costs of exit and some of these costs are such that the state neither can nor ought to seek to ameliorate. First, there is what Barry calls the 'intrinsic cost' of exit. In order to retain their character, churches, for instance, must be able to control who is to join and who is to be excluded. Excommunication is a cost that exiting church members might well have to bear, that is if the church is to retain the character that its remaining members wish it to have. Second, there are the 'associative costs' when members of the community cease to recognize those who leave; again, says Barry, there is nothing that the state can or should do to relieve this burden. It is in the third area of what he calls 'external costs' that Barry requires the state to act. Taking as his example a case where a Hutterite colony in Canada expelled several apostate members[3] Barry argues that, while the community has the right to expel these members, there ought to be some mechanism by which these exiting members are compensated for the contribution they will have made, possibly over a long period of time, to the shared property of the community. Compensation would enable members to exit and function in an alternative community; and so it is, says Barry, the absence of external costs that should be taken as the criterion of the voluntariness of continued membership. These are the costs that the liberal state must do something about.

Despite the kind of costs that exit is bound to require Barry (2002: 223) is optimistic about the possibility of exit and therefore the justification for liberal abstention from interfering in the internal workings of illiberal groups. He refers to both rural–urban and inter-country migration as part of a dynamic whereby individuals regularly leave their communities for another kind of life. Barry accuses those who advocate greater interference with the affairs of voluntary groups of exaggerating the extent to which group membership is constitutive of identity. While there are costs in leaving, 'history shows that when benefits outweigh the costs people behave rationally and leave' (*ibid*: 223).

Also drawing on the same Hutterite case Jeff Spinner-Halev (2000: 72–77) comes to similar conclusions and recommends much the same remedies. Spinner-Halev seeks some principle for liberal non-intervention in communities that have to be seen as constraining the lives of their members; the principle he chooses is that of right of exit. As long as members retain the possibility of leaving their community the liberal state should desist from intervening in community affairs. Against Green, with whose concerns about minorities within minorities I began this chapter, Spinner-Halev is more accepting of the risks and psychological difficulties that exit entails. Difficult though it may be for these individuals many do manage to leave; all that is required of the liberal state is to ensure that leaving is an option and that members know that this is so.

Spinner-Halev, like Barry, argues for the Hutterite community making available a small fund to facilitate the exit of members who so choose. This ought not to be enough to provide an incentive to leave, just sufficient to make exit an option for those who have decided they no longer wish to live as Hutterites. Additionally the liberal state ought to provide advice and support for exiting members starting new businesses and coming to terms with life outside the community. Spinner-Halev seems to suggest that no steps need be taken to highlight alternative ways of life as options for children from religious groups; it is inevitable, he argues, that these children will become aware of the alternatives that surround them.[4]

Chandran Kukathas (2003) sees the right of disassociation as the liberal right to repudiate authority and one which is complementary with the individual right of association. Unlike Barry and Spinner-Halev, who both hold illiberal groups responsible for bearing at least some of the costs that exiting members incur, Kukathas argues that although individuals must be free to leave, they have no right to require remaining members to bear any of the costs of their departure. Nor, says Kukathas, is there any responsibility on members of an illiberal group to take steps to facilitate the capacity of members to leave. All that is required, says Kukathas (1992), is that communities do not coerce members into remaining and that there exists a wider society which dissenting members may freely join.[5]

Susan Moller Okin (2002), like Shachar, focuses on exit rights as they affect women. Women's rights of exit are more constrained than those of men, says Okin, because of the key role of women in reproducing cultural identity. Girls receive less education and are often married at an early age. Okin also draws attention to the messages of inferiority that are communicated to girls in some patriarchal cultures; here girls learn specific roles within their communities. The outcome of these socialization patterns is said to be a loss of the kind of self-esteem necessary if individuals are to be the authors of their own lives. Such women, says Okin, can hardly conceive of exit from their communities let alone manage to do so. Nevertheless Okin notes that Raz, Galston and Kukathas all rely on exit rights to defend the liberal credentials of their respective theories of group and individual rights. Joseph Raz is criticized for failing to specify the conditions that would make exit the 'viable' option he requires it to be and while Galston has more to say about the conditions necessary to make right of exit meaningful these conditions ultimately prove inconsistent with the degree of freedom from interference that Galston seeks for illiberal groups in his 'diversity state'. Okin is concerned for those women who are deeply attached to their communities but prefer to work towards reforming aspects of those cultures; for them right of exit has little to offer. Kukathas's support for 'substantive' rights of exit fails to persuade Okin because he shares the problem with Galston that once attention is given to capacitating individuals to make use of that right then exit rights come into conflict with the kinds of illiberal practices that both Galston and Kukathas want to protect from liberal intervention.

Shachar (2001) is critical of the both the cruelty involved in forcing women to choose between their citizenship rights and their cultural identity and of the failure of advocates of exit rights to recognize the very real difficulty that women face in implementing that right. The so-called right of exit, she says, 'throws upon the already beleaguered individual the responsibility to either miraculously transform the legal-institutional conditions that keep her vulnerable or to find the resources to leave her world behind' (*ibid*: 43). Shachar's resolution is to favour joint governance between state and group with individuals able to opt for state authority in those aspects of their lives where group norms and practices require reform. Rather than facing an all-or-nothing choice either to stay and lose rights or leave and lose identity this 'partial exit' enables vulnerable individuals to exert pressure on group leaders so that their interest in group preservation becomes an incentive to protect rather than exploit individual members (*ibid*: 149 n. 2).

In a recent response to critics[6] of her earlier work on vulnerable 'minorities within minorities' Okin (2005) makes a distinction between liberal and democratic responses to group rights that reinforce gender inequalities within cultural groups. Liberalism, she argues, demands that intra-group inequalities based on gender be addressed but, where there is evidence of full and proper consultation with women and girls who belong to communities that have experienced domination and oppression at the hands of colonial powers, a democratic response might include acceding to an expressed wish to retain discriminatory practices. So, while Okin sees no good reason as to why the Catholic Church should enjoy tax exemptions while discriminating against women, she agrees with Deveaux (2005) that the compromises achieved by South African women with tribal elders, albeit that they retain some aspects of discriminatory practice, ought to be respected. Okin now describes her 'more considered view' to be that where groups have experienced oppression at the hands of colonial powers there may be a case for respecting the wish to continue cultural traditions that retain some aspects of women's traditional status.[7]

Clearly exit rights play a very significant role for liberal philosophers concerned with the relationship between liberal society and its constituent communities. While there is considerable disagreement about the role that exit rights might play there does seem to be agreement that, if exit rights are to play a part in liberal multicultural theory, then the right of exit must be meaningful, and, if that is to be so, some attention must be paid to the kind of education that makes exit a real possibility. It is to education that I now turn.

Education and making exit rights meaningful

While Galston (2002: 51) has reservations about '[cultivating] the awareness and reflective powers that may stimulate the desire to leave', Barry insists that 'children must be brought up in a way that will eventually enable them to leave behind the groups into which they were born, if they so choose' (Barry, 2001: 149). Barry's argument for a public stake in the education of future citizens requires resisting those parents who seek to limit the educational opportunities of their children in the interests of cultural survival. This is illustrated by Barry's comments on both the Gypsy and Amish communities and their concerns about schooling. Barry challenges the way that Kukathas (1992) argues both that Gypsy communities should be allowed to educate their own children as they wish rather than enrol them in public schools while continuing to claim liberal credentials for this case on the grounds of right of exit. Barry insists that a meaningful right of exit from the Gypsy community requires education that prepares children for a range of occupations and citizenship responsibilities that goes well beyond what is provided for within the community. Turning to the Amish case Barry dismisses claims that the number of Amish children exiting their community is enough to remove fears that they are disabled from doing so by their limited education; instead he focuses on the voluntariness of continued membership. Community control over individual members is so strict, says Barry, as to require a real right of exit before those who remain can be said to do so voluntarily.

This was the concern of Judge Roger Elmer in the original *Yoder* trial in the Green County Court in April 1969. Judge Elmer found against those Amish parents who kept their children out of high school because of his concern that an 'appreciable number of Amish-reared youth may decide to subsequently adopt a different faith, join a different church, or leave the Amish community to become part of a different culture' (cited in Peters, 2003: 99). These young people would, said this judge, suffer significant disadvantage, and so despite his sympathy with the Amish way of life, he came to the conclusion that school attendance laws quite properly existed to support the interests of such children. Judge Elmer was very clear that his finding in this case would have been very different had it not been for this particular interest of children. When this case came to appeal before the Wisconsin Supreme Court, Assistant Attorney General John Calhoun acting for the state of Wisconsin reiterated Judge Elmer's concern when he said: 'These Amish kids have no other options than to stay and join the order; it's hard for them to get into the mainstream without a high school education' (cited in Peters, 2003: 106). The Wisconsin Court, however, remained unmoved by this argument and in his majority opinion finding in favour of the Amish parents Chief Justice Hallows argued that it was folly to burden the religious liberty of the Amish on the grounds of what he called the speculation that some children would become adults who wanted to leave the community. Hallows did not regard the protection of the exit rights of these children as a compelling state interest that could override the claims of religious liberty.

In fact Hallows used another kind of exit argument to bolster his ruling in favour of the Amish parents. These Amish families had moved to Wisconsin as a result of a series of conflicts with the education authorities in neighbouring Iowa over the issue of school attendance. In the event of all other states including Wisconsin taking a similar view of the implications of the school attendance rules then the Amish would be left with nowhere to exit to. For Hallows it served religious liberty across the United States that some states allowed Amish exemptions from country-wide legislation on school attendance. But there was not unanimity among the members of this court and Justice Nathan Heffernan was moved to write a dissenting opinion that stressed the way that the court ruling limited the liberties of individual Amish members and failed to distinguish the interests of parents and children.[8]

In writing his opinion on the *Yoder* case for the United States Supreme Court, Chief Justice Warren Burger focused on the rights of parents and the threat to the religious liberty of the Amish that school attendance rules presented. In arguing that Amish vocational training for 14 to 16 year olds was adequate to ensure that exiting Amish would not be a burden on the state Burger appeared to be more concerned with protecting the state from welfare burdens than supporting the individual career options of any young people choosing to leave their community and make their way in the wider world. Again there were dissenting voices. Justice Byron White indicated concern that children's interests were being relegated in favour of those of their parents and Justice William O. Douglas translated the concerns of Heffernan and White into a note of partial dissent which regretted that so little attention had been given to the views of Amish children and worried about the religious liberty of any who chose to leave their community. In his review of the arguments presented in this case Peters (2003: 155) notes that, while Burger was quite right to insist that children were not parties to the legal case, children were clearly centrally involved and this left the ruling open to the criticism that it failed to distinguish the interests of parents and children, seriously neglecting those of the latter.

It is this kind of consideration that has forced Galston to acknowledge that in order to make the right of exit meaningful a number of conditions must hold and these conditions have significant educational implications. The conditions are that individuals must have knowledge of alternative ways of life; they must have the capacity to be able to evaluate these alternatives and the psychological freedom to be able to do so; and they must have the ability to participate in another way of life. It is difficult to see how these conditions can be met without re-introducing the education for autonomy that Galston wants to avoid imposing on illiberal communities. This is a problem that Galston first identified in his widely cited article *Two Concepts of Liberalism* (1995) and it is one that it appears he has yet to resolve.[9]

The educational dilemma presented by diversity liberal reliance on rights of exit is also evident in Jeff Spinner-Halev's argument for non-interference with illiberal religious communities. Spinner-Halev (2000) regards these religious groups as both enabling and constraining in their influence on members and, while he agrees with Green that exit from such groups is 'risky, wrenching and disorienting' (*ibid*: 72), he does not regard this as a matter for state interference. For Spinner-Halev the right of exit remains central to the case for diversity liberal tolerance of illiberal groups. In order to make the right of exit realistic Spinner-Halev concedes the need for what he describes as 'rudimentary schooling'. Without some kind of account of what this would entail it is difficult to judge whether it is going to be sufficient to overcome the psychological and practical difficulties to which he refers. There is only the briefest of descriptions of the kind of education being proposed and this refers only to reading and rudimentary maths and science. The matter is clouded even further when he argues both for including within science some teaching about evolution (*ibid*: 130) while at the same time making a case for exempting pupils from these lessons where parents request this (*ibid*: 138). Spinner-Halev goes on to suggest that, since pre-marital sex offends some people's religious beliefs, parents should be able to exempt their children from these lessons because '[this] will not harm the academic education of any child'.

There is some further hint of what a rudimentary education might mean when the possibility is accepted that parents will need to manipulate their children; for example, Spinner-Halev accepts that religious parents seeking to influence the behaviour of their children may rely upon the threat of damnation as the outcome of wrongdoing. Unlike Galston, Spinner-Halev is willing to acknowledge the possibility that community restrictions will be disabling rather than enabling and he is suspicious of what he sees as an attempt by Galston to reinstate liberal citizenship through the inculcation of state-sponsored liberal virtues. This, he argues, is trying to have it both ways; tolerance of diversity and the inculcation of liberal virtues. In Spinner-Halev's version of the diversity state there is an acceptance that some individuals living worthwhile but illiberal lives will be very bad citizens. It is difficult to argue with the conclusion of Ben Spiecker and Doret De Ruyter (2005) that Galston and Spinner-Halev fail to take exit rights seriously enough. Galston, they suggest, is at best ambivalent about exit while Spinner-Halev appears to be 'half-hearted' in claiming support for a 'real' right of exit while defending an education that is simply not up to the job.[10]

Reich (2002) examines two further diversity liberal accounts of exit rights and finds both wanting insofar as both rely on rights of exit while failing to require the kind of education necessary to make that right meaningful. Referring to Avishai Margalit and Moshe Halbertal's (1994)[11] defence of a separate education for Orthodox Jews that denies both boys and girls the kind of education that would facilitate exit into another way of life, Reich argues that no theory of group rights that fails to provide adequate preparation for those who choose to exit their own community can be counted as a liberal theory. For Reich it is only those members with the capacity to review and revise their own way of life who can be said to have *chosen* to remain.[12]

In the case of Kukathas (1992) Reich finds the emphasis on right of exit incompatible with the argument for leaving cultural groups free of government intervention in the kinds of education provided for their children. Gypsy children cannot be said to enjoy a right of exit if government stands back allowing parents to deny to their children the kind of schooling that would be necessary for them to survive outside the confines of their own community. Summing up his review of these political theorists Reich (2002: 73) concludes that 'the educational implications of their respective multicultural theories demonstrate the impossibility of calling either theory consistent with liberal values'.

Reich's own positive proposals for education are designed to facilitate exit. On this view of what Reich calls liberal multicultural education children are to be educated in such a way as to be minimally autonomous. Minimalist autonomy falls short of being a comprehensive way of life in the Rawlsian sense but it does say something about how an individual relates to her way of life. Because this must involve a degree of critical reflection, minimalist autonomy, while allowing for a range of cultures, is not tolerant of all ways of life. Reflection of the kind that Reich favours requires that children are educated about diverse ways of life and while this does not require being educated to live any kind of life, it must provide for a range of choice that extends beyond the culture of birth. Reich's account of minimalist autonomy combines the Berlinian negative liberty argument for freeing the individual from external coercion with that aspect of positive liberty that is about being the master of one's own life.[13] It is left up to individuals whether they become 'cultural purists' or 'cultural mongrels' (*ibid*: 118) and while Reich clearly favours a kind of cosmopolitan identity he accepts that some individuals will choose a way of life that includes very little autonomy. What matters is that the way of life is chosen and this requires there to have been some reflection. Multicultural education aids this critical reflection by allowing individuals the opportunity to step back from their own way of life and to see it as one among several possibilities. In a passage that resonates with Berlin's thinking about inter-cultural understanding Reich says, 'students do not view themselves or their cultural worldview as an impenetrable cocoon, as if no effort at understanding could ever succeed'(*ibid*: 185) and, in the context of a study of dialogue between Native and non-Native Americans (*ibid*: 259 n. 39), Reich refers to worldviews as being like distant but open horizons. The terminology resonates again with Berlin's own when Reich refers to his model of liberal multicultural education as '[generating] a common or shared horizon of intelligibility' (*ibid*: 186).

Conclusion: types of groups and their exit possibilities

Central to any discussion of the role of exit rights in liberal versions of arguments about the appropriateness of state interventions in the internal workings of communities is some kind of distinction between different types of cultural identity group. I have already made some reference to my discussion of liberal arguments for conditional support of faith-based schools where I used Kevin McDonough's categorization of moderate and strong cultural identity groups in order to argue that the communities most inclined to want their own schools were the same ones that would find liberal conditions most intrusive. Weinstock (2005) adopts a very similar argument in relation to exit rights and he begins by indicating some characteristics of groups. According to Weinstock there are groups that we are born into and there are groups we choose to join; there are groups that are issue-specific and others whose concerns are more general; there are groups that confer on the individual a very significant identity while others can be called 'identity-neutral'; groups may be democratic in their internal workings or undemocratic; and finally, groups may be broad or narrow in the reach they have into individual lives. While these characteristics may be combined in different ways it is possible to recognize what McDonough called strong identity groups as belonging to a type that is ascriptive rather than chosen in its membership. In Weinstock's terms these ascriptive groups tend to be identity-conferring and have norms and practices that reach into many aspects of people's day-to-day lives. These groups are often constituted in ways that are undemocratic and strictly hierarchical. These are the kind of groups that look most likely to give liberals greatest cause for concern about the vulnerability of internal minorities yet they are the kind of groups from which exit is most difficult.

The problem for liberals, says Weinstock, is that in these cases neither liberal abstention nor liberal interference appears to work. This is so largely because of what Shachar (2001: 35–37) calls 'reactive culturalism' which occurs when a group intensifies its adherence to its traditional laws, norms and practices as a kind of active resistance against pressures for change that originate outside the group. In particular it is noticed that '[w]hen a group's assertion of its identity becomes inlaid with elements of reactive culturalism, some of its more hierarchical practices may gain heightened significance as manifestations of the group's difference from mainstream society' (*ibid*: 36). Faced with outside interference the leaders of illiberal groups are pushed in the direction of greater illiberal control of their members. In earlier chapters I have made reference to Berlin's account of how members themselves may acquiesce in this push towards fundamentalism as part of a 'search for status'. Recall that Berlin recognized that individuals might feel unfree in two ways; one way of feeling unfree is the absence of self-government but another is to experience one's own group as neither recognized nor respected. In the absence of group recognition and respect, minorities within oppressed minorities have sometimes preferred to be governed badly by their own leaders than governed in benign fashion by outsiders:

> Although I may not get 'negative' liberty at the hands of my own society, yet they are members of my own group; they understand me, as I understand them; and this understanding creates within me the sense of being somebody in the world.
>
> (Berlin, 2002a: 203)

In a radio broadcast given in 1959[14] Berlin expanded on this passage from *Two Concepts of Liberty* by insisting that, although members of oppressed groups might refer to their search for status as a fight for liberty, there was an important distinction to be made. The broadcast opened with these remarks:

> We often speak of the demands for liberty made by oppressed classes or nationalities. But it is not always individual freedom, nor even individual equality, that they primarily want ... What they want, as often as not, is simply recognition – of their own class or nation, or colour or race – as an independent source of human activity ... and not to be ruled, educated, guided, with however light a hand, as being not quite fully human, and not therefore quite fully free.
>
> (Berlin, 2000a: 195)

Berlin continues by saying that this is not about freedom, but about 'solidarity, fraternity, mutual understanding, [the] need for association on equal terms' (*ibid*: 196) and, although it is close to the desire to be an independent agent, Berlin insists that status and liberty are to be distinguished.

Given the danger of a 'reactive culturalism' and the acquiescence of vulnerable and internally oppressed individuals that answers to this search for status

Weinstock advocates an approach that seeks to get beyond the liberal dilemma of choosing between abstention and intervention. Although he does not refer here directly to Berlin, there are aspects of Weinstock's approach that are distinctly Berlinian.[15] Weinstock argues that the ultimate goal of policies for dealing with illiberal groups within liberal societies must be minimization of harm to individual members of groups. There is a pluralist recognition of the range of goods that individuals enjoy together with agreement that a particular package of goods might include a degree of inequality and paternalism. Cultures will be judged, however, in terms of the contribution they make to individual (and therefore to some extent group) well-being and this will mean proscribing certain norms and practices that result in harms. In order to avoid 'reactive culturalism' Weinstock advises an indirect approach to liberalizing cultural groups, one that is designed to avoid the risk of pushing groups in the direction of fundamentalism.[16] This is to be achieved by addressing two significant problems. First, there is what Weinstock calls the 'problem of number'. Minorities fear for their survival as a group and what often exacerbates this fear is concern about the apparently assimilationist policies of the dominant group; a language policy that requires exclusive use of the dominant language, for example, will be seen as a major threat to the culture of the minority group.

The second problem Weinstock identifies is that of history. Minority and majority groups do not just happen to share the same space; 'we are here because you were there' is a slogan used by minorities to remind majorities of the history of colonial domination that explains much of the settlement patterns of minority groups in Western European liberal democracies. Public recognition of previous oppression is therefore recommended as going some way to relieving this burden.[17]

Because it is not possible for members of identity-conferring groups to measure their interests in terms of a cost-benefit analysis, exit offers little to those 'minorities within minorities' that experience maltreatment at the hands of their peers. With Berlin, Weinstock seeks to minimize the harsh treatment that these individuals receive and his approach is to reduce the amount of 'reactive culturalism' by addressing some of the key concerns that members of minority groups have. Consistent with his pluralism Weinstock acknowledges that what is required is that the well-being of individual members is the touchstone of acceptability of particular cultural norms and practices and that well-being comes in a variety, but not infinite variety, of ways. Where groups continue to treat their own members badly a liberal society has a duty to intervene.

Weinstock's recommendation of a strategy of indirection in responding to the need to balance the claims of identity groups and the interests of their individual members appears to offer a way of reducing the 'reactive culturalism' that Shachar has identified as problematic for vulnerable community members and which Berlin sought to explain and warn against in his account of what he called 'the search for status'. I will return to Weinstock's strategy of indirection as it can be applied to education in my concluding chapter but before doing so I turn to the important question of education for national identity.

6   National identity and education

Introduction

Liberal nationalism has been subjected to criticism by cosmopolitan philosophers worried that nationalisms of any kind neglect moral obligations to fellow human beings who happen to reside in other countries and by communitarians who argue that nationalists inevitably seek to impose a monolithic national identity and common culture onto the various cultural minorities typically found living within the modern nation-state. In England the introduction of citizenship education as a national curriculum subject and more recent initiatives that involve educating new immigrants about life in the United Kingdom represent the kind of liberal nation-building projects that are of such concern to both cosmopolitan and communitarian critics of nationalism.

This chapter argues for the relevance of Isaiah Berlin's distinctive liberal pluralism to contemporary debate about the place of education for national identity in fostering social cohesion around liberal institutions and I will seek to show how this philosophy, founded as it is on commitments to both individual freedom and value pluralism, suggests the possibility of a liberal approach to national identity that avoids at least some of the dangers that worry cosmopolitans and communitarians alike.

Prior to the 1990s few political philosophers had much good to say about nationalism and nationalists (Archard, 2000) but the publication of David Miller's *On Nationality* (1995a) and Will Kymlicka's *Multicultural Citizenship* (1996a) precipitated a revival of interest on both sides of the Atlantic in a specifically liberal version of what Miller preferred to call 'national identity' and what Kymlicka has come to call 'nation building'. In philosophy of education John White (1996, 2001) offered a liberal defence of education for national identity, while Nicholas Tate, Chief Executive of the School Curriculum and Assessment Authority, made a series of widely reported speeches during the late 1990s advocating a school curriculum designed to foster a sense of national identity. Liberal nationalists, often tracing their philosophical roots back to Berlin's writing, began to distinguish good and bad nationalisms and, in doing so, made a case for the particular importance in multi-ethnic societies of a national identity strong enough to provide the social cohesion necessary to underpin liberal institutions and feelings of mutual concern among citizens. Determining the appropriate nature of that shared identity, however, proved to be very problematic; too 'thin' an identity has seemed inadequate for the work of social cohesion while too 'thick' an identity risks excluding those minority groups who do not share the ethno-cultural character and history of the majority group. As Ronald Beiner (1999: 9) puts it: 'how to privilege the majority cultural identity in defining civic membership without consigning cultural minorities to second-class citizenship' remains the problem facing the liberal nationalist. Balancing the claims of social cohesion and cultural diversity in the context of the debate about national identity is the theme of this chapter. The tensions between social cohesion and cultural diversity will be explored in the context of current developments in citizenship education. I consider Sir Bernard Crick's liberal proposals for citizenship education (Qualifications and Curriculum Authority, 1998) together with Mark Olssen's (2004) response which calls for the 're-visioning' of citizenship education informed by the pluralist insights of Lord Parekh's report (Runnymede Trust, 2000). The examination of these important contributions to the debate about national identity provides a context for considering the wider debate about what kinds of pluralism can be reconciled with liberalism.

Berlin is identified by both Alain Dieckhoff (2004) and Pierre Birnbaum (2004) as one of the few philosophers who does not underestimate the power of nationalist sentiment and one who has become a major source for contemporary liberal nationalists such as Charles Taylor, Michael Walzer and Yael Tamir. According to Avishai Margalit (1997) Berlin's interest in Counter-Enlightenment and Romantic thinkers came from his appreciating that their insights into the psychology of human belonging and its particularistic tendencies were more predictive of the emotions and behaviour of human groups than the universalist faith of the Enlightenment *philosophes* and their rationalist descendants who mistakenly expected group belonging, whether ethnic, national, or religious, to be eroded in modern societies and eventually to give way to cosmopolitan identities.

The chapter begins by examining some recent developments that provide context for the debate about national identity and education in England. I then go on to discuss Berlin's account of nationalism(s) before considering how contemporary philosophers influenced by Berlin have developed a liberal nationalist version of the case for national identity. I then go on to examine cosmopolitan and communitarian critiques of what might be seen as nation-building educational projects before concluding by examining the possibilities of using Berlin's benign version of nationalism as a basis for reconciling liberalism and nationalism.

National identity in the United Kingdom: recent developments and issues

During the 1990s New Labour sought to reclaim national identity as a political project from those right-wing political parties that assumed an exclusive claim on nationalist ideologies and sentiments.[1] I have already noted Tate's contribution to this debate through regularly speaking about the role of schools and the national curriculum in fostering a strong sense of national belonging (for example, Tate, 1997a, 1997b). In response to concerns about levels of citizenship and political participation Crick was given the responsibility of leading an advisory group to work on a new citizenship curriculum for schools and he was subsequently asked to undertake a similar role in advising on the kind of civic education that would benefit new immigrants seeking British citizenship. Chapter 4 made reference to reports about the inter-ethnic disturbances in 2001 in several northern towns; these government reports talked of the need for greater social cohesion and the role that schools and the curriculum ought to play in fostering the kind of shared identity thought necessary to underpin such cohesion. In one of these reports the Home Office Community Cohesion Review Team concluded by saying that 'there has been little attempt to develop clear values which focus on what it means to be a citizen of a modern multi-racial Britain' (Great Britain: Home Office, 2001: para 2. 6). Launching this report the then Home Secretary David Blunkett talked about immigrants needing to accept certain 'norms of acceptability' that would serve to identify minority customs which ought to be accommodated within the wider national community (such as arranged marriage) and those which ought not (such as forced marriage).[2] The impact of the terrorist attacks on the United States in September 2001, subsequent reactions to British involvement in the Iraq war, and recent debates about Islamic fundamentalism in the light of the London attacks of 2005 have served to further divide opinion about, and focus minds on, issues of social cohesion and national identity.

It was in this climate of concern about the loyalty and citizenship potential of minority culture members that in December 2004 the Life in the United Kingdom Advisory Group announced the publication of its handbook entitled *Life in the United Kingdom: A Journey to Citizenship* (Great Britain, Home Office: Advisory Group on Life in the United Kingdom, 2004).[3] The handbook, aimed at teachers of English as a second language (ESOL), sets out what it considers to be useful information for new immigrants about life in the United Kingdom; the sections on British history and government were written by Crick himself. Although new immigrants are not to be tested on history and government they will be expected to be able to communicate in English (or Welsh or Scottish Gaelic as appropriate) and demonstrate some knowledge of life in the United Kingdom in order to qualify for British citizenship.

Pursuing the theme of national identity and achievement Gordon Brown spoke in November 2004 about the role he saw for a proposed institute for 'Britishness studies', an organization that would celebrate British achievement and values. Nations, according to the Chancellor, need to know who they are, and citizenship lessons, he said, provide an important means of doing this.[4] In similar vein, Charles Clarke, having succeeded David Blunkett at the Home Office, announced a proposal that 18 year olds take a pledge of citizenship that was described by Home Office Minister, Fiona Mactaggart, as a voluntary 'rite of passage' modelled on the Australian practice. This announcement came in the context of reports of the success of the citizenship ceremonies for new British citizens that were begun in 2004 and the suggestion of a Citizenship Day to be celebrated annually from October 2005.[5] Having been responsible for the initiation of the school citizenship curriculum and subsequently citizenship education, tests, and ceremonies for new immigrants, Blunkett returned to the theme of national identity, specifically English national identity, in a speech given to the Institute for Public Policy Research in March 2005.[6] Blunkett spoke about the importance of feelings of attachment and solidarity when groups are faced with rapid technological and global change; this was said in language, and expressed sentiments, in a way that would be very familiar to readers of Berlin. He rejected cosmopolitan arguments that strong national sentiment threatens both foreigners without and 'immigrant' communities within and, like Berlin, he warned that neglecting those sentiments risked 'creating a festering, resentful national identity'. Blunkett concluded by calling for an inclusive national identity that is both open and pluralistic, in his words: 'mongrel, multi-national, and multiethnic', an identity he saw as best served by education in citizenship education for national identity.

In January 2005 the Chief Inspector of Schools, David Bell, joined the debate about national identity when he called for all schools to prepare children for life in a culturally diverse society. Bell's speech to the Hansard Society drew particular attention to evidence in the OfSTED Annual Report (Office for Standards in Education, 2005) which claimed that at least some independent faith-based schools were failing to deliver the kind of citizenship education necessary for a strong sense of national identity.[7] In particular Bell directed his criticism at Islamic schools when referring to intolerance and illiberalism that particularly disadvantaged women as well as people living in non-traditional relationships. Within 24 hours of Bell's speech Trevor Phillips, Chairperson of the Commission for Racial Equality, added his voice to the debate agreeing that the growth of separate faith schools threatened the cohesion of society.[8] These criticisms of a failure to educate children properly for living in a pluralistic society were by no means limited to Muslim schools and several commentaries on Bell's speech pointed to evidence in reports by Office for Standards in Education inspectors that indicated deeper concerns about the growing number of evangelical Christian schools that failed to address cultural and social diversity in their teaching. It is quite clear that by Spring 2005 issues of national identity in the context of a diverse society had come to occupy an important place in debates about the role of education in preparing both children and new immigrants for participation in the civic culture. These debates were to be overtaken by events when the terrorist attacks on London in July 2005 ensured that issues of security and civic identity would remain at the top of the national agenda for the foreseeable future. Much of the subsequent reporting of attitudes within the British Muslim community has focused on the continuing struggle by moderate Muslim organizations for the hearts and minds of young Muslims opposed to British foreign policy in the Middle East.[9]

Isaiah Berlin's benign and malignant nationalisms

Benign nationalism: an expression of the need to belong

> I do not wish to abandon the belief that a world that is a reasonably peaceful coat of many colours, each portion of which develops its own distinct cultural identity and is tolerant of others, is not a utopian dream.
>
> (Berlin, 1991b: 814)

This benign version of nationalism is, for Berlin, consistent with liberalism, and what it expresses most clearly is the need felt by human beings for belonging to a community and the sharing of a particular culture. In his book, *Berlin*, John Gray (1995) talks about Berlin as being part of a pre-Enlightenment tradition of liberal thought that recognized the importance of belonging to a cultural group. Berlin knew that it is one thing to enjoy equal opportunities as a citizen who happens to be Jewish but it is another to be recognized as a Jew and enabled to live as a Jew. Enlightenment thinkers underestimated this desire for, and feeling of, group membership and expected, therefore, that group identities would weaken with time. Adopting Herder's cultural and non-aggressive version of nationalism Berlin often wrote about national consciousness as an expression of this human need to belong; to be recognized and understood by others sharing the same group identity (Berlin, 2000d: 179–189). Berlin saw nothing in this kind of nationalism that was inconsistent with his own liberal ideals and he cited England together with Holland and the Scandinavian countries as good examples of a specifically liberal nationalism.

Developing his own version of Berlinian nationalism Margalit distinguishes three senses of what it is to belong. First, membership of a group enables an individual to express herself in a particular way; just as painters representing different traditions or schools paint in a particular way so human beings who are French express themselves 'Frenchly' and Koreans 'Koreanly' (Margalit, 1997: 84). Second, membership of this kind cannot be denied to an individual because it is not a matter of achievement: 'To be a good Irishman, it is true, is an achievement. But to be an Irishman is not' (Margalit and Raz, 1990: 446–447). Third, membership in a group is about feeling at home; this means not having to explain oneself to others, being able to take a great many things for granted. The national self-determination advocated by Margalit and Raz is Berlinian because it identifies individual well-being with the experience of group membership. Nations, as 'encompassing groups', are valuable because they provide for this important human need. The emphasis on the *individual* benefiting is crucial because this kind of nationalism repudiates any tendency to reify or glorify the nation, to treat the nation as an end in itself. Berlin, says Margalit (1997: 78), was never a 'blood and soil' nationalist, a combination he always dismissed as causing 'only tetanus'. The cultural and non-aggressive nationalism of which Berlin approved is most clearly described in his essay on the Bengali poet Rabindranath Tagore who, Berlin said, understood that Bengalis needed their own cultural identity and language in order to flourish but Tagore's was a balanced nationalism that also recognized the value of studying other cultures and languages, and therefore saw English as a window onto the world.[10]

Earlier I made reference to Tate's series of speeches on national identity and education. To make his point about the importance of national attachment Tate draws freely on Berlin who he sees as a liberal who resisted Enlightenment cosmopolitanism because he appreciated the importance of national identity and attachment. Like Berlin, Tate (1995: para 34) sees the need for such attachment coming in response to feelings of alienation which he attributes to the experience of rapid change and he talks about cultural knowledge as 'the cement that helps to hold together the consciousness of a community and provides continuity across generations'. Returning to this theme in 1997 Tate argued the importance of shared texts and stories of national events and myths that provide a sense of identity in the face of uncertainty. Again Berlin is identified as the key source for relating attachment to self-esteem and in criticizing Enlightenment cosmopolitans for their disregard of this important human need (Tate, 1997b).[11]

Malignant nationalism: a response to humiliation and defeat

In his frequently cited essay *Nationalism: Past Neglect and Present Power*[12] Berlin wrote about another kind of nationalism; this is a nationalism that is qualitatively different from the benign version of national identity as belonging. This much more dangerous nationalism is the product of humiliation by others; in Berlin's words it is the outcome of 'wounded pride' (Berlin, 1979: 346). Borrowing from Schiller, Berlin (1991a: 246) describes German national resistance to the influence of France after the defeat at the hands of Napoleon as a 'bent twig . . . lashing back and refusing to accept alleged inferiority'.[13] When nations face humiliation, either through rapid technological change threatening traditional ways of life or through military catastrophe, there is the potential for extreme forms of nationalism where belonging becomes the supreme value and individuals are expected to identify with their nation first and foremost. In this form of nationalism the nation is reified to such an extent that it comes to be thought of as having a personality and any action, including the use of force, is justified in terms of the needs of the nation. The outbreaks of nationalist violence during the post-communist period have been taken to provide more recent empirical support for Berlin's vision of this extreme nationalism brought about through 'wounded pride' (Crowder, 2004).

Berlin's biographer Michael Ignatieff (1994b) has written about belonging and solidarity as human needs that are important yet difficult to satisfy within the terms of liberal rights theory. Ignatieff shares Berlin's concern for satisfying the human need to belong but when he came to draw together his own thoughts about nationalism following a series of journeys in those parts of the world most directly affected by nationalist violence, Ignatieff found himself re-thinking the need for belonging. As a Canadian of Russian origin living in London, Ignatieff claimed to know something of what it was to need to belong but he went on to say: ' I have been to places where belonging is so intense that I now recoil from it in fear ... Being only yourself is what nationalism will not allow. When people come, by terror or exaltation, to think of themselves as patriots first, individuals second, they have embarked on a path of ethical abdication' (Ignatieff, 1994a: 188). This form of nationalism, says Ignatieff, emerges when the collapse of state power persuades individuals to join 'communities of fear' based on, often fictitious, ethnic identities. Recalling a journey to the former Yugoslavia Ignatieff (1998b: 38) writes:

> Before the war, he [the Serb] might have thought of himself as a Yugoslav or a café manager or a husband rather than as a Serb. Now he sits in his farmhouse bunker, there are men two hundred and fifty yards away who would kill him. For them he is only a Serb, not a neighbour, not a friend, not a Yugoslav, not a former teammate at the football club. And because he is only a Serb for his enemies, he has become only a Serb to himself.

Berlin, we have seen, often described anti-imperialist nationalist movements as expressing a desire for status rather than freedom. This desire to have one's people given recognition was so strong, said Berlin, as to result in a willingness to be bullied by one's own group rather than be ruled by another, however benign that rule might be. Responding from the perspective of one such status-seeking nationalism Chisanga Siame (2000, see Chapter 1, note 25) takes Berlin to task for distinguishing status and freedom in this way. For Siame there is no distinction between the freedom of one's country and the freedom of the individual; Zambians, he said, see national independence as their own individual freedom even when this independence comes with the repression of freedoms such as restrictions on the movement of Zambian women. Siame's argument seems to bear out Berlin's observations about the search for status and a willingness to sacrifice individual freedoms in the interests of group solidarity. Berlin, however, unlike Siame, would still regard this as a loss of freedom.

These psychological insights into what might cause individuals of oppressed groups to relinquish their individual rights in favour of the status of their group suggest some lessons for contemporary liberals interested in questions about the appropriateness of national curricula in multinational societies. Kevin McDonough (2003) appears to have the dangers of wounded pride in mind when asking whether it is always right from a liberal perspective to seek to undermine illiberal practices within minority cultural groups. Liberal responses that threaten the status of groups and therefore the self-esteem of their members might only serve, he suggests, to strengthen cultural identities and the illiberal practices that liberals seek to constrain. Sometimes it is better, says McDonough, to delay projects that support federal civic loyalties in multinational societies so that liberal developments internal to illiberal groups are not stifled.[14]

Liberal nationalism and multi-ethnic societies

The policy implications of Berlin's writing on nationalism and belonging for multi-ethnic societies have been interpreted in very different ways. Birnbaum (1996, 2004) sees Berlin as making strong arguments for nations as political communities sharing a homogeneous culture; this is an interpretation that offers little support for the cultural claims of sub-state communities. Tamir (1998) draws very different conclusions and claims Berlin as a 'liberal of the fringes' whose recognition of the importance of group identity requires a separation of state and nation that allows space for cultural communities to flourish. In this section I consider both the liberal nationalism of David Miller, which suggests the need for a pan-state sense of national identity, and the cultural nationalism of Yael Tamir which calls for multi-national recognition and support within the state.

David Miller and national identity

Miller's liberal nationalist thesis has been the focus of considerable debate about national identity and the implications for minority groups.[15] Like Berlin, Miller (1997) sees nationhood as providing what he calls the 'social cement' that enables liberal institutions to function. In *On Nationality* Miller (1995a: 22–27) sets out in some detail the qualities that define what it is to be a nation. First, co-nationals must recognize each other as belonging together. This recognition does not depend on ethnicity, physical characteristics or anything to do with biology and Miller is often at pains to make the case that national identity can be, and usually is, multi-ethnic. Brian Barry's (2001: 88) notion of 'common national identity' as 'commitment to the welfare of the larger society made up of the majority and the minority (or minorities)' also captures this idea of nation as a community of individuals who believe they belong together and share mutual interests best realized through co-operative activity. Barry and Miller both qualify as civic rather than ethnic nationalists by employing 'community' in terms of residence (Brown, 1999), in other words people who have come to live together, rather than people who claim their homeland as a place of origin.

Second, nation provides historical continuity, an identity that stretches both back and forward. Recognition of this continuity is claimed to provide an emotional dimension to feelings of attachment which serve to strengthen civic engagement (White, 1996). Barry (1999) argues that this concern with the historical continuity that features regularly in those cultural nationalist accounts that are derived from Herder can be defended as consistent with liberal individualism because individuals have interests in the kind of culture available to their children and grandchildren.[16] Individuals of the present generation have a legitimate interest in what happens to their culture after they have gone.

In response to this kind of argument Michael Freeman (1994) queries how immigrant communities and their British-born children can be asked to share the history of, and shoulder obligations to, the descent-majority's forebears. Andrew

Vincent (1997: 23) also describes as 'highly dubious' Miller's attempt to distinguish his civic nationalist project of obligations to forebears from the more exclusive versions of ethnic nationalism. For all his talk of an inclusive national identity does Miller's concern with the past not serve to exclude the very people he is so determined to include? Miller's critics also point to the incompatibility of liberal commitments to rationality and truth-seeking with the kind of mythologies that nationalists accept in the interests of winning civic engagement.[17]

Liberal nationalists wrestle with the problem of how to balance liberal commitments to a multicultural curriculum that will inevitably teach minority children that their community has suffered at the hands of the majority group while still managing to win the allegiance of minority children to the national project. Recognizing that minority groups share an interest in social stability Eamonn Callan (2002b) asks how members of communities that have experienced oppression at the hands of the dominant group can, nevertheless, be encouraged to engage positively with the state? Callan's nicely balanced response calls for nations to use the best of their traditions to interrogate those occasions when the nation failed to live up to its best. Inevitably there will be a tension between the need for unity and teaching a historical narrative that has the potential to undermine that unity but Callan remains committed to the idea that learning that one's ancestors have not always lived up to their ideals is not to give up on those ideals. Robert Fullinwider (1996: 221) provides an example of how this might be achieved when he writes that the story of the Pilgrims' survival with the help of the Pemaquid people through the winter of 1620–1621 'pictures the cross-racial comity that *might have been and that might yet be* if students commit themselves to it' (emphasis added).[18] In support of his claims for the importance of the historical continuity that underpins national identity Miller argues that it is rational to retain a belief in stories about the past that are known to be myths; because myths of this kind can serve social purposes, they deserve liberal support.

Third, Miller turns to the active dimension to national attachments; members of a nation, he says, must act together, take decisions collectively, engage each other in debate, and accept that when they fail to persuade their co-patriots on a particular matter this does not mean that on another occasion they cannot succeed in doing so.[19] As a community of fate, members of a nation will recognize special responsibilities for the welfare of co-nationals with whom they 'wish to continue their life in common' (Miller, 1995a: 23). As a socialist, Miller argues that acknowledging membership of a community of fate requires a commitment to the redistribution of wealth for egalitarian purposes. This superordinate identity to which liberal nationalists are committed still worries Spinner-Halev and Theiss-Morse (2003) who are rather more concerned about the potential of collective identities for violence; their solution is to stress the importance of the sub-national identities that Miller accommodates: 'If many people have several salient identities, and if their collective self-esteem is not mostly tied to their nation, then the collective self-esteem that many find in their nation may not promote violence' (*ibid*: 525).

Fourth, members of a nation will identify with, and have feelings for, a particular geographical space, a homeland. While it is not necessary for all members to inhabit that space, this territory will continue to hold a special significance in the thoughts of members of that nation. Finally, and perhaps most controversially, Miller makes a claim for the importance of a shared public culture. Given Miller's strictures about the multi-ethnicity of national identity it matters greatly how this common public culture is defined. According to Miller citizens need shared understandings about how they live together but this is limited to the public culture leaving space for a diversity of cultures in the private context. This means, for example, that members of a nation must share a common language for communication in the public domain but this is perfectly compatible with a diversity of languages in the home and within local communities.

Miller's account of national identity, a term which he prefers to nationalism, has attracted a good deal of criticism from cosmopolitans who challenge the significance of national boundaries in determining ethical obligations. Miller's thesis fares no better with communitarians who doubt that any state could meet a commitment to a multi-ethnic national identity while incorporating the kind of historical and common culture elements that are required. Miller does acknowledge that the public culture will inevitably be influenced by the history of the ethnic majority community and that there is at least potential for conflict if and when the cultures of ethnic minority or religious groups differ significantly from the majority-influenced public culture. In his discussion of Islam, for example, Miller (1995b) suggests that a British identity founded on religious beliefs that privilege individuals' own experience and interpretation of sacred texts will conflict with the values of other religious traditions that are founded on revelation and the authority of religious leaders. Nevertheless, Miller believes that ethnic minority citizens have much to gain from a strong national identity and he criticizes the Swann Report (Great Britain: Department of Education and Science, 1985) for limiting the political education of minority pupils to a utilitarian curriculum for political participation; Miller wants to see more of an effort to get minority ethnic children to identify with a common citizenship and in Crick's approach to citizenship education in schools (Qualifications and Curriculum Authority, 1998) he sees and welcomes a commitment to that project (Miller, 2000b). On this view national identity can be thought of a hyphenated identity or, as Miller prefers to think of it, a nested identity, because pupils are encouraged to identify with the national political culture without any requirement to abandon more local and particularistic identities.

In more recent work Miller (2005: 101) is more explicit about the potential he finds in Berlin for an account of nationalism that coheres with liberalism when he contrasts the two metaphors that Berlin so often uses to refer to diversity and nationalism: 'If the Crooked Timber metaphor presents nationalism as a natural expression of human diversity, the Bent Twig metaphor presents it as a blind, irrational response to collective humiliation'. That Berlin offers such different perspectives on nationalism is not, says Miller, due to sloppy or lazy thinking but rather a genuine recognition of the tensions involved in marrying the concern with individual negative liberty and feelings of group belonging. Miller considers both the way that Berlin characterizes nationalism and the way that he accounts for its genesis and subsequent development. From this material Miller is able to arrive at a kind of nationalism he believes to be consistent with liberalism. This is a nationalism that stresses the cultural dimension of the nation without requiring political self-determination for all nations as long as the political unit provides protection for the different cultural groups that belong within its boundaries. This kind of nationalism is pluralist rather than unitary insofar as it allows for individuals to have multiple loyalties that accommodate subnational groups such as those based on community or religion. This nationalism is morally restricted in recognizing that, as well as observing what are national values, members of the nation are committed to universal values based on what it is to be human. Finally, this version of nationalism is reiterative rather than singular in that its claims for national self-determination are always subject to being consistent with the similar claims of other nations. The legacy that Berlin leaves with liberal nationalists is that there is a benign version of nationalism that responds to the proper recognition of human diversity but this is an unstable condition which, especially in conditions of oppression, is always likely to strike back with violent and illiberal consequences.

Miller's liberal account of national identity is Berlinian insofar as it discriminates between defensible and indefensible versions of nationalism. While recognizing that any national identity comes with 'the sediment of historical process' (Miller, 1995a: 42) this is an identity that is both inclusive in admitting immigrant communities and dynamic in acknowledging that immigrant groups will influence the national identity over time. It is an approach that allows for multiple identities that are shaped by individuals themselves. Miller's example of Jewish identity as one that is inescapable in the sense that a person is born into that group yet remains open in the equally important sense that there are many, individually chosen, ways to be Jewish is very close to Berlin's own account of Jewish identity and the right of the individual to choose. For Miller there is more than one way to be British but being British has to be more than a political identity if it is to provide the kind of 'social cement' required for liberal institutions and social justice.

Yael Tamir's liberal and cultural nationalism

Berlin is identified by Yael Tamir as the key source for a version of liberal nationalism which connects nation with cultural groups rather than with the state.[20] This cultural form of nationalism responds to the human need to belong that Tamir takes from the communitarian strand within Berlin's writing. The nation in this sense is defined in terms of 'feelings of fraternity, substantial distinctiveness and exclusivity, as well as a belief that [members] have common ancestors and that their community exhibits a continuous genealogy' (Tamir, 1995a: 425). On this view a nation is more like a group of friends than a set of people linked by objective characteristics because the existence of the nation depends on 'feelings of communion among its members' (*ibid*: 422). Where Miller focuses on the nation-state and the kind of citizenship education necessary to hold together disparate ethnic groups, Tamir collapses 'nation' and 'ethnicity', advocates a 'thin' civic education and focuses on the sub-state nations and the needs of individuals to express their own culture in the company of their co-nationals. Where Miller emphasizes the civic rights of individual members of liberal democracies, Tamir follows Berlin in explaining why members of minority nations will often choose the value of belonging in an illiberal group to the civic rights available to those who accept 'foreign' rule. The difference between the liberal nationalisms of Tamir and Miller is well captured by the distinction that Chaim Gans (2003) makes between culturalist and statist nationalisms: 'Cultural nationalism is concerned with the services that states can and ought to provide for nations, while statist nationalism is concerned with the services which a common national culture could provide for states' (*ibid*: 25).

This kind of cultural nationalism mirrors the way that Berlin contrasts the attitudes towards Zionism of some successfully assimilated Jews in Western countries with those of the Russian and Polish Jews of the Pale of Settlement. In his essay *Chaim Weizmann*[21] Berlin (1998: 37) describes how Western assimilated Jews often found it difficult to think of Jews as a nation 'as the Italians or, at least, the Armenians were a nation, and had just claims ... to a territorial existence as a nation organised in the form of a State'. With these Jews Berlin contrasted those of Russia and Poland who lived together in ways not dissimilar to their medieval forebears; sacred and secular were not distinguished, they lived isolated from the wider society, speaking their own language and developing their own institutions so that, 'as time went on [they] came to resemble more and more an authentic national minority settled upon its own ancestral soil' (*ibid*: 40). These Jews, moreover, thought of themselves as a coherent group and, although they lived often in poverty, 'they did not feel outcast or rootless' (*ibid*: 41), nor needed to ask themselves whether they were Jews.

Tamir defends the liberal credentials of this kind of cultural nationalism by insisting that national identity is not simply ascriptive; individuals can, and often do, choose their national identities. Here Berlin's account of Vico is cited in support of the ability of individuals to use their imaginative insight to understand the value systems of other national cultures; this plurality of cultural possibilities from which choices can be made is then identified as a condition for the exercise of individual autonomy (Tamir, 1993a: 27). What matters, however, is that individuals choose – this matters more than the actual choices they make. Sometimes individuals will choose non-liberal cultures and these choices must be respected. Some critics of this position have charged Tamir with failing to discuss in detail the illiberal practices, such as clitoridectomy and the denial of education, that characterize some of the cultural groups that she regards as properly choosable by individuals. This remains so for Tamir even when these practices are chosen by parents on behalf of their children (Levey, 2001). While Tamir defends these group rights because of the benefits that individuals gain from their group membership, she fails to acknowledge, say these critics, the harms that groups often do to their own members. For Geoffrey Levey the right to group self-determination that Tamir defends disregards an individual's right to choose assimilation into the dominant cultural group, a right that Berlin himself always defended. Despite her concern to make a case for a specifically liberal nationalism that respects both the rights of individuals and those of other nations, Tamir sometimes appears to favour group identities at the expense of individual agency in the way that cosmopolitan critics suggest any form of nationalism is bound to do. To the communitarian charge that nationalism fails to recognize internal cultural diversity Tamir appears much less vulnerable. Beiner (1999) has an explanation for this; he does not think that Tamir is really a nationalist at all. No real nationalist would say, as Tamir does (1993a: 150), that the ideal of the nation-state should be abandoned. On his view Tamir offers not nationalism but 'a form of liberalism that is not indifferent to concerns about national identity' (Beiner, 1999: 9). This suggests that liberalizing nationalism inevitably removes what is distinctive about nationalism or as Russell Hardin (2000: 206) puts it: 'Liberal nationalism is too good to be true, and ordinary nationalism is too true to be good'.

Distinguishing nation and state in the way that cultural nationalism does has consequences for education. Tamir identifies educational aims that serve state interests and those that are directed towards national interests. In the service of the state Tamir (1992) calls for civic education in legal and political matters designed to encourage commitment to public institutions; in a multi-national state the children of minority national groups are to be 'coached', rather than taught, in the majority political culture without adopting this culture as a way of life. National education(s), on the other hand, will aim to help children to become good members of their respective national groups; in a diverse society it follows that there will be as many national educations as there are cultural, that is national, groups. Tamir concludes by recommending a three-part curriculum which, for any particular child, will include civic education, a national education specific to her own group, and education about the other national groups that make up the state.[22]

The Crick Reports: education for nation-building

Liberal democracies and nation-building

Liberal democracies have nation-building needs, says Wayne Norman (2004: 98), because:

> Immigrants will not be seen as 'one of us' simply by being in the territory or by espousing certain values; but to the extent that they seem loyal and committed to the national project ... and begin to share memories and knowledge of at least recent social and political events, then they will come to be seen as members of the national community even if they cannot shake thick accents and awkward syntax.

There are several types of nation-building. There is 'reprioritization' of national identity that calls for members of sub-national groups to identify more closely with the wider national community. While Norman does not see this reprioritization requiring the abandonment of other identities, it does call for some level of identification with a pan-state national identity. Then there is 'reconfiguring' which aims to make an existing national identity more inclusive and therefore more hospitable to immigrant minorities. This reconfiguring is evident for example when in 1997 the then Secretary of State for Culture, Media and Sport, Chris Smith, said: 'When we try to understand our national culture and sense of identity, let us remember first and foremost that diversity is one of the key ingredients of both that culture and that identity'.[23] In the Blunkett and Brown speeches cited earlier it is possible to detect this kind of reconfiguration in the emphasis both give to the diverse origins of the English/British people making 'difference' a characteristic of the national identity. This appears to be an attempt to protect the liberal foundations of New Labour's civic nationalism from an association with ethnic nationalisms that celebrate common ancestry.

For Norman nation-building is inevitable and the task facing liberals is to distinguish and support its better forms. Any national identity is likely to include an ethnic-descent group component that will help shape what Miller called the 'common public culture'. Cultural traits such as the language, customs, tastes, and memories that enable members to recognize each other will fall along a continuum that extends from ethnically derived elements at one end to the more politically derived elements at the other. To the extent that politically derived traits come to dominate nation-building projects new members will be more easily accommodated. In what follows I aim to show how two recent reports might be considered as examples of nation-building projects with both reprioritization and reconfiguring dimensions and to gauge the extent to which each might be seen as a benign version of nationalism. I consider *Life in the United Kingdom: A Journey to Citizenship* briefly before going on to consider in more detail *Education for Citizenship and the Teaching of Democracy in Schools.*

Life in the United Kingdom: A Journey to Citizenship

The Advisory Group on Life in the United Kingdom was asked to identify how best to prepare new immigrants with the language skills and knowledge of life in the United Kingdom that would foster their sense of national identity and citizenship status. *Life in the United Kingdom: A Journey to Citizenship* (Great Britain, Home Office: Advisory Group on Life in the United Kingdom, 2004) is the outcome of the group's deliberations; it is a curriculum to be used by English language tutors working with new immigrants. The document was produced with the help of the Citizenship Foundation with the chapters on British history and government being prepared by Crick himself. Candidates for citizenship through naturalization will be required to show language skills and knowledge of life in the United Kingdom but will not be tested on the history and government sections. The document defines 'Britishness' as respect for law and democratic institutions and procedures, commitment to the values of equality and tolerance, and an allegiance to the state. Crick's brief history of the United Kingdom chronicles the invasions, dynastic rivalries and developments in forms of government; the formation of a multi-national state and its history of empire; the growth of democracy and the welfare state, and the emergence of a multicultural society, that together make up the national story. The most recent aspects of multiculturalism are covered in more detail in a section devoted to migration post-1945.

With reference to the debate about teaching the history of multicultural societies in a way that uses the best of the tradition to interrogate the sins of the past Crick's brief history acknowledges 'the evil of the slave trade' (*ibid*: 31) while also claiming that 'the British Empire brought more regular, acceptable and impartial systems of law and order than many had experienced under their own rulers' (*ibid*: 32). Crick continues: 'Public health, peace, and access to education can mean more to ordinary people than precisely who are their rulers' (*ibid*: 32). Here Crick is some distance from Berlin's observations about what he called the search for status that characterized the response of colonized peoples to foreign rule. Interestingly it was Berlin's own travels in Palestine that, in part, led him to this very different conclusion.[24]

Subsequent chapters deal with the profile of the British people, modern government and everyday life, and there are sections that provide guidance to further sources of information. While it is too early to judge how effective the handbook will be in supporting a citizenship curriculum for new immigrants it is possible to detect aspects of Norman's nation-building project. There is clearly both 'reprioritization' in seeking to win the allegiance of individuals whose identities are founded in their own ethnic and religious groups; it is also possible to detect 'reconfiguration' in the way that the document seeks to establish the United Kingdom as a multi-national, multicultural and multi-faith society where diversity is regarded as a key component and major strength.

Education for Citizenship and the Teaching of Democracy in Schools (The Crick Report)

Communitarians are critical of liberal nationalism because of the demands for cultural conformity it is claimed to make of minority cultural groups; these perceived demands have been seen as colonialist and racist (Osler and Starkey, 2001). Olssen (2004) considers Crick's account of citizenship education and national identity from this perspective and finds the report wanting in its approach to minority communities. Crick's shortcomings are to be made good, says Olssen, by 're-visioning' its recommendations along the lines of Lord Parekh's pluralist account of Britain as a 'community of communities' (Runnymede Trust, 2000).

There are three elements to Olssen's reasoning: first, what is of value in Crick's version of citizenship is the liberal defence of the civil rights of individuals; second, when it comes to the equally important claims for recognition by cultural groups Crick's liberal universalism is found wanting; and, third, this weakness can be ameliorated by drawing on the more culturally sensitive recommendations in Parekh's report. In this section I will respond by arguing: first, that Olssen's acceptance of Crick's liberalism limits him to versions of pluralism that are consistent with liberalism; second, that Parekh has been associated with both strong and more limited versions of pluralism; third, that only Parekh's limited pluralism is compatible with liberalism; and finally that Crick's approach to citizenship is already sufficiently pluralist in this limited and liberal sense thus rendering any 're-visioning' unnecessary.

Olssen's pluralist re-visioning of liberal citizenship education

According to Olssen (2004) Crick's citizenship education report is inadequate in its treatment of citizenship in a culturally diverse society because it ignores cultural difference by treating members of minority groups in just the same way as the majority. By ignoring difference this 'universalist citizenship' (Young, 1997, 2000) is just as exclusionary and discriminatory as unequal treatment on the basis of irrelevant differences such as skin colour. With Audrey Osler and Hugh Starkey (2001) Olssen regards Crick's version of liberal social democracy with its singular notion of national identity and its uniform conception of moral values as vulnerable to charges of colonialism and institutional racism. In reply Crick (2001) reminds his critics that his report argues for 'a national identity that is secure enough to find a place for the plurality of nations, cultures, ethnic identities and religions long found in the United Kingdom' (Qualifications and Curriculum Authority, 1998: 17). While Olssen clearly accepts the need to balance the requirements of unity and diversity he appears unconvinced by this response and concludes instead that Crick favours unity at the expense of diversity. Olssen justifies this interpretation by referring to the way the report calls for minority group members to respect the laws, codes and conventions of the wider society in a way that Olssen considers patronizing and culturally arrogant.

Parekh is said to improve on Crick on grounds of greater cultural sensitivity and a better balance between unity and difference while retaining an advantage over more radical multiculturalist positions in recognizing that difference only becomes meaningful within a wider context of some shared values. The superiority of Parekh's account is said to be founded in its key principles which recognize: the equal worth of all people; that citizens are both individuals and members of cultural identity groups; that same treatment is not necessarily equal treatment; that social cohesion is an important good requiring the sharing of some values, not least human rights; and that racism has no place in a decent society.

Liberals would not argue with any of these principles which are clearly endorsed by Crick (2000) in his own commentaries on the work of his committee. There is scope, however, for disagreement about how these principles relate to each other and how they are to be applied in practice. These disagreements come about as a result of the tensions increasingly appreciated between the equal civil rights of individuals as citizens and the recognition of cultural differences between community groups. Olssen accepts Kymlicka's liberal defence of minority group rights limited to cultural groups that acknowledge the rights of their individual members, a defence that is in conflict with Parekh's stronger version of pluralism. This tension is not lost on Parekh and Kymlicka themselves. Parekh (2000) devotes a substantial section of his book, *Rethinking Multiculturalism*, to a critique of liberal responses to cultural diversity and Kymlicka is chosen as one of his major targets. Kymlicka is criticized for the distinction he makes between what he calls national minorities such as 'First Peoples' of North America and immigrant communities such as Pakistani migrants to the UK. According to Kymlicka it is only the former type of minority that is owed group rights; having chosen to migrate to liberal democracies immigrant groups are owed the less substantial 'polyethnic rights' designed mainly to ease integration into the majority culture. Where Kymlicka (2003) argues for accommodating immigrant groups it is on the consequentialist grounds that tactically this is the most effective way of liberalizing illiberal groups. Parekh challenges both Kymlicka's distinction between national minorities and immigrants and his liberalizing agenda. For the pluralist Parekh there is more to human well-being than individual choice and Kymlicka is guilty, along with liberalism generally, in privileging the examined life over non-liberal but equally satisfying lives.

Parekh's pluralist response to the liberal theory of minority group rights indicates a tension between liberalism and pluralism that is potentially damaging to Olssen's project of reconciliation between the Crick and Parekh reports. This is the same tension that can be found throughout Berlin's liberal pluralism and it is interesting to see how differently Crick and Parekh draw upon Berlin's version of liberal pluralism.

Liberal political philosophy, national identity and the Crick Report

Crick (2000) regards freedom as an important procedural value of citizenship education and his discussion of freedom is articulated in response to Berlin's account of negative and positive liberty. He agrees with Berlin about the fundamental importance of negative liberty as the absence of constraints and the opportunity to make choices. Crick (2001) also acknowledges the potential dangers of positive liberty when it comes in the form of the idea that there is but one true freedom which is the serving of a particular cause and that those who fail to see this 'truth' are to be 'saved' by being forced to be free. However, having agreed the importance of negative liberty and the danger of the kind of positive liberty associated with monistic philosophies, Crick goes further than Berlin in arguing for a more active sense of freedom, something more than the passive notion of liberty as being left alone. It is because he prefers to think of freedom in this way that Crick links freedom to citizenship. In fact Crick (1969) has suggested that for all Berlin's insistence on the primacy of negative liberty, by valuing non-conformity in the way that he so often does, and in his recognition that negative liberty will sometimes have to be positively defended, Berlin himself acknowledges that freedom involves more than the opportunity for choice, it requires actually choosing. This is consistent with the two major themes in Berlin's work, the defence of freedom and the recognition of value pluralism; if there are many human values, some of which are incompatible, then humans must be free to choose between them.

Most importantly it is the freedom of individuals rather than that of groups that Crick defends, and in doing this he claims to be following Berlin who he described as 'humanist through and through, sometimes in the almost reductionist sense that individuals alone move or personify events, but also in the moral sense that it is the happiness or dignity of individuals that counts, not the pride and power of nations or ethnic groups' (Crick, 2001: 170). He goes on to recall that, although Berlin taught that we need group identities, he also insisted that 'individuals can and sometimes should take on other identities or challenge the dominant beliefs of the group in the name of freedom' (*ibid*: 170–171).

Crick (2000) describes the philosophy of his report as both civic republican and pluralist in its recognition of citizens both as individuals and as members of groups. Although he acknowledges the danger of the language of group rights in that groups can sometimes limit the freedoms of their own members, Crick does want pupils to see themselves as both members of particular cultural groups with values and identities and as members of a wider society within which there is a plurality of identities. There are benefits to be gained from diversity but these are best enjoyed within the context of a wider citizenship culture. Writing about national identity Crick (1991, 1995) distinguishes British and English identity and argues that while 'immigrant' communities need to become British in the political sense of shared rights and obligations, there is no requirement to become English in the cultural sense.[25] It is because he recognizes that a multicultural society will include a plurality of values that Crick makes tolerance one of the core values of the citizenship curriculum.

This brief review of Crick's attempt to bring together the claims of liberalism and pluralism, an attempt inspired in part by his response to both strands within Berlin's political philosophy, reveals a more positive account of the importance of ethnic and religious identities than some criticisms of the Crick Report would suggest.

Pluralist political philosophy and the Parekh Report

It is the pluralist dimension in Berlin's philosophy with which Parekh engages, so much so that *Rethinking Multiculturalism* (Parekh, 2000) has been described as 'an embroidery on Isaiah Berlin's argument for value pluralism' (Horton, 2001: 308). Where Crick urges thinking of freedom in individual terms Parekh is more inclined to the communitarian concern with group identity. This is most clearly expressed in Parekh's account of community which is clearly influenced by Berlin's view of community as feeling at home:

> A community gives its members a sense of belonging, and therefore of their identity and dignity. Here in my community I am among my own people, I

am at home, I know them and understand them, and they know me and understand me. . . . We speak the same language (including often the same body language), smile and laugh at the same jokes, know the same stories and music, have shared memories. I am recognised and respected. I am a somebody not a nonentity.

(Runnymede Trust, 2000: 50)

Parekh's own account of Berlin focuses on the critique of the Enlightenment belief that reason must lead to one true way of life; for Parekh (1982) and for Berlin, this is a denial of the truth of value pluralism. But Parekh is much less enthusiastic about Berlin's account of negative liberty with its focus on the rights of the individual rather than the attribution of rights to groups. Less concerned than Berlin about the totalitarian potential of positive liberty Parekh argues that there are forms of freedom, such as spiritual freedom, which actually require an authoritarian context.

In *Rethinking Multiculturalism* Parekh examines the attempts of contemporary liberals to reconcile their liberalism with the claims of cultural pluralism. He argues that liberals fail to recognize the culturally embedded nature of their commitments to individual rights. Much the same is said of international instruments such as the Universal Declaration of Human Rights and, along the lines of the 1993 Bangkok Declaration, Parekh stresses the incompatibility of Western human rights values with Eastern traditions and he argues for the *local* interpretation of human rights. This concern for group rights is most clearly seen in Parekh's approval of the religious toleration extended to different religious groups within the Ottoman millet system of government. While it is true that this system recognized the rights of such groups, it is also the case that it did little for the individual rights of dissenting individuals within these groups (see Chapter 3, note 30). In his determination to set himself apart from contemporary liberals Parekh appears to be arguing for a strong version of pluralism, one that insists against liberalism that individual rights should not always trump group rights. This is the political philosophy that informs what the Parekh Report refers to as a 'community of communities'; it is difficult to see how this is to be reconciled with Crick.

But there is another strand to *Rethinking Multiculturalism* and this also appears throughout the Parekh Report. This is the view that a multicultural society, like any other society, requires a 'broadly shared culture' – one that is bound to be related to a character and identity that has been historically acquired. Although Parekh (1995: 256) is unhappy with the term 'national identity' he does talk about the 'collective identity' of a polity, an identity that is defined by 'its deepest tendencies, impulses, ideals, values, beliefs, dispositions and characteristic ways of thought'. It is acknowledged that, although this identity ought to be defined in terms that are politico-institutional rather than ethnocultural, any such identity is likely, for historical reasons, to find itself tied to a particular ethnic group. Furthermore this historic community is entitled to disallow any cultural practices that offend its core values thereby threatening to change the nature of that society. Although Parekh favours achieving consensus through a dialogue between the groups that make up the multicultural society, he argues that such dialogue must start from what he calls society's 'operative public values' (Parekh, 2000: 267). If a minority group fails to persuade the majority of the value of a practice of which the society disapproves it is the operative public value that must prevail because 'while a society has the obligation to accommodate the minority way of life, it has no obligation to do so at the cost to its own ' (Parekh, 2000: 273). What is more, 'immigrants' being unfamiliar with the wider society ought to defer to the majority on contentious matters. This appears to be just the kind of thinking that so concerns the multiculturalist critics of the Crick Report yet it is to Parekh that Olssen turns for a more culturally sensitive account of citizenship.

There is a tension between Parekh's reluctance to interfere with the operative public values of a society and the reforming agenda of his report. Although it is the Crick Report that Olssen finds wanting in his treatment of cultural minorities, it is difficult to see how Parekh's requirement that minority cultural claims be subject to examination in the context of the operative public values of the majority community provides any advance on Crick's proposals for a shared citizenship culture. As Paul Kelly (2001) says, it is because Parekh refuses liberal universalist values that he is left with no resources to challenge the 'operative public values' of a society that discriminates. There appears to be no strategy for translating the report's reference to a new and more inclusive sense of Britishness into ways that minorities can challenge the terms of that inclusion.

The Parekh Report attempts to reconcile the claims of liberalism and pluralism by calling for a community of communities and it is in its balancing of these two dimensions that Olssen claims that this offers a resource for re-visioning Crick's liberal approach to citizenship and national identity. What Olssen seeks is a pluralism that is sensitive to the differences between cultural groups without prejudicing the rights of individual group members. Given his commitment to individual freedom the strong version of Parekh's pluralism that speaks of the need to go beyond liberalism in order to meet the needs of cultural minorities is unavailable to Olssen. In this mode, Parekh's pluralism is incompatible with liberalism and, as a liberal who rejects cultural separatism, Olssen must reject it. Where Parekh's pluralism is of the more moderate kind limited by the requirement of congruence with the operative public values of society it appears to offer no advance on Crick's civic republicanism. In fact Crick's recognition of a dynamic national identity properly influenced by the impact of migration appears more accommodating of cultural difference than Parekh's prioritization of whatever public values a majority happens to hold. Either way it is difficult to see the Parekh Report as providing the kind of resource for re-visioning Crick in the way that Olssen requires. In what follows I will conclude that a more appropriate resource is to found in the liberal, therefore limited, pluralism of Isaiah Berlin.

Liberal pluralism and national identity

Graham Day and Andrew Thompson (2004: 165) ask whether nationalism 'which displays an interminable preoccupation with difference' can ever be liberal. The preoccupation with difference, they say, is revealed in beliefs by members about the uniqueness and superiority of their own nation and an intolerance of difference within the nation. Nationalists, then, are said to behave illiberally towards those perceived as 'foreigners' both within and without and so '[a]t best, this means that outsiders will be viewed as requiring some degree of cultural transformation or control, rather than as individuals to be valued in their own right' (*ibid*: 165). This chapter has been concerned with exploring the potential for rescuing nationalism (or national identity) from these criticisms and considering what role Berlin might play in such a mission.

National identity and cosmopolitanism

Cosmopolitans question the moral significance of national boundaries and the special obligations that liberal nationalists claim are owed by members to co-nationals. Arguing for the recognition of the human good that members get from their belonging to a cultural group Berlin has often rejected the 'emptiness' of cosmopolitanism but, recalling Berlin, William Waldegrave said:

> [I]f you had asked me to show you what I meant by the ideal of Englishness, I would have taken you to see a Latvian, Jewish, German, Italian mixture of all the cultures of Europe. I would have taken you to see Isaiah Berlin.[26]

It could be argued that cosmopolitan ideals and civic, as opposed to ethnic, nationalism do not have to be seen as necessarily coming into conflict. Ignatieff, for example, calls for national symbols to be linked to justice rather than ethnicity saying, '[i]f a society no longer teaches its children that Britishness has a connection, not to ethnicity, but to justice, then its symbols are bound to figure on the placards of hatred' (Ignatieff, 1994a: 185). This is a reference to events in Northern Ireland and the significance there of the Union flag but it might just as easily have been said about the newspaper images of Muslim youths burning the same flag in protest against British policy in Iraq, images which led the Chairperson of the Commission for Racial Equality to question the policy of multiculturalism and call for a stronger and more inclusive national identity.[27]

Despite his own frequent rejections of cosmopolitanism Berlin's ethical outlook has been called 'deeply cosmopolitan'; on this view Berlin is no defender of extreme cultural particularism because, in cosmopolitan fashion, he wants us to understand our own choices 'against a background of very different, incompatible yet valuable alternatives' (Zakaras, 2003: 497). Other cultural groups have different values but outsiders can understand these values because they answer to shared human needs. What Berlin adds to our understanding of

freedom, says Alex Zakaras, is the recognition that it is the cosmopolitan awareness and engagement with a range of values that we might choose to live by that
allows us to think of choosing our own way of life so that '[t]he moral virtue of
empathy turns out to have special significance in opening avenues for self-
creation' (*ibid*: 515).

Judging both extreme nationalism and empty cosmopolitanism as equally
dangerous Brett Bowden (2003) seeks a reconciliation between what he calls
these two 'ideals-cum-ideologies' and he identifies Berlin as a potential source
for mediation. For Bowden nationalism represents the communitarian response
to liberalism being founded as it is on the belief that it is the grounding within a
particular community that enables human beings to flourish and maximize their
potential. The liberal cosmopolitan side of the debate resists tying individuals to
any kind of primordial community preferring to think of the individual in terms
of autonomous agency. I have argued throughout this book for recognizing both
of these perspectives in Berlin's writing.

Bowden, like Berlin, distinguishes good and bad nationalisms. Civic nationalism, he says, both allows the individual to care more for co-nationals without
neglecting the claims of non-nationals and to identify with the wider community
without prejudicing individual freedoms. On this view patriotic feelings are conditional on the ethical behaviour of the nation and a true patriot will not be slow
in pointing out when the nation fails to live up to its best self. With Thomas
Pogge (1992) and cosmopolitans from Diogenes and Marcus Arelius through
Erasmus, Kant and Paine to the contemporary work of Martha Nussbaum,
Bowden identifies cosmopolitanism with individual agency rather than group
identity. Resisting a perception of nationalism and cosmopolitanism as incommensurable paradigms Bowden agrees with Ignatieff's observation that
cosmopolitan cities succeed best within the boundaries of secure nation-states.
Like Stephen Macedo (2000), Ignatieff and Bowden clearly prefer a Sydney to a
Sarajevo.[28] All of this suggests the need for some reconciliation between nationalism and cosmopolitanism and it is to Berlin that Bowden turns in order to consider this possibility.

Noting Berlin's warnings against the dangers of a 'wounded Volkgeist'
Bowden moderates cosmopolitan claims. It was the anthropologist Ulf Hannerz
(1990) who once remarked that cosmopolitans keen on cultural borrowing
needed locals to maintain their respective cultures, and Bowden makes much the
same point when he says that it is the contrast with others that allows us to see
the distinctiveness of our own traditions.[29] Civic nationalists and cosmopolitans
alike can see the benefits of cultural borrowing and individuals with a secure
sense of belonging are best placed to appreciate what others have to offer. It is
by following Herder's non-aggressive nationalism that Berlin teaches the possibility that individuals can feel a sense of belonging in their own nation while at
the same time appreciating what other nations mean to their own nationals.

National identity and cultural diversity

Liberal nationalism is one version of communitarianism, one where the nation-state represents the community around which individuals are asked to identify, but communitarianism might equally be taken as a call for the recognition of those cultural groups that exist within the nation-state (Vincent, 2002). Tamir, it will be recalled, believes that Berlin's recognition of the importance of the human value of belonging and cultural identity leads to a cultural nationalism where nation and cultural group come together to force the separation of nation and state, whereas in Miller's liberal nationalism a distinction between public and private realms seeks to create the space for both a shared public culture and a multiplicity of community cultures. Where Berlin stands on this relationship between the nation-state and the cultural identities of sub-state communities has become the subject of considerable debate.

George Crowder (2004) concedes that in much of what he wrote and said Berlin seemed to favour the mono-cultural state as the most secure political environment for liberal institutions and values. This is certainly the argument that Birnbaum (1996) offers against Gray's 'internal pluralist' interpretation of Berlin when he says that, in his concern to resist global cultural homogeneity, Berlin emphasizes the differences between national cultures at the expense of internal heterogeneity. Crowder cites the interview given to Nathan Gardels in 1991[30] where Berlin referred to ethnic minority claims for academic recognition on American university campuses ('Black studies, Puerto Rican studies, and the rest') as potentially disruptive of the kind of common culture that any stable society requires, and to the *Jewish Slavery and Emancipation* paper where Berlin (2000a: 180) describes as 'sorry absurdities' those Jews who favour the idea of a nation as 'a motley amalgam of highly diverse and quasi-autonomous communities'. While Berlin always argued for the right of Jews to choose to live as Jews in whatever nation-state they resided, he did not believe that this justi-fied the political autonomy of sub-state communities; letters to his parents from 1940s New York describing his visits to Jewish religious courts suggest that Berlin was no more accepting of legal autonomy for cultural groups (Berlin, 2004a: 394–395). These passages notwithstanding, Crowder (2004: 185) describes Berlin's position as one of integration rather than assimilation, one 'where members of the group maintain their distinct identity within the family and in voluntary associations, while accepting the same public rights and duties as other citizens'. This is suggestive of a model of liberal cultural nationalism where members of immigrant communities operate within both a (minority) culture of origin and another (majority) culture where many aspects of their lives take place (Gans, 2003). On this model of national self-determination a national group is granted self-government rights, representation rights, and the right to cultural preservation within its homeland territory. This means that national groups can control their own culture and live their lives within its framework; national group members will be supported in the maintenance of their own culture as the public culture. But Gans is clear that these rights do not extend to ownership of the state which might be shared by more than one national group. Equally national group members who reside in a national diaspora retain national rights on matters that concern them, such as rights of return. The protection of the rights of a national group in its own homeland is important to all national group members irrespective of where they reside.

The ideal society on this view is multicultural and significantly more pluralistic than the nation-state. Individuals can reside in one state while retaining loyalty to, and some rights within, another. This also accommodates cosmopolitans who enjoy the opportunity to operate within a culture that draws on a range of local cultures. Gans recognizes that the privileging of citizens resident in their own homeland is likely to create other groups of citizens who, living outside their own homelands, lack full self-determination rights and this might be regarded as a domestic injustice. Gans answers this by arguing for the separation of individuals' interests in freedom and identity. Members of a national group residing outside their own homeland do enjoy citizenship rights in the wider society where they will live much of their lives (their culture of endeavours); additionally they enjoy polyethnic rights that protect their adherence to their own culture. Unlike Kymlicka whose account of minority rights appears to consign immigrant groups with polyethnic rights to a second-class status Gans claims that in his own version polyethnic rights are appropriate rather than second class. These citizens enjoy freedom within the wider society, opportunities to adhere to their own cultural group and the right to influence their own national culture in the homeland. Social cohesion is gained through a constitutional patriotism that falls short of requiring adoption of the majority culture while allowing for this should individuals so choose. This combination of citizenship rights in the wider society, cultural membership within the community of identity, and loyalty to the homeland state appears to mirror Berlin's argument against Arthur Koestler in *Jewish Slavery and Emancipation*. Koestler had argued that the founding of Israel provided Jews of the diaspora with a choice between complete assimilation into their country of residence or emigration to Israel to live as a Jew. Berlin famously resisted what he saw as this oppressive choice and replied by saying that 'individual Jews will surely claim their rights and perform their full duties as human beings and citizens in the communities in which, at last, they can freely choose to live – freely, because they are physically as well as morally free to leave them, and their choice whether to go or stay, being no longer forced on them, is a genuine choice' (Berlin, 2000a: 183). Like Gans, however, Berlin did not believe that Jews had any right to 'even an attenuated version of a State within a State' (*ibid*: 184).

Crowder does ask whether Berlin's communitarian strand does not push him further towards this kind of group political autonomy but concludes that the best of Berlin's arguments suggest that he resists such a move. Berlin's pluralism is of a limited kind, limited by a requirement of national unity in support of liberal institutions and by the commitment to individual liberty. Because he remains committed to individual liberty Berlin cannot find in favour of state support for cultural groups that fail to respect the freedoms of their own members. Berlin's pluralism is never a cultural pluralism but a pluralism that extends beyond groups to individuals and so for Crowder Berlin's liberal nationalism is akin to Kymlicka's 'multicultural citizenship' where liberty is ranked above belonging whenever these two important values come into conflict and where cultures are valued for the context of choice and the benefit of belonging that they provide but cultural groups must not be allowed to impede social unity nor prevent individuals exercising their autonomy.

7   In pursuit of an uncertain future

Wrestling with diversity[1]

> When someone is honestly 55% right, that's very good and there's no use wrangling. And if someone is 60% right, it's wonderful, it's great luck, and let him thank God. But what is to be said about 75% right? Wise people say this is suspicious. Well, and what about 100% right? Whoever says he's 100% right is a fanatic, a thug, and the worst kind of rascal.
>
> (Attributed to 'An Old Jew of Galicia' and cited by Milosz, 1985)

This opening quotation has been attributed to 'An Old Jew of Galicia' and it was chosen by Czeslaw Milosz as an introduction to his 1953 book *The Captive Mind.* Introducing the 1985 edition of the book the author describes its subject as 'the vulnerability of the twentieth century mind to seduction by socio-political doctrines and its readiness to accept totalitarian terror for the sake of a hypothetic future' (Milosz, 1985: vii). This book, much admired by Isaiah Berlin, warns against the 'longing for any, even the most illusory, certainty' (*ibid*: vii) that is characteristic of the totalitarian mind; against this it suggests a place for some healthy doubt. Berlin understood the nature of what Aileen Kelly (1978: xvi) calls this 'craving for certainties' but we have seen how Berlin always rejected what he referred to as this 'pursuit of the ideal'. More recently it has been suggested that Berlin's own critique of the totalitarian mind and the quest for certainty has a particular relevance in the context of the emergence of new fundamentalist utopias in the twenty-first century (Hatier, 2004). In attempting to bring together what lessons educators might learn from Berlin I take heed of these warnings about the dangers of certainty; wrestling with the dilemmas posed for education by cultural diversity points not to definitive solutions but rather to the necessity and value of the kind of compromises and trade-offs that Berlin saw as the inevitable outcome of pluralism. In his more contemporary novel, *Saturday*, which like *The Captive Mind* takes as one of its main themes the danger of certainty, Ian McEwan (2005) reflects the fears he shares with Berlin and Milosz when he says: 'No more big ideas. The world must improve, if at all, by tiny steps' (*ibid*: 74).

In drawing together the themes of this book I argue that an education that prepares individuals for life in culturally diverse societies will need to attend not only to all three of the strands that have been identified within Berlin's liberal pluralism (Chapter 1) but it will also need to take account of the significant tensions that exist between them. This means recognizing the enduring significance of those universal Enlightenment values to which Berlin remained committed while acknowledging the significance to individuals of the communities within which they are able to live well and flourish. Education must recognize both the importance of cultural context and the sense of belonging that children gain from their cultural membership as well as acknowledging those universal human rights that set some limits to the diversity that any truly liberal society is able to accommodate. To acknowledge the value of cultural membership, however, is not to accept cultural determinism and any education based on Berlinian liberal pluralism will be committed to supporting individual agency in the face of the coercive pressures and constraints of any particular culture. Drawing on what Jacob Levy (2000), following and adapting Judith Shklar, calls the 'multiculturalism of fear', I have argued for the priority of avoiding cruelty and fear as a means for evaluating the kinds of compromises that continuing commitments to liberalism and pluralism require. It is by recognizing each of these strands and the tensions between them that Berlin can be shown to provide an important contribution to contemporary debate about the value of liberal education for culturally diverse societies.

In the late summer of 2005 the British Home Secretary, Charles Clarke, was reported to be about to set up a commission which would be asked to investigate ways to improve the integration of faith groups into the wider British community.[2] This initiative came in the wake of extensive debate post-July 2005 about social cohesion and especially the civic identity of young Muslim citizens in the United Kingdom. Beginning with responses to the widely reported disturbances of 2001 in northern England (Chapter 4), and seen more recently in the debate surrounding the motivation for the terrorist attacks of July 2005 in London, it is possible to detect a growing shift of centre-left opinion away from the multicultural orthodoxy of the 1970s towards a community cohesion agenda which has been interpreted by some critics as representing a return to the assimilationist language and policies of the 1960s (Abbas, 2005; Back *et al.*, 2002; Kofman, 2005).[3] Tariq Modood (2005a) regrets this movement of centre-left opinion away from multiculturalism and warns against majority community assimilative pressure that risks antagonizing moderate Muslim opinion. Modood seeks a balance between societal cohesion and a recognition of difference that is integrative rather than assimilative. This requires, he argues, a sense of national identity that is strong but one that remains openly pluralistic. Muslims on this view must be included in the compromises between religion and the state that are part of everyday life in a modern but moderate secular state. By including Muslims in this way, says Modood, this pluralist British identity 'can be as emotionally and politically meaningful to British Muslims as the appeal of *jihadi* sentiments [and] critical to isolating and defeating extremism' (*ibid*: 7).

Elsewhere Modood (2005b) is optimistic about this balanced approach to diversity and cohesion. He remarks on the way that minority ethnic identities in the United Kingdom have come to be less oppositional and are beginning to be seen as simply different ways of being British; Modood holds out the hope that the religious identity of Muslims can also come to be yet another way of being British. This is most likely to be the case, continues the argument, if the majority community and public institutions such as education can become as open to ethno-cultural collective identities as they have come to be with hybrid cosmopolitan individuals. This will require of the British state that it resist the kinds of assimilative reactions to political contestation by Muslims that has recently characterized government policy in France and the Netherlands, reactions that risk turning 'identity assertions [into] walls of separation' (*ibid*: 209).

This optimistic view of plural Britishness is shared by the Chief Rabbi, Sir Jonathan Sacks, when he turns his attention to the attitudes of minority group members themselves. While he wants to celebrate 350 years of British Jewry as a distinctive community, Sacks is primarily concerned here to warn against Jews and Muslims turning inward as local communities without any identification with British society.[4] This is a call for minorities to maintain their cultural and religious identities while continuing to participate fully in the wider society. Sacks builds on a theme he developed in a lecture given earlier in 2005 when he argued that members of religious and cultural minority groups must live, not as guests in a country house or as clients of a hotel, but as co-nationals who share in the building of a home.[5] With Berlin, Sacks (2002: 57) recognizes both moral universals, such as the sanctity of life and the right to be free, along with the particular loyalties and obligations that come with group membership. When he cites Berlin's pluralism to support his own account of 'the dignity of difference' it is to Berlin's *Notes on Prejudice*[6] that Sacks turns where Berlin, echoing the quotation that appears at the head of this chapter, says:

> Few things have done more harm than the belief on the part of individuals and groups (or tribes or states or nations or churches) that he or she or they are in *sole* possession of the truth . . . It is a terrible and dangerous arrogance to believe that you alone are right; have a magical eye which sees *the* truth; and that others cannot be right if they disagree. This makes one certain that there is *one* goal and only one for one's nation or church or the whole of humanity, and that it is worth any amount of suffering (particularly on the part of other people) if only the goal is attained.
>
> (Berlin, 2002a: 345, original emphasis)

The liberal dilemma

Earlier I made reference to the way that Trevor Phillips, Chairperson of the Commission for Racial Equality, appeared to join the shift of left-centre political opinion away from multiculturalism. Phillips repeated his own concerns about increased segregation when in September 2005 he spoke about a multiculturalism that appeared to have gone too far.[7] In this widely reported speech Phillips warned against the erosion of shared values that he took to be taking place when, for example, Christians belonging to the African-British community carried out exorcisms on their children and when British Sikhs in Birmingham brought about the closure of a play that they found offensive to their religion. The kind of examples cited by Phillips point to the dilemma for theorists who seek a liberal response to cultural and religious diversity and for education policy makers and practitioners who are involved in considering the claims of those cultural minority groups whose members often feel marginalized within the larger society and alienated by the majority culture and its public institutions, not least the education system. The egalitarian liberalism of Brian Barry (Chapter 2) appears well placed to respond to liberal concerns for equality of opportunity and the individual rights of all citizens irrespective of cultural identity but stands accused by its communitarian critics of failing to appreciate what it is that individuals gain from their community membership. The dilemma goes deeper still when the community identity is of a religious kind.

Responding to Barry's liberal egalitarian critique of multiculturalism John Horton (2003: 32) echoes Berlin when he describes culture as 'an essential strand in the fabric of our experience and an expression of our situatedness as social beings, which locates us and helps us feel "at home" in the world'. Any liberalism that fails to recognize this aspect of human well-being runs the risk of leaving some citizens feeling both marginalized and alienated. On the other hand the variations on diversity liberalism articulated by theorists such as William Galston and Joseph Raz, and the multicultural citizenship of Will Kymlicka, which all claim to be more responsive to the claims of cultural groups, have been criticized for leaving vulnerable members exposed to group oppression. These fears continue to persuade liberals of the need for some restraint on group rights and support for realistic exit options for those individuals who choose to leave their culture of birth for another.

Liberals have usually responded to this dilemma by recommending the accommodation of non-liberal cultural minority groups subject to conditions designed both to foster social cohesion across the wider national society and to protect the citizenship rights of vulnerable group members especially women and children. Much has been said about exit rights as an important element in protecting individuals from the more damaging aspects of group membership but this emphasis on exit rights fails to appreciate what follows from the involuntary dimension of certain kinds of group membership. Growing up as a member of a community results in a kind of 'rootedness', says Horton (*ibid*: 35), that is 'almost axiomatically a quality that implies the difficulty of detachment, and a sense of loss when one is so sundered'. While acknowledging liberal fears about group oppression of individual members Horton (*ibid*: 32), again echoing Berlin, continues by saying that 'even where a culture does contain practices that harm some of its members, it does not *necessarily* follow that even those so harmed do not derive overall benefit and value from that culture' (original emphasis).

This suggests the need for a response to the liberal dilemma that incorporates the insights of both egalitarian and diversity liberalisms. In Chapter 1 I referred to a third strand of liberalism, one that Levy identifies in Berlin as being concerned primarily with minimizing cruelty and fear. This pluralized liberalism attends to the importance that individuals attach to their groups but without neglecting the dangers that group identities represent if they become perverted as they so frequently are. I have argued throughout this book that Berlin provides both a corrective to those liberals who deny any communal dimension to human well-being and to those communitarians who give insufficient attention to the multiplicity and complexity of individual identity.

Tensions within Berlin's liberal pluralism

Speaking in 2000 the American philosopher Martha Nussbaum suggested that the existence of tensions within a theoretical perspective ought not to be taken as necessarily indicating weakness. Rather than suggesting a defect, inconsistencies might simply indicate the extent to which a theory is in touch with the difficulties and complexities of life.[8] From what has been said already it is clear that there are tensions running through Berlin's writing on liberalism and pluralism but, if Nussbaum is right, it is possible to see these tensions, even inconsistencies, as fruitful rather than problematic. A particular tension in liberalism identified by Nussbaum, and one that is especially relevant to Berlin, is the tension that exists between the liberal preference for non-interference with the ways that individuals choose to live their lives and the need for the state to intervene when it appears that failure to do so will result in group tyrannies and fear.

If genuine tensions are not to be eliminated and if one set of values is not to be totally abandoned in favour of another, then we must learn how to achieve compromises that are sensitive to the context of which these tensions are an ineliminable part. Berlin's liberal pluralism points to the need to recognize that it is an inevitable outcome of pluralism that not all legitimate concerns can be reconciled. What matters is that individuals are able to believe that a failure to persuade others of the legitimacy of a particular claim does not imply that all subsequent claims will meet the same fate. Social cohesion ultimately depends on all groups feeling that there will be occasions when they will be successful in their legitimate claims. Berlin warned against the dangers inherent in the utopian search for perfection; better that societies learn to live with their internal tensions. Reflecting on what this aspect of Berlin's anti-utopianism might mean for tensions within the Christian church the theologian and philosopher Michael Jinkins (2004: 137) says: 'It is possible to imagine a society (and I would argue a "good society") in which conflict over values and ideas, interests, aspirations, needs and ends, rages in a lively social and political praxis'. Attempts to build heaven on earth by eliminating these tensions are more likely, says Jinkins, to result in hell. For Berlin (2000b) it is not only rare but dangerous for a society or an individual to be dominated by any one thought-determining model.[9] Dangerous because the more totalistic the model the more violent the outcome if and when it is seen to fail. Much healthier is the society or individual able to draw on a range of models with less regard for internal consistency. When right clashes with right, and good with good, Berlin advocated the solution that mini-mized the harm or loss that choice between incommensurable goods always entails.[10] As Berlin (1991a: 18) himself says, this utilitarian calculus of the bene-fits and losses associated with rival courses of action is hardly the kind of answer to inspire idealists but, as John Gray (1995: 168) observes, it is this exis-tential and tragic quality of Berlin's liberalism that sets it apart from all others and, 'in refusing with a passion the pretence that there is peace when our lives abound in deep conflicts and hard choices', it does ring true with our daily experience. In what follows I consider separately the lessons that might be learned from Berlin's liberalism and pluralism before considering how what Levy identified as the third strand – a multiculturalism of fear – indicates how liberalism and pluralism might be combined so that each works to moderate the other.

Some lessons from Berlin's liberalism

Against those who claim Berlin as a key source for a radical multiculturalism or identity politics I have argued for seeing Berlin's liberal pluralism as having limits that are set by an enduring commitment to Enlightenment values; values that Judith Shklar (1996: 275) regarded as 'our best hope for a less brutal and irrational world'.[11] Berlin's version of pluralism has to be distinguished from the more contemporary politics of identity because of the significance he gives to the differences between individual members of groups as well as to those that exist between groups. Berlin's account of the relationship between community and individual identity strikes a chord with that of Peri Roberts (2003) who resists any identification of the boundaries of justification for beliefs with those of any particular community identity and argues that while '[w]e must stand somewhere . . . we can always later stand somewhere else to look more closely at our initial footing'(*ibid*: 152). Roberts is able to get to this point by regarding our background assumptions as points of departure for deliberation rather than 'givens' that are 'immune from revision'. This is the view of identity to which Edward Said comes in concluding his book *Culture and Imperialism*:

> No one today is purely *one* thing. Labels like Indian, or woman, or Muslim, or American are no more than starting points, which if followed into actual experience for only a moment are quickly left behind [and] just as human beings make their own history, they also make their cultural and ethnic identities.
>
> (Said, 1994: 407–408, original emphasis)

The motivation for the revision of these background assumptions to which both Roberts and Said point can come entirely from within the identity group (see MacMullen, 2004) but, as Berlin so often says, there is much to be said for the creative potential of culture contact in encouraging this critical perspective. In stressing the important role of those individuals who ask the difficult questions (and in encouraging children to ask these questions) Berlin took the opportunity during an interview with Bryan Magee to articulate his dislike of dogma:

> Societies can decay as a result of going to sleep on some comfortable bed of unquestioned dogma. If the imagination is to be stirred, if the intellect is to work, if mental life is not to sink to a low ebb, and the pursuit of truth (or justice, or self-fulfilment) is not to cease, assumptions must be challenged – sufficiently, at any rate, to keep society moving.
>
> (Berlin interviewed by Magee: 1978: 17)

I have argued that negative liberty as described by Berlin rules out liberal support for any community or form of education that is so coercive as to prejudice the ultimate capacity of individuals to choose their own projects in life. It has been argued that negative liberty defines the outer limits of Berlin's communitarianism with only benign forms of community compatible with negative liberty (Garrard, 1997: 291). This view is shared by Roger Hausheer when he remarks on the significance and implications of Berlin's work which show, he says, the need 'to cast off the chains of any one monolithic system which threatens to foreclose open and in principle unpredictable human developments' (1983: 59). On this view individuals are most likely to gain new knowledge when they are encouraged to expose themselves to different perspectives and when they are able to resist certainty and embrace doubt. Nowhere is this put more clearly by Berlin than in the introduction to his essays on Russian thinkers when, by way of disclaiming unshakeable confidence in his own opinions, he describes the burden of these essays as 'distrust of all claims to the possession of incorrigible knowledge about issues of fact or principle in any sphere of human behaviour' (Berlin, 1994a: viii).

In arguing for an education built on negative liberty that aims for open-mindedness and a fallibilism that recognizes the provisionality of knowledge I do not wish to rule out a form of early schooling that seeks education for young children in an environment that is culturally coherent such as that described by Michael Merry (2005b). Merry's point is that education for cultural coherence contributes both to achieving the *eventual* autonomy of children as well as valid educational aims other than autonomy facilitation.[12] Education for cultural coherence especially in the early years may be a necessary component of a liberal education but Merry is clear that it will not be sufficient and it is quite possible that children educated for open-mindedness will ultimately reject the world of their parents. This is an outcome that Berlin as the 'liberal philosopher of pluralism *par excellence*' is happy to recognize (Ellett and Ericson, 1997) even when the loss of inter-generational reproduction of a particular culture results in a society of less internal diversity; for Berlin there was no social world that did not involve some loss.

Communitarian accounts that neglect the darker side of community fail to register the dangers of positive liberty to which Berlin pointed. Nel Noddings (1996) draws on Berlin when she warns against perverted versions of liberty that identify freedom with immersion in strong 'normocentric' communities. Borrowing Berlin's words from *Two Concepts of Liberty* Noddings says that positive liberty 'renders it easy for me to conceive of myself as coercing others for their own sake, in their, not my, interest' (*ibid*: 255; Berlin, 2002a: 179). Schooling then becomes a form of character education aligned with a singular model of the ideal citizen. For Noddings an education that takes Berlin's warning seriously must combine negative liberty with the benefits of a collective orientation and this is best achieved by teaching children about what is both good *and* bad about community. Berlin was always clear that groups were to be valued, not for themselves, but for what they gave to individuals; those groups that fail to benefit their own members are undeserving of liberal support.[13]

Tensions within liberal nationalism: crooked timber or bent twig?[14]

In Chapter 6 I identified the different concerns of cosmopolitans and communitarians about liberal nationalist proposals for education for citizenship. In the United Kingdom recent initiatives aimed at both school pupils and adult new immigrants have been taken to suggest a monolithic national identity and community that is both socially exclusive of cultural minorities within the nation-state and insufficiently cognizant of moral obligations to other human beings resident outside that state. I have attempted to show how Berlin's version of liberal nationalism seeks to avoid these problems while warning of the dangers of failing to do so.

So-called 'thin' national identities have been seen as falling short of what is required for social cohesion while 'thick' identities based on a national ethnocultural past have the potential to exclude members of cultural minority groups. What Berlin recognized and what appears to inform the language of politicians such as David Blunkett and educational policy makers such as Nicholas Tate and Bernard Crick is that any failure to address national sentiment is to invite a much more dangerous version of aggressive nationalism. The nationalism of both majority and minorities has the potential to be no more than the benign face of cultural diversity (Berlin's 'crooked timber') but might equally become the resentful backlash to wounded pride that led Berlin to refer to this kind of nationalism as a 'bent twig'.

I have already discussed how David Miller observes a tension between, on the one hand, Berlin's commitment to the claims of negative liberty against collective versions of self-determination, and on the other, his lifelong support for Zionism and other national independence movements (Chapter 6). Miller (2005) agrees with Nussbaum about the potential productivity of tensions within theories and for him it is the tension between individual freedom and collective identity that allows Berlin's benign version of nationalism to cohere with modern welfare-based liberalism. This is possible because the recognition of universal values based on what it is that humans share limits what can be done in the name of nationalism. Miller calls this a 'morally restricted nationalism' because it recognizes both the claims of nations to self-determination as well as the claims of any sub-national communities to which individuals also owe loyalty and from which they gain an important dimension of identity.

From Berlin's central commitment to individual freedom Miller hypothesizes about how Berlin might have reacted to nationalist policies such as those designed to protect French Canada. While acknowledging the support that a super-ordinate identity gives to liberal politics and while cognizant of the fragmentation threat that some claims by sub-national communities might present, Berlin's concern to protect individuals from state interference would, says Miller, make it unlikely that Berlin would have supported the kind of policies that some liberal nationalists require such as constraints on English language usage in Quebec designed to ensure the survival of French. Miller (ibid: 114) writes:

> So although Berlin sees and accepts the argument connecting national unity to liberal democracy, he would have been reluctant to draw from it the practical conclusion that many liberal nationalists have wished to derive – namely that nation-building goals, justified in the past by their contribution to liberty in the long run, may nonetheless in the short term justify restricting individual freedom of some individuals and some groups to live as they wish.

What was said in Chapter 1 about Berlin's reluctance to favour constraints in the present on the often spurious grounds of protecting liberties in the future does offer support for Miller's view here. Despite all Berlin's criticisms of 'rootless cosmopolitans' Miller puts Berlin closer to Jeremy Waldron's (1995) notion of 'a cosmopolitan alternative' that draws from a range of cultural materials than to Will Kymlicka's external protections designed to protect societal cultures from erosion by outside influences. Again in Miller's own words: '[Berlin's] liberalism . . . is then about protecting individuals from outside interference, rather than about using the state to protect the cultural conditions under which people can lead autonomous lives' (Miller, 2005: 115).

For Berlin national self-determination has to be an instrumental rather than intrinsic good; it serves to enable individuals to live freely. Miller claims that the nationalism he derives from Berlin remains liberal and he describes it in terms of six theses. In large mobile and potentially anonymous societies national identity and the education designed to sustain it provides for a trans-generational community that is open to new members because it is not defined by either race or ethnicity. While this national identity provides for a sense of shared living, it does not do this at the expense of commitments to other group identities and, while there are special obligations to co-nationals, these are not to be insisted upon at the expense of the wider obligations that cosmopolitans identify with being human. The political self-determination that nations claim is only justified instrumentally in protecting ways of life that are valued by individuals and these national claims are not to be made by one nation without regard for the claims of other nations. Finally, Berlin's legacy is recognized by Miller not only for providing this liberally constrained nationalism but also for providing a salient and timely warning about the fragility of this version and its potential for perversion.

Some lessons from Berlin's pluralism

Avoiding 'reactive culturalism' by educating for trust

There are some clear links between the kind of Counter-Enlightenment thinkers who fascinated Berlin so much and the more contemporary politics of identity but, while there appears to be considerable agreement that Berlin's focus on the value that individuals gain from their attachments to identity groups provides a useful corrective to the universalising claims of the French Enlightenment, there is some disagreement about whether Berlin's version of communitarianism favours the protection of cultures at the level of the nation-state only or whether it is comprehensive enough to take in the identity claims of sub-state community groups. Berlin has been seen variously as a defender of the cultural identity of the homogeneous nation-state (Birnbaum, 2004) and as a resource for challenging those assimilationists who see in diversity a clear threat to social cohesion and national identity (Kenny, 2004). In this section I will explore the tensions between nation and cultural group and suggest what might be learned from Berlin's treatment of these tensions that is relevant to education in culturally diverse societies.

In previous chapters I have stressed the significance of what Berlin called the 'search for status' that he saw as such a strong motivating force for members of those cultural groups that are experiencing or have recently experienced oppression. Berlin often observed how the desire for self-government on the part of oppressed groups can be enough for members of groups who experience double oppression – from outsiders and from some of their own group – to accept the internal oppression rather than submit to rule by outsiders. In the course of this book I have noted several liberal philosophers who now agree that these kinds of circumstances are to be taken onto account before ruling against illiberal practices internal to oppressed groups. In Chapter 5 I discussed how the liberal emphasis on exit rights to counter internal group oppression falls down when it transpires that it tends to be those groups where liberal interference can be most easily justified from which exit proves to be most difficult. In the light of this Daniel Weinstock (2001, 2004a, 2004b) recommends an alternative approach aimed at reducing what Shachar (2001) called 'reactive culturalism', a process whereby groups experiencing external interference react by turning inwards to a more orthodox and often more repressive version of their own culture.

I want to consider Weinstock's arguments and recommendations in the context of the debate about British Muslim identity and the education of Muslim children to which I refer at the start of this chapter. I begin by referring back to Weinstock's case first introduced in Chapter 5 and showing how this relates to Berlin's psychological insights about the 'search for status'. Cultural groups, says Weinstock, face two problems. First, they fear loss of their group identity through the assimilation of their members into the cultural mainstream, what Weinstock calls 'the problem of number'. Second, they reject those elements of the majority culture's version of the past that they see as misrepresenting their own part in that story, what Weinstock calls 'the problem of history'. Avoiding reactive culturalism, and the harms to vulnerable group members that this often entails, involves policies designed to address these two problems thereby avoiding pushing minority groups into their more fundamentalist versions. What I want to suggest here is that that Weinstock's recommendations for educational policy provide a useful way forward in the context of what Berlin teaches about the psychology of minority group membership.

To avoid 'reactive culturalism' Weinstock (1999, 2001, 2004b) opposes the kind of identity-shaping and nation-building projects that some liberal nationalists recommend. Facing up to the problem of number, minority groups are likely to resent assimilatory projects of this kind. In a recent discussion that makes the important distinction between assimilationist policies and the choices of individuals to assimilate, Eamonn Callan (2005) has observed how resentment at assimilationist policy is turned against those members who choose to leave their minority group for the mainstream culture. Such individuals are often perceived and then portrayed as complicit in the oppression of their original (unchosen) culture by appearing 'to have given at least small victories to their oppressors' (*ibid*: 491). While Callan rejects this charge of complicity on the grounds that there are many valid grounds for an assimilatory response that is chosen, he notes that the charge of complicity is more likely to be brought against individuals when the group they are choosing to leave is under strong assimilationist pressure from the dominant group. In this respect, at least, assimilationist pressures are counterproductive and, if Weinstock is right in arguing that a shared identity is neither necessary for social cohesion purposes nor likely to be achieved, then liberal nationalists would be well advised to contain any assimilationist impulses. What does matter, says Weinstock, is gaining the kind of trust between communities that is required if groups are going to make the kind of compromises that shared living in a pluralist society entails. It follows that policy makers need to look to the interests of groups and the kinds of compromises and accommodations that allow minority group members to feel confident that meeting their economic and political interests is a matter of importance and concern to the majority group. Failure on this count results in group members turning to identity interests of a kind where compromises will be that much more difficult to achieve. As Weinstock (2004a: 110) puts it: '[A]spects of our identity become salient when the interests which we come to have as occupiers of this or that station are not satisfied [and] they become politically salient when we perceive that the source of our frustration is intentional'. Pointing to states such as Canada that enjoy considerable shared commitment to redistribution of wealth Weinstock claims that it is mutual trust that motivates citizens in this direction rather than shared identity.[15] Members of a minority group need to feel that their fellow citizens are not ill-disposed towards them realizing their own conception of the good life. Attempts to impose a common culture are likely to destroy this kind of trust and, citing the French approach to the headscarf issue, Weinstock advocates a less directly assimilationist stance on these matters, a stance that is less likely to result in the turn to identity about which Berlin warns.[16]

If it is trust rather than shared identity that holds together the citizens of a diverse society, what are the implications for education? In relation to the problem of history Weinstock (2004a) notes both that children will tend to reject attempts by their teachers to instil particular values and that children have access to versions of history from sources other than the school. On both counts a strategy of indirection is recommended. Taking the children of British Pakistani-origin families as his example Weinstock points out that community accounts of their own history, and in particular the relationship with the dominant majority culture, are likely to conflict with the 'official' version of the school. Nor, he says, are children likely to accept teaching about the value of national institutions if their own experience of those institutions is a negative one.[17] The kind of patriotic education favoured by some liberal nationalists is likely to sit uneasily with pupils who come from a community that currently experiences material disadvantage, relatively high levels of unemployment, low wages, inadequate housing and poor health (Abbas, 2005). This suggests the need for a curriculum such as that outlined by Callan which, while avoiding any sentimentalizing of the past, employs the best national traditions to interrogate occasions when the nation has failed to live up to its best (see Chapter 6). In the light of these comments it is worth noting that one of the fundamental recommendations of the Parekh Report (Runnymede Trust, 2000) was for some reckoning with Britain's imperial past. Unfortunately the enraged reaction of the British media to this suggestion does not augur well for any willingness to move in this direction (Fortier, 2005).

With reference to the problem of number and concerns about assimilationist policies Weinstock recommends close consultation with minority culture parents about accommodations that encourage parents to keep their children in public schooling. To this end he challenges Meira Levinson's support for the detached liberal school (Chapter 2). Sharing Levinson's liberal aim that children eventually become autonomous Weinstock argues that this is best achieved by keeping children from non-liberal communities in autonomy-facilitating public schools.[18] This concern for children to learn to trust each other through experiencing a shared schooling leads Weinstock to favour the common school yet he is uncomfortably aware that refusing faith-based schooling to religious minorities is also likely to undermine the social trust he seeks. Schools that are differentiated along lines of religious difference are unlikely to foster social cohesion and so Weinstock would discourage parochial schools except at the elementary level where there is something to be said for schooling within an environment that supports the development of a secure self-concept.[19] That said, there is a dilemma for liberals and Weinstock (2004a) acknowledges that curriculum designers face what he calls:

> [A] difficult, perhaps even tragic choice, between the requirements of indi-
> vidual identity and those of social trust. In a nutshell, the problem facing the
> designers of educational institutions for multicultural societies is that trust
> might require that the young be taught in structures that defy the various
> dimensions along which distrust tends to develop, but that other worthy
> moral and pedagogical goals might require that such lines of division be
> taken into account.
>
> *(Ibid*: 122)

Where Weinstock departs from other liberal accounts of how to respond to illiberal groups is in his recognition that the way that groups treat their own
members is often responsive to the situation of the group within the wider
society. Assimilationist policies 'have exacerbated rather than moderated the
tendency of groups to adopt a hierarchical and illiberal understanding of their
own cultures' (Weinstock, 2005: 240).[20] But then the opposite extreme of grant-
ing extensive group rights to illiberal groups only gives group leaders further
reason to present the so-called 'authentic' version of group culture thereby
leading to a narrowing of the group's self-understanding. It follows that reactive
culturalism is best avoided by policies that enable members of minority
communities to feel secure and trusted in such a way that the pressure to organ-
ize their internal affairs in such an authoritarian fashion is reduced. Weinstock
seeks to minimize the harm that members of illiberal groups experience whether
it comes at the hands of outsiders or their fellow group members. What is
required, says Weinstock (1998), is an approach to diversity that weighs the contribution that each group makes to the well-being of its members. This approach
is pluralist insofar as it recognizes that there are more groups that contribute
effectively to the well-being of their members than there are groups that liberals
would want to join. What matters is not whether a group prioritizes individual
autonomy but whether the group is reasonable in providing for the welfare of its
members. Here well-being is pluralized so that the pursuit of 'a life privileging
individual autonomy and placing a high premium on individual accomplishment
will probably require trade-offs with those values involved in more community-
or family-based lifestyles' (*ibid*: 294).

A liberal and limited pluralism: context and compromise

Contemporary liberal pluralists such as Weinstock and Levy, as well as Galston
and Baumeister in their most recent work, challenge Gray's radical pluralist and
anti-liberal interpretation of Berlin by insisting on a more limited pluralism.
Galston (2005) now agrees with Levy when he talks about not two liberalisms,
but one liberalism drawing on two strands, one of which is designed to protect
individuals from the coercive pressures of their groups. Levy (2003) criticizes
Gray for his failure to do justice to this more nuanced liberalism to be found in
Berlin. Baumeister (2003) also now qualifies her support for 'deep cultural
diversity' by warning against cultural practices that harm individuals, practices

that she goes on to describe as often peripheral to the culture and which can, therefore, be abandoned without damage to the cultural integrity of the group.

Berlin, recall, identified himself as both a liberal and a pluralist but claimed no logical connection between the two. As both are 'elements of our cultural birthright [both] deserve our allegiance [and] so much the worse for consistency if it requires that we abandon one for the sake of the other', says Weinstock (1997: 494). In Chapter 1 I sought to show how a concern with what Judith Shklar called 'the liberalism of fear' led Berlin to the conclusion that the claims of liberalism and pluralism must be balanced in the context of particular circumstances.[21] Wherever pluralism requires a choice the choosing should aim to prioritize the minimization of cruelty and fear.

In answer to questions about what is to be done when choices have to be made between competing values Berlin (1991a: 17–19) replies that claims have to be balanced against each other and compromises reached – and in this balancing '[t]he concrete situation is almost everything' (*ibid*: 18).[22] None of the factors impinging on a situation are to be ignored. There are, of course, limits to the kind of compromises that can be made, because some things – slavery, ritual murder, torture – must never be tolerated, but in rejecting the possibility of the perfect society as a recipe for bloodshed Berlin opts for a model of society as 'an uneasy equilibrium, which is constantly threatened and in constant need of repair' (*ibid*: 19).

This commitment of Berlin's to compromises achieved with full and proper attention to context strikes a clear chord with the contextualist approaches favoured by many political philosophers interested in issues of justice in culturally diverse societies. In what I have had to say about the issues surrounding faith schools (Chapter 4) I have followed this contextualist line in focusing on the 'hard cases' of what I called strong cultural identity schools. This approach requires that liberal principles such as individual autonomy be examined in the context of a range of issues. As Veit Bader and Sawitri Saharso (2004: 109) put it: 'numbers matter, power asymmetries matter, history matters, constitutional, political, socio-economic and cultural contexts matter, and consequences matter'. Once these contextual issues are factored in, the process of finding compromises between values that conflict has to go beyond monist solutions that require one 'morally permissible or optimal institutional setting' (*ibid*: 111).

Joseph Carens (2004) notes how dealing with a 'hard case' such as immigration policy in Fiji made him think again about the way that his liberal principles favouring open borders failed to take account of some issues to do with community and culture. He goes on to say: 'I have not abandoned my liberal commitments . . . on issues such as immigration, but I now have a more complicated view of the ways in which the claims of culture and community should be taken into account and a deeper appreciation of their moral weight' (*ibid*: 126). I would say much the same about the position I have taken in Chapter 4 on the question of faith schools. As Carens himself concludes, although it is always difficult to steer a course between some universal values that must remain beyond compromise and the more local values of particular communities, this remains the only option for liberal pluralists.

There are dangers both in the kinds of group identity that resentment against marginalization and oppression generates and in any liberal failure to acknowledge the benefits that individuals gain from their collective identities (Kenny, 2004). It is in recognition of these twin dangers that I have given so much attention to Weinstock's recommendations for education that seek to reduce the culturalism that feeds these dangerous and harmful versions of identity. In an earlier work Kenny (2000: 1034) described Berlin's liberalism as a politics of negotiation and compromise, one that taught its citizens 'that the achievement of any moral order necessarily involves the loss and defeat of some fundamental human values'. As such, liberalism must remain imperfect but it is able 'nevertheless [to] sustain a civil society in which basic fears and insecurities are kept at bay' (*ibid*: 1037).

It has been noted with some surprise that 'one of the greatest intellectual champions of diversity of our century' should be so neglected by today's advocates of diversity (Mack, 1996: 100). Why is this? According to Eric Mack it is both the way that Berlin draws back from a complete rejection of universal values and the way that he warns against the dangers of a wounded pride that can translate into some of the less benign forms of the 'particularist, group-defined modes of thought and feeling which today's friends of diversity want to license and empower' (*ibid*: 109) that excludes him from the pantheon of multiculturalist heroes. It is his commitment to negative liberty together with his recognition of the value of belonging that makes Berlin so relevant to debates about the contrasting claims of assimilation and accommodation in culturally diverse societies. Berlin would have agreed with Callan (2005: 475 n. 8) when he said that 'a culture makes possible good lives for many of its members [while] making good lives impossible for other members'. In the biography that brings together Berlin's life and work Michael Ignatieff concludes with a picture of Berlin as a hedgehog who knew one big thing – that freedom is both important and in danger of betrayal. What Berlin's balanced treatment of diversity suggests is that the betrayal may come in the forms of both assimilation and accommodation. The challenge is how to reap the benefits of the Enlightenment attack on dogma without falling into the trap of believing that reason reveals the one true way to live and that those who fail to see must be made to do so in order to be free. Genuine liberals will follow Berlin in recognizing that human beings have to accept the absence of certainties and learn to live with pluralist doubt.

In what he had to say about education Berlin consistently argued for openness in the way that knowledge is sought and values held. Although he understood very well the psychology of group attachments, especially in circumstances of oppression by outsiders, Berlin was always clear that, while certainty might bring happy obedience, this fell short of an understanding of what it is to be human. From what he had to say in his original introduction to his essays on liberty (Berlin, 2002a: 46) to his more recently published essays on the repression of thought in the Soviet Union (Berlin, 2004b) it is clear that negative liberty demands a liberal education if individuals are to be able to live their chosen lives well. This suggests an education such as that described by Mike Degenhardt (2005) which aims to incorporate both the hedgehog-like virtues of commitment and integration that relate to having a single vision with the more fox-like virtues of openness that are needed to prevent that vision becoming a prison.[23] In his rejection of determinism and warnings against the reification of cultures, nations and ages Berlin clearly speaks for the individual. I began this final chapter with a quotation that warns against those who claim certainty for their beliefs; Berlin's refusal to be blinded by the reality of the difficult choices we face between incompatible goods means acknowledging the importance of education that allows students to live their chosen lives well and to do so while enjoying the company of those who have chosen differently.

Notes

1 Isaiah Berlin and liberalism

1 *Four Essays on Liberty* was published in 1969 and included *Two Concepts of Liberty* which was Berlin's inaugural lecture as Chichele Professor of Social and Political Theory at Oxford given in 1958 (Berlin, 1969). In 2002 Henry Hardy edited a collection of Berlin's writing entitled *Liberty* (Berlin, 2002a) which incorporates the original four essays and adds other relevant material. All page references to *Four Essays on Liberty* will be to the expanded 2002 edition.

2 For biographical detail on Berlin's life see Ignatieff (1998a). For the view that Berlin's personal history is intimately related to his intellectual output see, for example, Anderson (1992) and Ryan (1999).

3 Other writers on Berlin who have stressed the value pluralist dimension include Baumeister (2000), Crowder (2002), Galston (2002) and Parekh (1982).

4 See Kelly (2003) for an account of the influence of Berlin's thought through his supervision of the many of his students who took up key university posts throughout the world.

5 See, for example, the tributes by Noel Annan, Stuart Hampshire, Avishai Margalit, Bernard Williams and Aileen Kelly in Berlin (1999).

6 After initial publication in four separate parts in the *Jewish Chronicle* this controversial essay was published with some omissions in a 1952 collection edited by Bentwich. The original version is restored by Hardy in *The Power of Ideas* (Berlin, 2000a).

7 Here Collini is borrowing the wording that Berlin himself used to describe his Montenegrin-origin Oxford colleague, John Plamenatz. Berlin (1998: 146) goes on to say of Plamenatz: 'He was never wholly assimilated either to England or to Oxford: when he said "we" – "This is the way we think", or "This is how it is with us" – he usually meant Montenegrins'.

8 For a review of critiques of Berlin's account of the distinction between negative and positive liberty and a rebuttal of those views see Crowder (2004: 68–94).

9 On the great impact on political philosophy of Berlin's most famous lecture see Barry (2003).

10 Jinkins (2004) and Wokler (2003) share this view of Berlin as a friendly critic of the Enlightenment and as a truly enlightened philosopher. A view that is also shared by Hobsbawm (2003: 130) who, in his autobiography, refers to Berlin as his friend who 'with his visceral commitment to a non-negotiable Jewish identity, which made him defend, or at least try to understand, critics of the Enlightenment, found it impossible not to behave like an Enlightenment liberal'.

11 Crowder (2004: 76–93) accuses Berlin's critics of transmitting a number of myths: among these are (i) that negative and positive liberty are exhaustive categories of liberty and (ii) that Berlin favours only negative liberty to the complete exclusion of

positive liberty. In his own reply to one of his critics Berlin (1993: 297) begins with these words: 'I should like to begin with a rebuttal of Mr West's allegation that I imply that any conception of positive freedom must involve a potentially tyrannical "reification" of the self. This is not so. I did not say that the concept of positive freedom itself, only that perverted interpretations of it can lead, and indeed have led, to such consequences. Positive freedom or liberty is an unimpeachable human value'.

12 *Political Ideas in the Twentieth Century* was written in 1949. *Historical Inevitability* was the Auguste Comte Memorial Trust Lecture given at the London School of Economics in 1953 and first published in 1954.

13 *From Hope and Fear Set Free* was originally given as a paper to the Aristotelian Society in 1964 and Berlin sought unsuccessfully to have it included in the original *Four Essays on Liberty*. Hardy took the opportunity with the publication of *Liberty* to honour Berlin's wish (for details see *The Editor's Tale* which is Hardy's editorial introduction to *Liberty*).

14 Somewhat surprisingly Berlin (2002a: 158 n. 1) exempts Durkheim from this criticism. For my own account of determinism in Durkheim and its impact on English education through the work of Sir Fred Clarke see Burtonwood (1981).

15 In his essay *Is Nothing Sacred?* Rushdie makes much the same point when he uses the metaphor of a house with a number of different rooms. Rushdie's house contains rooms where people go to hear voices that say things unheard of in the rest of the house. Imagine, he says, waking up one morning to find all the voice-rooms have disappeared and there is no way out of the house: 'It becomes clear that the house is a prison. People begin to scream and pound the walls. Men arrive with guns. The house begins to shake. You do not wake up. You are already awake' (Rushdie, 1992: 428).

16 In another interview Berlin bases his commitment to the idea of a shared human nature on the mutual intelligibility between members of different human cultures (Lukes, 1998).

17 In a television interview first broadcast in 1992 (BBC2 *The Late Show*) and repeated in 2003 Berlin suggested to Michael Ignatieff that it was on the basis of certain cross-cultural human values that the British were justified in the suppression of *sati* in India. See also the interview with Nathan Gardels (*Guardian*, 5 November 1991) when Berlin said: 'Unless there is a minimum of shared values that can preserve the peace, no decent societies can survive'. For Roach (2005) this ensures the consistency of Berlin's value pluralism with the work of the International Criminal Court in defending universal human rights against the abuses of national customs.

18 Ignatieff (1998a: 81) describes Berlin as a Humean sceptic about religion but one who always saw the value of keeping the Jewish festivals. Jewishness for Berlin, says Ignatieff, was an identity that might be questioned but could never be transcended. Although Ignatieff agrees that Jewishness defined Berlin's ultimate commitments, he says this was always combined with a cosmopolitan awareness and a belief that it was for each Jew to decide how to live as a Jew. Reflecting on Berlin's relationship with Judaism, Jonathan Sacks (Credo, *The Times*, October 1998) refers to Berlin in his own words as 'tone deaf to God' but religious in the sense that he remained committed to those Jewish institutions and rituals that expressed belonging to the group – a loyal, if not a believing, Jew (available online at: www.chiefrabbi.org/articles/credo/octb98. html, accessed 10 January 2006).

19 *Three Strands of My Life* was delivered as an address that Berlin gave in Jerusalem in 1979; it was published the same year in the *Jewish Quarterly* and included by Hardy in the 1998 edition of *Personal Impressions*. Hardy explains that Berlin resisted publication of these autobiographical reflections during his lifetime because he felt it too personal a piece of writing.

20 See for example Berlin's *Jewish Slavery and Emancipation* (1952) where, in response to Arthur Koestler's view that Jews must assimilate into whatever society they reside

or else emigrate to Israel, Berlin defended the right of Jews to live as Jews in any society but without implying any requirement that they choose to do so.

21 Ignatieff (1998a: 89) refers to a letter written in 1933 by Berlin to Elizabeth Bowen which includes an early statement of Berlin's value pluralism (see Berlin, 2004a: 70–73 for the letter). Hardy cites this letter as Berlin's earliest use of what became a favourite quotation from Kant: 'Out of the crooked timber of humanity no straight thing was ever made' (Berlin, 2004a: 72 n. 4). Crowder (2004: 27) shows how Berlin (1939) develops his opposition to monism in his early writing on Marx who was to become Berlin's 'archetypal critical target'. Kelly (2002: 31) agrees when saying that it was Berlin's reading of Marx that set 'the contours of an opposition between pluralism and monism'.

22 *The Originality of Machiavelli* was first read as a paper at the Political Studies Association in 1953; it is included in the collection *The Proper Study of Mankind* (Berlin, 2000b).

23 *The Pursuit of the Ideal* was read in Turin on the occasion of Berlin receiving the Agnelli Prize and is included in the collection *The Crooked Timber of Humanity* (Berlin, 1991a).

24 *The Search for Status* was broadcast in 1959 and is published in Berlin (2000a).

25 Siame (2000: 62) responds to Berlin on this point by arguing that in Zambia citizens do regard national independence as individual freedom although this is described as cultural freedom rather than individual freedom: 'The nationalist struggle in Zambia was about the Africans' desire to assert their own cultural autonomy ... They were once more free to be themselves ... This became possible because both rulers and ruled shared the same culture'. Penny Enslin (2003) notes that Thandabantu Nhlapo makes much the same point about support for customary law in South Africa being the outcome of people seeking forms of government that acknowledge their own traditions, however discriminatory they may be.

26 *My Intellectual Path* was written by Berlin to be published first in Chinese. For details see Hardy's Preface to Berlin (2000a) which includes the English version of what is Berlin's final essay.

27 Hardy suggests that Berlin is responding to a call by Cecil Roth, then President of the Jewish Historical Society of England, for Jews to retain their religious identity.

28 In his editorial Preface to Shklar (1998) Stanley Hoffman notes Judith Shklar's friendship with, and admiration for, Berlin. Like Berlin, Shklar was from a Jewish family of Riga; she fled from Riga to Sweden in 1939 before settling in the United States.

29 Zakaras (2003) and Kenny (2000) also remark on this common grounding of the liberalisms of Berlin and Shklar in the prioritization of avoiding cruelty.

30 This story *The Purpose Justifies The Ways* appears as the first piece in *The First and Last*. It is based, says Hardy, on the murder of Uritsky, Soviet Commissar and Chairman of the Petrograd Cheka, by Kunnegiesser, a member of the Russian gentry, in 1918.

31 *Cultures in Search of their Countries* is an interview with Nathan Gardels published in the *Guardian*, 5 November 1991.

32 An address delivered at the Commemoration in the Sheldonian Theatre, Oxford, on 21 March 1998 and published in Berlin (1999).

33 This was a conference organized at the New York Institute for the Humanities in 1998 which aimed to identify Berlin's intellectual legacy. The Aladdin's lamp thought experiment was raised by Margalit during a discussion that came after a series of papers on Berlin's contribution to thinking about nationalism and Israel (see Dworkin, Lilla and Silvers, 2001: 183).

34 Wollheim's recent memoir of childhood reveals his own feelings about identity. As the child of a German father growing up in England he relates how he preferred to think of himself as a 'citizen of the world' and how his Jewish father told him that

classification in terms of ethnicity represented the first step on the road to persecution (see Wollheim, 2004: 106). Wollheim and Margalit disagree both about the significance of Jewish identity and about Berlin's view of this. See their debate in Dworkin, Lilla and Silvers (2001: 177–198).

35 After recalling how Berlin witnessed the Petrograd policeman being dragged away by the mob Annan (1999: 217) observes how the intense horror of violence extended to Berlin's taste in music: 'With all his love of opera he disliked Tosca and Turandot, Wozzeck and Peter Grimes: they were too cruel'.

36 An incident that Ignatieff (1998a: 234) reports taking place in the lift of the King David Hotel, Jerusalem.

37 See Margalit's account in Dworkin, Lilla and Silvers (2001: 157) where he relates the content of a letter sent to him in 1997 by Berlin which included a statement headed 'Israel and the Palestinians' that argued for partition of Israel as a compromise designed to avoid 'a savage war which could inflict irreparable damage on both sides'. For a critique of Berlin's Zionism from the Palestinian perspective see Edward Said's reflections on Berlin in Said (2001).

38 For an account of how Ignatieff's own version of limited pluralism draws on Berlin see Plaisance (2002).

2 Political philosophy, cultural diversity and education

1 *Wisconsin* v. *Yoder* (406 U. S. 205 1972). The *Yoder* case was initiated in New Glarus, Wisconsin, in 1968 when the school authorities prosecuted three Amish families (including the Yoder family) for refusing to send their children to school for the last two years of compulsory education. In 1969 the Green County Court found in favour of the state authorities and the parents were fined and directed to send their children to school. This decision was reversed by the Wisconsin Supreme Court in 1971 and the reversal was approved in the United States Supreme Court in 1972. For a detailed account of the case and the individuals involved see Peters (2003).

2 *Pierce* v. *Society of Sisters* (268 U. S. 510 1925). In *Pierce* the Supreme Court found in favour of Catholic parents who resisted state legislation in Oregon that required children to attend public schools rather than private religious schools. *Pierce* came to be regularly cited in cases where government was perceived to have overextended its authority in attempting to determine the *kind* of education that children received. That the state had the right to ensure that children were provided with some kind of education was never questioned.

3 *Mozert* v. *Hawkins County Board of Education* (827 F. 2d Sixth Circuit Court 1987).

4 The United States District Court for the Eastern District of Tennessee had initially found in favour of the *Mozert* parents but this decision was overturned on appeal.

5 In a telling example Macedo (2000) acknowledges that a society without the Spanish Inquisition is necessarily less diverse but would, he says, be none the worse for that.

6 Following the same line of reasoning Bromwich (1995) warns communitarian critics of liberal commitments to individual freedoms that their support for illiberal groups creates a danger of 'hatching dragons'.

7 See Shachar (1999) and Okin (2002) for warnings against strong versions of multicultural citizenship that leave cultural groups free to oppress some of their own members, especially women. Cultural conventions, Shachar observes, usually serve the interests of powerful members of a community but these conventions never go uncontested. Reich (2003) agrees with Shachar but he feels that her recognition of 'multicultural vulnerability' gives insufficient attention to the particular oppression of children.

8 Barry notes the paradox that the 20 per cent exit rate has been regarded as both small (and therefore justifying the limited education that Amish children get on the grounds that few appear to need it) and large (and therefore justifying the same situation on

the grounds that, however limited, it appears to be enough to facilitate the exit of those who choose to leave).

9 From what has already been said it is clear that rights of exit constitute a very important element of liberal arguments for accommodating non-liberal communities. These rights and the difficulties involved in their implementation are considered in more detail in Chapter 5.

10 In *Adler* v. *Ontario* (1996) the Supreme Court of Canada found against religious conservatives who claimed funding for denominational schooling. Justice L'Heureux-Dub dissented by accepting an argument based on community survival. Callan (2000) counters by rejecting group recognition based claims and insisting that admissible arguments must be based on the children's interests. Arneson and Shapiro (1996) dismiss the Amish claims on similar grounds; by admitting that their claim was about community survival the Amish acknowledge that their primary concern is not the children.

11 In a recent discussion about the right to participate in extreme, risky and potentially harmful leisure pursuits and 'extreme sports' Olivier (2006: 102) identifies his own view of the autonomous individual as 'someone capable of deliberation about personal goals, beliefs, values and decisions, and who is capable of choosing and acting under the direction of such deliberation' as one that is founded on Berlin's account of negative liberty.

12 In 1974 the anthropologist Edmund Leach gave a public lecture at the University of Birmingham on the relationship between education and culture. Challenging the anthropological consensus that schooling should reflect the culture of the home, Leach reflected that such congruence would breed conformity. Arguing for the creativity of a contrast between home and school Leach (1975: 96) said that, 'the significant innovator is nearly always, in my experience, very close to being "a mixed up kid"'. See Burtonwood (2002a) for a fuller account of the implications of Leach's argument.

13 Wolterstorff (1993), Yale philosopher and theologian, describes his religious upbringing in the Dutch Reformed Church that included both induction into the faith through exposure to, and participation in ritual and tradition, as well as what he called 'disputatious family gatherings'. Callan (2002a: 128) summarizes the role of tradition in Wolterstorff's religious upbringing in these words: 'Within the received boundaries of the tradition, the intellect could move freely, unhampered by any social hierarchy, and for Wolterstorff at least, the boundaries were experienced as no constraint'.

14 In *Diversity and Distrust* Macedo (2000: 208) concludes that even 'grudging tolerance' goes too far in accommodating the Amish and therefore, '*Yoder* should at some point be overruled'.

15 See Coleman (2002, 2003) for the argument that teenage children should be allowed much greater involvement in decisions about their own education. Judge Boggs, it has already been noted, regretted the almost total absence of children's views in the *Yoder* hearing.

16 Brighouse accepts Schrag's example of Lisa Aiken, a woman who converts to Orthodox Judaism and chooses a life of obedience, as one of autonomy (see Aiken, 1992). For Schrag, Aiken's account serves as testimony to the value of a life of obedience and the goodness of this life stands whether or not it is autonomously chosen. Where Schrag's argument proves wanting, says Brighouse (2003a: 73), is in failing to recognize that, 'people have different personalities, characters, or internal constitutions, that suit them differently well to different ways of life; and these differences do not correlate perfectly with the demands of their parents' or their communities' religious commitments'.

17 This section of the chapter is based on my earlier account of diversity liberalism and education (see Burtonwood, 2003a).

18 Mill (1962 [1859]: 161) argued against the silencing of opinion on the grounds that if

the opinion is right we are robbed of the truth and, if it is wrong, we are robbed of the clearer perception of truth that we get when it is compared with error.

19 *Ohio Civil Rights Commission* v. *Dayton Christian Schools Inc.* (477 U. S. 619 1986).

20 Kateb (1994: 535) also voices a willingness to tolerate the 'vices' of identity groups where oppression requires 'solidarity' as a tactical response. Macedo (2003: 422) is less enthusiastic; having noted the tactical significance of 'writing positive scripts' such as black power and queer identity, Macedo is still bothered by the way that such scripts can thwart individuality.

21 Sacks (2002) notes that 'religion' comes from the Latin *'religare'* meaning 'to bind'; religion, says Sacks, binds people to their communities.

22 Kymlicka (for example, 1996a) remains the most widely referenced instrumental defence of cultural groups in terms of their role in providing a context for choice-making.

23 This American example of cultural sensitivity is contrasted by McConnell with the French model exemplified by Napoleon when he required Jewish citizens to attend a ceremony pledging allegiance to the Republic. The event took place on the Jewish Sabbath.

24 Reports from Pennsylvania in October 2004 suggested some shifting of the Amish position as many Amish turned out at rallies to support George Bush's presidential election campaign. See 'Hats off to Bush as he calls on Amish country', *The Times*, 28 October 2004.

25 Political liberalism is Rawls's attempt to adjust his theory of justice in response to those of his critics who claimed that his earlier work failed to recognize the role that cultural attachments played when individuals deliberate about the kind of society that they wish for. Political liberalism separates the public sphere where all citizens are expected to operate according to shared principles and to give reasons that can be understood by all and a private sphere where citizens are free to live according to their own diverse, often illiberal, ways of life.

26 In an earlier article (Burtonwood, 1995) I make reference to a story told by a Canadian arts educator, Anna Kindler, who tells how her own son, five-year-old Jan, developed an interest in native Canadian art and, when asked by his teacher to bring to school some example of his own culture, Jan brought his drawings produced in the style of the Haida sculptor he so much admired. Because Jan was of Polish family origin (though born in Canada) this teacher complained that she had expected something Polish from Jan. The boy's mother makes the case that Jan's culture is still evolving and what becomes of Canadian culture will be the outcome of people like Jan. This story provides some support for the Brighouse response.

27 See the account in Kukathas (2003: 113–114) of Fatima, the Muslim wife of a Malay fisherman living in Malaysia. Here Kukathas argues that Fatima remains free despite neither choosing her way of life nor ever having been made aware of the possibility of leaving for another way of life. Kukathas also stresses the importance of exit rights but, unlike Barry, he would not require that Fatima's community make any provision to facilitate her exit should she be minded to do so. Brighouse's criticism of Schrag holds good here; Kukathas makes no provision for a Fatima whose personality is ill-suited to the life of a fisherman's wife.

28 White is particularly troubled by what he sees as the dominance of a kind of religious communitarianism in British philosophy of education. For responses see the replies to White's thesis by Wilfred Carr, Richard Smith, Paul Standish and Terence McLaughlin in *Journal of Philosophy of Education*, 37, 1: 161–184.

29 First published in 1969 this paper also appeared in *Oxford Review of Education* in 1975 and is included by Hardy in the collection *The Power of Ideas* (Berlin, 2000a).

30 *Woodrow Wilson on Education* was originally commissioned by the Woodrow Wilson Foundation for inclusion in a book entitled *Education in the Nation's Service: A Series of Essays on American Education* published in 1960 by Praeger. It was not in

fact included in that collection as planned but has been made available by the Isaiah Berlin Literary Trust through the Isaiah Berlin Virtual Library (posted October 2002). I am grateful to Henry Hardy for alerting me to this piece.

31 Notes on Prejudice was written by Berlin in 1981 and was first published by Hardy in the *New York Review of Books* in October 2001 in the aftermath of the terrorist attacks on the United States. It has since been included by Hardy in the collection *Liberty* (Berlin, 2002a).

3 Cultural diversity, value pluralism and the curriculum

1 On the nature of Berlin's pluralism see Weinstein (2004: 236–237 n. 2) and also Macedo (1990: 236–239) who contrasts Charles Taylor's cultural pluralism with Berlin's more far-reaching value pluralism. Macedo notes that, for Taylor, once a perspective is chosen value conflict for the individual is over; for Berlin it never ends. This concurs with Berlin's own comments on the differences between Taylor's thinking and his own (Berlin, 1994b). For a critique of Taylor's neglect of the interaction between culture and the self see Jonathon Seglow (1998: 975) who says, 'No member of an oppressed group would deny the saliency of the collective level of recognition ... But, very often, we want to use our cultural or other identities as symbolic material with which to construct, precisely, our self'.

2 Dworkin (2001) argues against Berlin that the values of equality and liberty can be harmonized. In a value pluralist reply to Dworkin, Galston (2005: 173–176) refers to the British National Health Service as an example of the conflict between liberty and equality. Any restriction on private health care in the interests of equality would, says Galston, be opposed by many citizens on the grounds of protecting the individual freedom to provide and to choose private health care.

3 *Saxe v. State College Area School District*, 77F. Supp. 2d 621 (M. D. Pa. 1999).

4 *Saxe v. State College Area School District*, 240 F. 3d 200 (3rd Circuit 2001).

5 The case was presented by the Woodring College of Education Center for Educational Pluralism as the subject for discussion in its new journal *Teaching and Learning in a Pluralistic Society: Dilemmas, Perplexities and Tensions.*

6 Galston borrows the term 'civic totalist' from Macedo (2000) who uses it to refer to an over-extension of state authority such as that attempted by the Oregon state authorities in the *Pierce* case discussed in Chapter 2. Although he warns against such over-extension of state authority Macedo remains committed to a kind of pluralism that is constrained by liberal conditions. In a recent account of his own position and its relationship to Berlin's thought Macedo (forthcoming) argues that although Berlin's pluralism does not in itself justify liberal political institutions there is much else in Berlin that does so, not least the prioritization of avoiding cruelty. I am grateful to Stephen Macedo for making his forthcoming work available to me.

7 Talisse (2004) argues in much the same way that both Berlin and Galston commit the naturalistic fallacy in deriving value from fact. For Galston's reply see Galston (2005: 190–192).

8 In his conversation with Jahanbegloo (2000: 44) Berlin seems to acknowledge this when he says: 'I believe in both liberalism and pluralism, but they are not logically connected'.

9 Although Crowder rejects the way that some of Berlin's critics have wanted to characterize *Two Concepts of Liberty* as a total denial of any benefits of positive liberty, he clearly believes that it remains necessary to go further than Berlin in making a case for some aspects of positive liberty. See also Chapter 1, note 11.

10 The Statement of Values is published in Great Britain: Department for Education and Employment/Qualifications and Curriculum Authority (1999) *The National Curriculum: Handbook for Secondary Teachers in England Key Stages 3 & 4* pp. 195–197 and it also appears in Talbot and Tate (1997: 10–14). For a summary of the develop-

ments that culminated in the publication of the Statement of Values see Halstead and Taylor (2000: 11–16). A preamble to the Statement of Values reminds readers that the values which are arranged in four groups (self, relationships, society, and environment) are ones that are agreed across society; that they are not intended to be exhaustive; and that they allow for disagreement about the sources of the values as well as disagreement about their specific application.

11 Nicholas Tate was speaking as Chief Executive of the School Curriculum and Assessment Authority (SCAA). See Tate (1997a, 1997b, 1997c).

12 The National Forum for Values in Education and the Community (NFVEC) included 150 representatives from a range of communities; it was charged with finding what consensus could be achieved on moral values that teachers could feel confident in teaching and with making recommendations about how schools might approach values education.

13 Tate made the attack on relativism central to his speech opening the 1996 SCAA Conference 'Education for Adult Life: The Spiritual and Moral Development of Young People'.

14 For a critique of the MacIntyre argument that draws on the findings of the NFVEC see Katayama (2003: 332) who argues that 'the SCAA Forum's results provide *prima facie* evidence for a shared morality in a plural society like ours, based on recognition of certain shared virtues'.

15 Kunzman (2005) proposes a middle ground which identifies the political as a sub-set of the broader civic realm. In the civic realm Kunzman encourages a moral conversation that welcomes religious perspectives among others; he identifies the common school as the most appropriate civic institution for such conversations to take place. In the more limited political sphere which brings into play the use of coercive power by the state Kunzman recognizes that 'public reason', which draws only on reasons that all citizens can share, must prevail. For the contrary argument that religious citizens ought not to be required to privatize their religious commitments when debating coercive legislation see Eberle (2002).

16 Heyting quotes Berlin (2000c: 87) who is commenting on the thought of the Romantics when he says: 'This introduces for the first time what seems to me to be a crucial note in the history of human thought, namely that ideals, ends, objectives are not to be discovered by intuition, by scientific means, by reading sacred texts, by listening to experts or authoritative persons; that ideals are not to be discovered at all, they are to be invented; not to be found but to be generated, generated as art is generated'. Mack (1993a) observes a shift in Berlin from this subjectivist view of values as expressed in the 1965 A. W. Mellon Lectures (published as Berlin, 2000c) and the view expressed by Berlin in 1988 when he again attributed this subjectivism to the Romantics but explicitly denied this as his own position (see Jahanbegloo, 2000: 158).

17 Pardales offers Charles Dickens's *Hard Times* and Richard Wright's *Native Son* as examples of literature rich in possibilities for stimulating the moral imagination.

18 The teacher may also find herself in the position of alerting her pupils to circumstances where there is no right answer. I am grateful to Colin Wringe for pointing to this additional difficulty.

19 Baumeister is following Galston (1995) here in distinguishing Enlightenment and post-Reformation liberalisms and placing Berlin in the second category. John Rawls, Joseph Raz and Will Kymlicka are offered by Baumeister as examples of liberals located in the Enlightenment tradition.

20 Baumeister refers here to the Swann Report (Great Britain: Department of Education and Science, 1985) and the critique published by the Islamic Academy (1985). Swann is criticized here, for example, for its autonomy-promoting approach to religious education which: '[presents] Islam as one of a variety of equally valid perspectives [and fails] to recognize the special significance for Muslims of the Qur'an as the revealed word of God' (Baumeister, 2000: 64).

21 In an earlier version of her argument Baumeister (1998) rests her case entirely on Gray's interpretation of Berlinian pluralism.

22 See Burtonwood (1996, 1998, 2000) for earlier responses to Halstead's series of articles on accommodating religious, specifically Muslim, minorities. See also responses to Halstead by Beck (1999) and Merry (2005a). In his most recent contribution Halstead (2005) describes himself as a 'cultural interpreter' of the Muslim world with 40 years knowledge of Islam.

23 Whether exit rights are up to the job of protecting dissenting individuals is an issue identified in Chapter 1 and discussed in greater detail in Chapter 5.

24 Halstead frequently takes Charles Bailey's (1984) use of the phrase 'beyond the present and particular' to characterize the aims of a liberal education.

25 Elsewhere Halstead (1990: 5) states that Islam 'unashamedly guides [children] into a predetermined way of life'.

26 Discussing the education of Muslims in Australia, Sanjakdar (2004) complains of a hegemonic Judeo-Christian heritage that discriminates against Muslims by treating as 'normal' what Islam regards as unnatural and sinful.

27 Halstead's 1998 article is co-authored with K. Lewicka.

28 Merry (2005a) queries Halstead and Lewicka's use of the term 'lifestyle' here because this implies a degree of choice that fails to capture adequately the nature of sexual orientation. Merry writes: 'No one doubts that heterosexuals experience heterosexual attraction. Few suppose that straights *choose* to be attracted to the opposite sex' (*ibid*: 26, original emphasis).

29 See Sarwar (1996) for an Islamic account of what Muslim children ought to be taught about sex education generally and homosexuality in particular.

30 On the millet system and its implications for individuals see Merry (2004: 131–132, 138–139 n. 46, 47).

31 Halstead (2005) responds that his use of the phrase 'the Muslim perspective', inferring singularity and homogeneity, is chosen for the sake of brevity and in order to 'set aside complexities'. Unfortunately this tendency to generalize Islamic views is replicated in some local authority guidelines for teaching about homosexuality which call for teachers to include *the* Islamic perspective in their teaching about this issue. See for example Kirklees Local Education Authority guidance for teachers on sex education with Muslim pupils (Kirklees Ednet, 2002).

32 Colleen Vojak (2003) makes much the same point when she offers the case of a young gay Mormon who committed suicide as evidence of the need for a liberal education that provides tools for self-understanding. She concludes: 'Had [the young Mormon] been able to link his sexual identity to a broader neutral or positive social perspective of what it means to be gay, he may not have ended his life' (*ibid*: 417).

33 Petrovic extends Taylor's (1994a) use of the term 'cultural group' to include groups based on sexual orientation and goes on to adopt Taylor's argument that respect for persons requires 'recognition' of identity-supporting groups.

34 For the wider debate about the perceived threat of Orthodox Islam to Dutch liberal values and institutions see Hekma (2002).

4 Faith-based and cultural identity schools: a liberal defence?

1 The 'School Question' here refers to the debate around the issue of public funding for religious education which has been an issue in the United States ever since Catholic immigrants resisted supposedly non-sectarian Christian schooling and argued for the right to their own parochial schools.

2 Iraq provides a more contemporary example. In September 2005 Archbishop Louis Sako of Kirkup and Bishop Andreas Abouna of Baghdad urged the case for a secular constitution, fearing as they did for the future of Christianity in Iraq if religion were

to dominate the emerging constitutional settlement. See 'Is there any place for Christians in the new Iraq?' *The Times*, 10 September 2005.

3 Relevant to this right of exit from American public schooling Brighouse (2005) reminds that the liberal state has responsibility for all its children regardless of where they are educated. Many American children educated in private religious schools are, says Brighouse, denied their right to autonomy-facilitating education (see Chapter 2). For this reason Brighouse doubts that the United Kingdom has much to learn from American state-religion separatism; better to fund religious schools thereby retaining some control over how they operate while reducing the scope for sectarian influence. See also Brighouse (2006: Chapter 5).

4 In 1983 Bob Jones University was famously denied federal tax exemptions because of its policy of disallowing inter-racial dating among its students.

5 In her defence of faith-based schooling in the United States, and in relation to the Bob Jones University case, Salomone (2000) argues that, because opposition to racial discrimination is a core American value around which there is a national consensus, it follows that no faith-based school should be allowed to compromise on that value. On gender discrimination Salomone doubts that there is any such consensus because many religious citizens put gender-specific roles at the centre of their faith. Schools therefore, she argues, should be allowed to determine gender issues locally.

6 In 2001 the Church of England supported a recommendation for an increase of 100 church secondary schools over a seven to eight year period (Archbishops' Council, 2001). In 1998 the General Synod of the Church of England had called for church schools to demonstrate a stronger degree of religious identity (General Synod, 1998).

7 A minority of the Swann Committee members added a note of dissent on this issue arguing that it was unjust to deny positive assistance to those minority faith groups seeking their own voluntary-aided schools (Great Britain: Department of Education and Science (1985: 515 n. 43). Commenting on Swann's recommendations the Commission for Racial Equality (1990) noted that some of Swann's justified fears about ghettoized schooling were rendered outdated by the introduction of a national curriculum in 1988 (a point which counts equally against my own critique of the secessionist implications of pre-1988 faith schools in Burtonwood, 1985). Nevertheless the Commission remained concerned about faith schools and called for a debate about the value of all faith schools in a culturally diverse society.

8 The Seventh Day Adventist, Greek Orthodox and Sikh religious communities have also acquired funding for their religious schools since 1997 (see Halstead, 2002 for details).

9 See '"Faith schools" scrutinised after Bradford riots', in the *Independent*, 17 July 2001.

10 See 'Union votes for end to faith schools', in the *Guardian*, 5 April 2002.

11 See 'Teachers lack faith in Muslim schools', the *Guardian*, 9 June 2004 where John Dunford, General Secretary of the Secondary Heads Association, is quoted as saying: 'To create a stable multi-cultural society we need successful multi-cultural schools and not a proliferation of single faith schools'.

12 See 'Two thirds oppose state aided faith schools', the *Guardian*, 23 August 2005. The Guardian/ICM poll reported in this article indicates public concern about government intentions to increase the number of faith schools. In pursuit of this government aim the Department for Education and Skills awarded £100,000 to the Association of Muslim Schools for research into how independent Islamic schools might be brought into the state sector.

13 See 'Forced marriages', Letters, the *Independent*, 5 June 1999.

14 For details of these empirical findings see Short (2003) and Short and Lenga (2002).

15 Halstead and McLaughlin (2005: 65–66) discuss the dangers of distinguishing between types of faith schools in this way. These authors, however, do adopt a similar approach when they distinguish between types of faith schools in terms of their 'dis-

tinctive non-common educational aims' and 'restricted non-common educational environments'.

16 There are clear similarities between the concerns of this community and those of the Wisconsin Amish involved in the *Yoder* case discussed in Chapter 2. The details of the Torah Maczikei Hadass School case are outlined in 'Wishes of their parents' in *Times Educational Supplement*, 20 September 1985, and for further discussion see Burtonwood (2000).

17 Parker-Jenkins (2002) identifies a difference between 'Muslim schools' where the entire ethos is permeated with Islamic values and 'schools for Muslims' where religious values are less far reaching; she suggests that schools of the former type would need to modify their programmes in order to meet the conditions of state funding.

18 Sanford Levinson (2003: 68) draws on his own experience of sharing schooling with friends belonging to different religious communities to make a very useful point here: 'We too often automatically sneer at the phrase "some of my best friends are Jewish (or any other given religion or race)," but surely it would be a profound social good if all of us could say, with conviction, that some of our best friends *are* from groups other than those with which we most centrally identify. No heterogeneous society can long survive if it becomes truly exceptional to develop the particular intimacies of friendship with anyone other than those who are exactly like oneself in most important aspects'.

19 Short and Lenga (2002) report that all the 15 Jewish primary schools in their sample employed teachers from outside the Jewish community.

20 Weisse reports on a religious education project in Hamburg that, untypically for Germany, involves teaching children from diverse communities together. Ipgrave describes the use of information technology to link pupils from Leicester with others from East Sussex.

21 Pring agrees that defenders of faith schools would do well to turn away from spurious and irrelevant arguments about academic results. If faith schools are to be defended, he says, it will have to be done through an exploration of the ways that faith schools can contribute to children's development of autonomy through initiation into 'the different forms of thought through which we have come to see, explain, appreciate and value the world' (Pring, 2005: 56).

22 For an earlier version of this argument see Snik and De Jong (1995).

23 It is not clear that Kymlicka would be as supportive of faith schools as De Jong and Snik imply. While it is true that Kymlicka (1999) acknowledges the 'alternative starting points to autonomy' thesis, he is very reluctant in accepting a role for faith schools in the primary sector and has often been taken to task by his critics for failing to support Islamic schools (see for example: Deveaux, 2000; Modood, 1993). Kymlicka's reservations about minority educational institutions follow from the distinction he often makes between national minorities such as the indigenous peoples of his native Canada and immigrant communities such as Pakistani-origin Muslims in the United Kingdom, who are, he insists, mainly concerned with assimilation.

24 For a fuller discussion of Williams (1998) and his conditional support for faith schools see Burtonwood (2000).

25 In a recent response to this argument Snik and De Jong (2005) agree that traditional religious communities would be unlikely to accept the liberal conditions that they attached to their defence of state funding for denominational education.

26 In earlier work written in reply to Gardner (1988), who questioned whether religious parents would accept the commitment to eventual autonomy that McLaughlin builds into his liberal developmental model of religious upbringing, McLaughlin (1990) appears to have been more willing to acknowledge that some religious communities would find this unacceptable. In this earlier work McLaughlin's approach is consistent with my own argument that liberal conditional support for faith schooling will rule out at least some religious communities.

27 Dagovitz (2004: 166) responds to my own account (Burtonwood, 2003b) of the way that many religious parents reject the kind of moderate schooling that liberals want to make a condition of their support for faith schools by arguing that political (as opposed to comprehensive) liberalism is able to accommodate the strong version of faith-based schooling by removing religion from those aspects of human living where individual autonomy ought to prevail.

28 For an argument that political liberalism, no less than comprehensive liberalism, must deny the right of parental choice of faith school to religious citizens who teach their children that theirs is a superior faith see Quong (2004). Political liberals, says Quong, must be prepared to limit the rights of what he calls 'unreasonable citizens' in the interests of social stability – unless these unreasonable citizens choose to live apart from society thereby reducing their threat to stability and cohesion.

5 Cultural communities, education and right of exit

1 Fagan (2004: 26) draws on an account of the way that a Dutch Hindustani woman experiences attachment to her culture (Saharso, 2000) to argue that liberal reliance on exit rights to justify non-interference in illiberal groups 'simply underestimates the extent to which individuals may be ontologically dependent upon continuing membership of the community'. The woman in question had taken her own life after frequent maltreatment at the hands of her husband because, claims Fagan, she had an attachment to her cultural group and its requirement that she stayed with her husband, that allowed her no other way out.

2 For a critical response to the model of cultural groups as voluntary associations see Addis (1997: 125) who says of the Kukathas (1992) argument: '[Toleration] comes in abundance only after the tolerated group has been redescribed so as to rob it of its significance and the nature of its complaints'.

3 The Hutterites live in small colonies and share their property. Although the Canadian courts (*Hofer* v. *Hofer*, 1970) found in favour of the Hutterite Church, Kymlicka (1996a: 161) agrees with Justice Pigeon who, in a note of dissent in this case, argued that the difficulty faced by exiting Hutterites served to limit their freedom of religion (*Hofer* v. *Hofer et al.* 13 dlr (3d)).

4 Benhabib (2002: 149) also distinguishes formal and informal costs of exit and restricts state responsibility to ameliorating formal costs: 'Ostracism and social exclusion are the informal prices of exclusion; loss of land rights and certain welfare benefits would be formal costs. With regards to the latter, the liberal-democratic state has the right to intervene and regulate the costs of exit in accordance with principles of citizens' equality'.

5 Kymlicka (1996a: 234–235 n. 18) argues that Kukathas is wrong to claim that liberals can regard the availability of an open society as a sufficient guarantee of exit rights and he urges education as the kind of precondition necessary to make exit a substantial right.

6 See Cohen, Howard and Nussbaum (1999) for Okin's essay *Is Multiculturalism Bad for Women?* and a series of critical responses.

7 Okin (2005: 87) adds: '[Women] should be taken seriously if, when consulted in truly non-intimidating settings, they produce good reasons for preferring to continue aspects of their traditional subordinate status over moving to a status of immediate equality within their group'.

8 On Heffernan's dissent see Peters (2003: 112–119) who expresses some surprise that Wisconsin was unable to make more of this line of argument in the subsequent appeal to the United States Supreme Court.

9 For an earlier and fuller response to Galston on education and exit rights see Burtonwood (2003a).

10 See also Swaine's proposals for liberal tolerance of, and semi-sovereign status for,

theocratic communities which include a restricted education along the same lines as those proposed by Spinner-Halev (see Swaine, 2001).

11 See also Halbertal (1996) who argues that while exit must remain an option, the cultural group is under no obligation either to make children aware of alternative ways of life or to prepare them for the possibility of adopting such alternatives.

12 For further arguments along these lines see Sunstein (1999: 88) who says: 'The remedy of "exit" – the right of women to leave a religious order – is crucial, but it will not be sufficient when girls have been taught in such a way as to be unable to scrutinize the practices with which they have grown up'. Gutmann (2003: 61) also argues that: 'at minimum, states would need to ensure that all children receive an education that enables them to exercise informed consent about membership in any given cultural group, which means being exposed to alternatives and taught the skills of critical thinking about them'.

13 See Reich (2002: 100) where Berlin is cited in support of this sense of freedom. Reich is also drawing from that part of positive freedom that Crowder (2004) relies on to make the link between Berlin's pluralism and liberalism.

14 *The Search for Status* was broadcast on 20 July 1959 on the BBC's European Service and was first published in Berlin (2000a). See Chapter 1 for further discussion.

15 Elsewhere Weinstock (1997) does offer an account of Berlin's philosophy and how it might be used to deal with the kind of issues that liberals face in pluralist societies.

16 Weinstock (2001) adopts a similar approach to the issue of secession in multi-nation states. Arguing that members of minority nations enjoy real benefits from continued membership of the multi-nation state, Weinstock observes nevertheless that any lack of the option to secede will taint the enjoyment of these benefits: 'because the fact of unfreedom unavoidably *dampens* the enjoyment we can derive from those goods that we are provided with in our captivity' (*ibid:* 201, original emphasis). A constitutional right to secede would serve to encourage a cost-benefit analysis that, with the absence of a feeling of captivity, would favour continued membership.

17 Weinstock (2005) gives as examples the work of South Africa's Truth and Reconciliation Commission and New Zealand's Waitangi Tribunal. Eisenberg (2005) also refers to the way that colonial relationships of domination and oppression push post-colonial subjects to prefer the protection of their cultural identity over individual rights.

6 National identity and education

1 See Grosvenor (1999) for details of a series of speeches on national identity given by Tony Blair to Labour Party conferences in the period 1995–1998. In 2001 the Labour Party tasked Michael Willis, an Education Secretary, with encouraging government ministers to address issues of national identity in their speeches and policy decisions (Fortier, 2005: 575 n. 24).

2 In an interview published in the *Independent on Sunday*, 9 December 2001, David Blunkett set out what he called 'norms of acceptability'. What Blunkett had to say here strikes a chord with a letter sent to Muslim leaders in 1989 by the then Home Office Minister, John Patten, spelling out those British values regarded as non-negotiable (Home Office Press Release 18/07/89 'On being British'). These values were said to include the freedom of speech denied to the author Salman Rushdie by some Muslim responses to the publication of his book, *The Satanic Verses* (Rushdie, 1988).

3 This handbook was the direct outcome of a recommendation in the Advisory Group's 2003 report, *The New and the Old* (Great Britain, Home Office: Advisory Group on Life in the United Kingdom, 2003). This called for citizenship lessons for new immigrants seeking British citizenship through naturalization.

4 Gordon Brown was speaking at the Political Studies Awards Ceremony on 30 November 2004. In his British Council Annual Lecture given in July 2004 the Chan-

cellor expressed regret that British identity appeared to have lost confidence and direction and he called for a stronger sense of national identity, one that is based on shared values rather than ethnicity.

5 See 'All teenagers face citizen pledge at 18', the *Guardian*, 20 January 2005.

6 See 'A New England: An English identity within Britain', 14 March 2005. Available online at: efdss. org/newengland. pdf (accessed 2 January 2006).

7 In the speech, *What Does It Mean To Be A Citizen?* given to the Hansard Society on 17 January 2005, Bell said, 'I worry that many young people are being educated in faith-based schools with little appreciation of their wider responsibilities and obligations to British society'.

8 Trevor Phillips was speaking at the Learning and Skills Development Agency Annual Lecture in London. See 'CRE Chief gives his backing to criticism of Muslim schools', the *Guardian*, 19 January 2005.

9 Media reports appeared in September 2005 indicating that advisory groups appointed by Prime Minister Blair to investigate the views of British Muslims would be recommending the reconfiguring of the recently introduced Holocaust Memorial Day as Genocide Day so as to ameliorate the feelings of those Muslims concerned to register what they regarded as the genocide of the Palestinian people. These reports created sufficient concern for the Home Secretary to write to the Holocaust Memorial Day Trust denying any such intentions and confirming support for the work of the Trust and its inclusive approach. Spokespersons for moderate Muslim groups also complained that anti-terrorism laws planned by the government risked further alienating Muslim youth and those moderate Muslim organizations whose co-operation was seen as essential to combating extremism. For an account of the educational implications of Holocaust Memorial Day including the debate about recognizing other genocides see Burtonwood (2002b).

10 I refer to the essay *Rabindranath Tagore and the Consciousness of Nationality* (Berlin, 1996) in Chapter 1 as an expression of the strand of Berlin's liberalism that recognizes belonging as an important human good.

11 Tate has often been criticized for a 'cultural restorationism' that is racist in excluding cultural minorities (see for example: Beck, 1996; Gillborn, 1997). Tate has responded to these criticisms by insisting that his view of national identity is both broad and inclusive and allows for individuals to retain multiple identities.

12 *Nationalism: Past Neglect and Present Power* was first published in 1978 and reprinted in Berlin (1979).

13 *The Bent Twig* was first published in 1972 and reprinted in Berlin (1991a).

14 McDonough does not go so far as to insulate cultural communities from liberal criticism. See, for example, his account of the Lester Desjarlais case. Here a 13-year-old aboriginal boy committed suicide at the Sandy Bay Ojibway Reserve in Manitoba after a history of abuse from his foster parents. An inquiry initiated by aboriginal feminists revealed that the boy's case had been mishandled by aboriginal child welfare agencies and that male aboriginal leaders had sought to shield those responsible on the grounds that the days of provincial interference in aboriginal affairs were over. McDonough criticizes those liberals who appear reluctant to intervene in minority affairs when justice and the avoidance of cruelty requires it.

15 Miller's thesis is presented in his 1995 book *On Nationality* (Miller, 1995a) and in a series of papers collected as Miller (2000a). More recently Miller (2005) has indicated how Berlin's work has helped shape his own specifically liberal version of nationalism.

16 Barry identifies Berlin as belonging to a group of Cold War refugee liberals who generally opposed any kind of collective means of achieving political ends, preferring always to think of society as the outcome of individual projects. Although it is Plamenatz that Barry identifies as the exception in avoiding an antipathy to nationalism he does describe Berlin's membership of this group of Central European intellectuals as a 'more shaded' commitment to individualism (Barry, 1999: 249).

17 There is an extensive literature on the question of liberalism and patriotic education; within this literature there is a particular focus on liberal responses to the role of myths in fostering civic attachments (Abizadeh, 2004; Archard, 1999; Brighouse, 2003b; Callan, 1997a, 1999, 2002b; Enslin, 1999; Fullinwider, 1996; Galston, 1991; Schrag, 1999). It was in this context that in his British Council Lecture (see Chapter 6, note 4) Gordon Brown called for history to be made a compulsory subject for all secondary school pupils. For the alternative view that history is the least appropriate school subject for this purpose see Brighouse (2003b: 168–173).

18 This optimistic version of liberal nationalism can be seen reflected in Kymlicka's choice of the Edward Hicks painting *The Peaceable Kingdom* for the cover of his book *Multicultural Citizenship* (Kymlicka, 1996a). Rather less optimistically Kukathas chose a version of *Le Massacre de la Saint-Barthelemy* for the cover of his book *The Liberal Archipelago* (Kukathas, 2003); this was to illustrate the difficulties of accommodating religious differences. Markell (2000) provides some grounds for optimism about the willingness of citizens to patriotically call their government to account for a failure to live up to the best of its traditions when he refers to demonstrations in Germany following the murder of a Turkish family in 1992. These demonstrators were criticizing not only the neo-Nazi perpetrators of this crime but also their own government that was seen to fail to deal with earlier attacks on Turkish people.

19 See Miller (2002) for an account of how deliberative democracy provides the means both for minority groups to make their case for changes in the society's rules that disadvantage minority members and for the majority community to seek explanations in order to be satisfied about any changes to the rules that justice requires.

20 Tamir's liberal nationalism is set out in her 1993 book of the same name and in a series of articles (Tamir, 1991, 1992, 1993a, 1993b, 1995a, 1995b, 1996, 1997). Tamir (1998) presents Berlin's liberal pluralism as compatible with more recent difference theory and the politics of identity.

21 *Chaim Weizmann* was first published in 1958 and is reprinted in Berlin (1998).

22 Tamir's three-part curriculum provides the model that Halstead uses for his own curriculum model designed to accommodate British Muslim children (Halstead, 1995). See Chapter 3 for a discussion of Halstead's proposals. For another account which seeks to combine education in a common republican politics with cultural education specific to national groups see Schwartzmantel (2003).

23 Chris Smith was speaking at a seminar *A Diverse Heritage* organized by the European Year Against Racism Unit at the Commission for Racial Equality, November 1997.

24 See, for example, Berlin's letter of 20 March 1935 to Felix Frankfurter where Berlin remarks about Arabs that, 'they prefer to be self-governed badly rather than *verjudet* (Jewified)' (Berlin, 2004a: 120).

25 Barry (2001) challenges the argument that immigrant groups cannot be asked to take on an English (as opposed to British) identity; he points out that both Roman Catholics and Jews have joined in a process of 'additive assimilation' that has enabled them to think of themselves as English without losing their distinctive religious identity. This can be accomplished because the 'cultural threshold' of Englishness has been lowered so that being Protestant no longer plays any role in being English. For Barry there is no reason to prevent members of other religious groups following this path. This matters to Barry because he believes that a British identity that means little more than passport holding falls short in the cohesion-facilitating stakes. For another recent account of assimilation and assimilationist policies see Callan (2005).

26 *Daily Telegraph*, 10 November 1997 (cited by Ignatieff, 1998a: 300). In their editorial preface to a recent collection of essays on Berlin's writing on the Counter-Enlightenment Mali and Wokler (2003: vii) also describe a cosmopolitan Berlin as:

'the most peripatetic scholar, at home in three continents . . . a firm Zionist and yet the most cosmopolitan nationalist of the twentieth century, himself a perfect personification of his own pluralist philosophy'.

27 'Forget colour – we're all British now', said Trevor Phillips in an interview published in *The Times*, 3 April 2004.

28 Macedo (2000: 26) says that, 'the celebration of peaceful diversity behoves us to try and understand what must be done from a political standpoint to keep Sydney from becoming Sarajevo, or Boston from becoming Beirut'. The recent conflict (December 2005) between Lebanese Muslim and white Australian youth on the beaches around Sydney highlights the significance of Macedo's point here.

29 For an account of how Hannerz contrasts local and cosmopolitan ways of relating to a world culture made up of interconnected and varied local cultures see Burtonwood (1995).

30 'Two concepts of nationalism: An interview with Isaiah Berlin', published in *New York Review of Books*, 21 November 1991. A shortened version of this interview appeared as 'Cultures in search of their countries' in *Guardian*, 5 November 1991.

7 In pursuit of an uncertain future

1 It is Levinson (2003: 317) who remarks that in the absence of definitive solutions 'wrestling with diversity is likely to be a permanent condition'.

2 See 'Agency set to encourage wider community ties for Muslims', *The Times*, 20 September 2005.

3 Back *et al.* (2002) identify Blunkett's introduction to the Home Office White Paper, *Secure Borders, Safe Haven: Integration and Diversity in Modern Britain*, as evidence of New Labour turning away from a celebration of diversity and returning to an earlier assimilationist rhetoric. Given that these authors appear to regard opposition to forced marriage and female circumcision as assimilation it is not clear that liberals would want to disown assimilation if it is to be defined in these terms. For a recent critique of the relativism that continues to be found in multicultural orthodoxy see Malik (2005).

4 The Chief Rabbi's warning comes in an article 'Giving and belonging: the lesson that Jews can offer new immigrants' published in *The Times*, 1 October 2005.

5 Sir Jonathan Sacks articulated his theme of multiculturalism as building a shared home in a lecture *How To Build A Culture Of Respect* given at King's College, London, 18 May 2005. It is interesting to note in this context that when Harriet Harman concluded a debate with members of Hizb ut-Tahrir by calling on them to play their part in British society they replied: 'We're not part of British society. We stay here like guests in a hotel' (for details see Nick Cohen, Comment, the *Observer*, 23 October 2005).

6 For details of *Notes on Prejudice* see Chapter 2, note 31.

7 Phillips was speaking to Manchester Council for Community Relations at Manchester Town Hall, 22 September 2005.

8 Nussbaum's speech *The Future of Feminist Liberalism* was given as her presidential address to the American Philosophical Association's Central Division Conference in Chicago, 22 April 2000 and it is reprinted in Kittay and Felder (2002; Nussbaum, 2002). See also Levy (2003: 297) and Levinson (2003: 5) on the significance of Nussbaum's observation on the creative potential of tensions within theoretical perspectives.

9 See, for example, Berlin's *Does Political Theory Still Exist?* first published in 1962 and reprinted in Berlin (2000b).

10 Berlin's recognition of the tragedy of choice and the inevitability of loss when different goods conflict has been referred to recently by Michael Hughes (2005: 199) when citing a letter written by Berlin which clearly expresses the need for compromise in

the face of tragic choices. The letter concerns the situation in Israel: 'That Arab rights have been trodden on – that a wrong to them has been committed – it seems to be morally shameful to deny. If you then ask me why I am a Zionist, it is because I think that where right clashes with right – or rather misery with misery – one must not think about rights, which always exist ... but of some calm utilitarian solution which produces on the whole the best or happiest solution in the end'.

11 Written in 1989, Shklar's 'A life in learning' is reprinted in *Liberalism Without Illusions* (Yack, 1996).

12 Merry's (2005b) account of the autonomy-facilitating potential of an early education carried out within a framework of cultural coherence is similar to a rare concession to dogmatism that Sir Karl Popper makes in his autobiography, *Unended Quest*. Here Popper (1976) refers to the way that a fundamental melody provides the foundation against which the counterpoint can develop. Referring to religious music he says: 'It was the established *cantus firmus* which provided the framework, the order, the regularity, that made possible inventive freedom without chaos' (*ibid*: 58).

13 See Willinsky (1998) for an interesting account of how children might be taught about how individuals come to be identified as belonging to particular identity groups. This kind of teaching, says Willinsky, is both valuable and risky: 'To make a study of the divisions by which we live is a risky education. It can leave one no longer unthinkingly at home with one's self or place' (*ibid*: 399).

14 In Chapter 6 I noted how Miller (2005) uses these two Berlin metaphors to describe the benign and dangerous versions of nationalism.

15 By way of an example Weinstock argues that the USA, with a stronger national identity than Canada, enjoys much less commitment to the sharing of wealth among co-nationals. See also Merry (2005c) who comments on the lack of mutual trust between communities in Belgium and the consequent social exclusion of Muslims.

16 For a recent account of the dispute in France over the rights of Muslim girls to cover their heads while attending French schools see Laborde (2005). The issue of trust in achieving good inter-community relations in the multi-nation state is taken up by both McDonough (2003) and Mason (2000). Mason believes that it is identification with the institutions of a polity rather than a shared national identity which wins the loyalty of a group to a state in which it finds itself a cultural minority. Verhaar and Saharso (2004) offer some support for Mason's point when arguing that enabling Dutch Muslim police and court officers to wear headscarves as uniform would strengthen minority group trust in the public institutions of justice in The Netherlands.

17 In the light of Prime Minister Blair's failure in November 2005 to persuade his parliamentary colleagues of the need for legislation that would have allowed the detention for up to 90 days of individuals suspected of involvement in terrorism, it is interesting to note what Waldron (2003b) has to say about balancing the claims of security and liberty. Waldron observes that the reduction of civil liberties at times of national threat is unlikely to be distributed equally between communities and he questions whether any increased threat to security is best ameliorated by compromising the liberties of citizens when the impact is likely to be felt unequally. Waldron writes: 'If security-gains for most people are being balanced against liberty-losses for a few, then we need to pay attention to the few/most dimension of the balance, not just the liberty/security dimension' (*ibid*: 203).

18 Brighouse (2006: Chapter 5) shows how the reality of parents withdrawing their children from public schools in favour of private religious schools must influence judgements about the kinds of accommodations to make with orthodox religious families in order to maximize the number of children attending autonomy-facilitating schools.

19 Merry (2005c) notes the particular significance of an education for cultural coherence when the self-concept of children is threatened by a majority culture that disparages their community.

20 Spinner-Halev (2005) notes how resistance to colonialism caused Hindu nationalists

to link their own freedom to the rejection of what were perceived as British values thus making it difficult for nationalists to reform inegalitarian Hindu practices. Following a similar line of argument Mahajan (2005) considers the progress made by Christian, Parsi and Muslim women in India in reforming the internal practices of their communities in the direction of women's equality. Improved prospects are noted when the community is not subject to external hostility: 'When the [Indian] state is viewed with mistrust, as has happened in the case of the Muslim community of India, protecting and consolidating the community identity becomes the primary concern' (*ibid*: 111). Mahajan observes how this works to the advantage of religious leaders seeking to protect the *status quo* and against the interests of women dissenters.

21 Shklar (1998) was no more concerned with consistency than Berlin and agreed with Emerson (1983: 265) that a 'foolish consistency is the hobgoblin of little minds'.

22 Galipeau (1994: 171) links contextualism as a methodology with Berlin's fundamental opposition to the sacrifice of individuals to abstractions: 'To be anything but concrete and historical is to risk prescribing the sacrifice of living people to theories, to abstractions'.

23 I am grateful to Mike Degenhardt for making this paper available to me.

References

Abbas, T. (2005) 'Recent developments to British multicultural theory, policy and practice: the case of British Muslims', *The Journal of Political Philosophy*, 9: 153–166.

Abizadeh, A. (2004) 'Historical truth, national myths and liberal democracy: on the coherence of liberal nationalism', *The Journal of Political Philosophy*, 12: 291–313.

Addis, A. (1997) 'On human diversity and the limits of toleration', in I. Shapiro and W. Kymlicka (eds) *Ethnicity and Group Rights*, NOMOS XXXIX, New York: New York University Press.

Aiken, L. (1992) *To Be A Jewish Woman*, Northvale, NJ: Jason Aronson Inc.

Alexander, H. and McLaughlin, T. H. (2003) 'Education in religion and spirituality', in N. Blake, P. Smeyers, R. Smith and P. Standish (eds) *The Blackwell Guide to the Philosophy of Education*, Oxford: Blackwell.

Anderson, P. (1992) *A Zone of Engagement*, London: Verso.

Annan, N. (1997) 'Foreword', in I. Berlin (2000a) *The Proper Study of Mankind: An Anthology of Essays*, edited by H. Hardy and R. Hausheer, New York: Farrar, Straus and Giroux.

—— (1999) *The Dons: Mentors, Eccentrics and Geniuses*, London: HarperCollins.

Appiah, K. A. (2003) 'Liberal education: the United States example', in K. McDonough and W. Feinberg (eds) *Citizenship and Education in Liberal-Democratic Societies: Teaching for Cosmopolitan Values and Collective Identities*, Oxford: Oxford University Press.

Applebaum, B. (2003) 'Social justice, democratic education and the silencing of the words that wound', *Journal of Moral Education*, 32: 151–162.

Archard, D. (1999) 'Should we teach patriotism?', *Studies in Philosophy and Education*, 18: 157–173.

—— (2000) 'Nationalism and political theory', in N. O'Sullivan (ed.) *Political Theory in Transition*, London: Routledge.

Archbishops' Council (2001) *The Way Ahead: Church of England Schools in the New Millennium (The Dearing Report)*, London: Church House Publishing.

Arneson, R. and Shapiro, I. (1996) 'Democratic autonomy and religious freedom: a critique of Wisconsin v. Yoder', in I. Shapiro (ed.) *Democracy's Place*, Ithaca, NY: Cornell University Press.

Asante, M. K. (1992) 'Afro-centric curriculum', *Educational Leadership*, 49: 28–31.

Ashraf, S. A. (1993) 'The role of religious education in curriculum designing', *Westminster Studies in Education*, 16: 15–18.

Ashraf, S. A. , Mabud, S. A. and Mitchell, P. J. (1991) *Sex Education in the School Curriculum: An Agreed Statement*, Cambridge: The Islamic Academy.

Back, L., Keith, M., Khan, A., Shukra, K. and Solomos, J. (2002) 'The return of assimilationism: race, multiculturalism and New Labour', *Sociological Research Online*, 7: 2 Available Online: www. socresonline. org. uk/7/2. back. html (accessed 3 January 2006).

Bader, V. and Saharso, S. (2004) 'Introduction: contextualised morality and ethno-religious diversity', *Ethical Theory and Moral Practice*, 7: 107–115.

Bailey, C. (1984) *Beyond the Present and the Particular*, London: Routledge and Kegan Paul.

Barrow, R. (1999) 'The higher nonsense: some persistent errors in educational thinking', *Journal of Curriculum Studies*, 31: 131–142.

Barry, B. (1999) 'Self-government revisited', in R. Beiner (ed.) *Theorizing Nationalism*, Albany, NY: State University of New York Press.

—— (2001) *Culture and Equality: An Egalitarian Critique of Multiculturalism*, Cambridge: Polity Press.

—— (2002) 'Second thoughts - and some first thoughts revived', in P. Kelly (ed.) *Multiculturalism Reconsidered: Culture and Equality and its Critics*, Cambridge: Polity Press.

—— (2003) 'The study of politics as a vocation', in J. Hayward, B. Barry and A. Brown (eds) *The British Study of Politics in the Twentieth Century*, Oxford: Oxford University Press.

Bauman, Z. (2001) *Community: Seeking Safety in an Insecure World*, Cambridge: Polity Press.

Baumeister, A. (1998) 'Cultural diversity and education: the dilemma of political stability', *Political Studies*, 46: 919–936.

—— (2000) *Liberalism and the 'Politics of Difference'*, Edinburgh: Edinburgh University Press.

—— (2003) 'The limits of universalism', in B. Haddock and P. Sutch (eds) *Multiculturalism, Identity and Rights*, London: Routledge.

Beck, J. (1996) 'Nation, curriculum and identity in a conservative cultural analysis: a critical commentary', *Cambridge Journal of Education*, 26: 171–198.

—— (1999) 'Should homosexuality be taught as an acceptable lifestyle? A Muslim perspective: A reply to Halstead and Lewicka', *Cambridge Journal of Education*, 29: 121–130.

Beiner, R. (1999) 'Introduction', in R. Beiner (ed.) *Theorizing Nationalism*, Albany, NY: State University of New York University Press.

Benhabib, S. (2002) *The Claims of Culture: Equality and Diversity in the Global Era*, Princeton, NJ: Princeton University Press.

Bentwich, N. (ed.) (1952) *Hebrew University Garland: A Silver Jubilee Symposium*, London: Constellation Books.

Berlin, I. (1939) *Karl Marx: His Life and Environment*, London: Oxford University Press.

—— (1952) 'Jewish slavery and emancipation', in N. Bentwich (ed.) *Hebrew University Garland*, London: Constellation Books.

—— (1969) *Four Essays on Liberty*, Oxford: Oxford University Press.

—— (1978) *Concepts and Categories*, edited by H. Hardy, London: Hogarth.

—— (1979) *Against the Current: Essays in the History of Ideas*, edited by H. Hardy, London: Hogarth.

—— (1991a) *The Crooked Timber of Humanity: Chapters in the History of Ideas*, edited by H. Hardy, London: Fontana.

—— (1991b) 'The ingathering storm of nationalism', *New Perspectives Quarterly*, 8: 4–10.

—— (1991c) 'Cultures in search of their countries', *Guardian*, 5 November, p. 25.

—— (1993) 'A reply to David West', *Political Studies*, 41: 297–298.

—— (1994a) *Russian Thinkers*, edited by H. Hardy and A. Kelly, London: Penguin.

—— (1994b) 'Introduction', in J. Tully (ed.) *Philosophy in an Age of Pluralism*, Cambridge: Cambridge University Press.

—— (1996) *The Sense of Reality: Studies in Ideas and their History*, edited by H. Hardy, London: Pimlico.

—— (1998) *Personal Impressions*, second edition (enlarged) edited by H. Hardy, London, Pimlico.

—— (1999) *The First and Last*, introduced by H. Hardy, London: Granta Books.

—— (2000a) *The Power of Ideas*, edited by H. Hardy, London: Chatto & Windus.

—— (2000b) *The Proper Study of Mankind: An Anthology of Essays*, edited by H. Hardy and R. Hausheer, New York: Farrar, Straus and Giroux.

—— (2000c) *The Roots of Romanticism*, edited by H. Hardy, London: Pimlico.

—— (2000d) *Three Critics of the Enlightenment: Vico, Hamann, Herder*, edited by H. Hardy, Princeton, NJ: Princeton University Press.

—— (2002a) *Liberty*, edited by H. Hardy, Oxford: Oxford University Press.

—— (2002b) *Freedom and its Betrayal: Six Enemies of Human Liberty*, edited by H. Hardy, Princeton, NJ: Princeton University Press.

—— (2002c) *Woodrow Wilson on Education*, Available Online: berlin.wolf.ox.ac.uk/lists/nachlass/woodrow.pdf (accessed 29 December 2005).

—— (2004a) *Flourishing: Letters 1928–1946*, edited by H. Hardy, London: Chatto & Windus.

—— (2004b) *The Soviet Mind: Russian Culture Under Communism*, edited by H. Hardy, Washington, D.C.: Brookings Institute Press.

Birnbaum, P. (1996) 'From multiculturalism to nationalism', *Political Theory*, 24: 33–45.

—— (2004) 'Between universalism and multiculturalism: the French model in contemporary political theory', in A. Dieckhoff (ed.) *The Politics of Belonging: Nationalism, Liberalism, and Pluralism*, Lanham, MD.: Lexington Books.

Bleher, S. M. (1996) 'A programme for Muslim education in a non-Muslim society', in Muslim Education Trust, *Issues in Islamic Education*, London: Muslim Education Trust.

Bowden, B. (2003) 'Nationalism and cosmopolitanism: irreconcilable differences or possible bedfellows?', *National Identities*, 5: 235–249.

Brighouse, H. (1998) 'Civic education and liberal legitimacy', *Ethics*, 108: 719–745.

—— (2003a) *School Choice and Social Justice*, Oxford: Oxford University Press.

—— (2003b) 'Should we teach patriotic history?', in K. McDonough and W. Feinberg (eds) *Citizenship and Education in Liberal-Democratic Societies: Teaching for Cosmopolitan Values and Collective Identities*, Oxford: Oxford University Press.

—— (2005) 'Faith-based schools in the United Kingdom: an unenthusiastic defence of a slightly revised status quo', in R. Gardner, J. Cairns and D. Lawton (eds) *Faith Schools: Consensus or Conflict?*, London: RoutledgeFalmer.

—— (2006) *On Education*, London: Routledge.

Bromwich, D. (1995) 'Culturalism, the euthanasia of liberalism', *Dissent*, 42: 89–106.

Brown, D. (1999) 'Are there good and bad nationalisms?', *Nations and Nationalism*, 5: 281–302.

Burtonwood, N. (1981) 'Durkheim, Sir Fred Clarke and English education', *Westminster Studies in Education*, 4: 105–113.

—— (1985) 'Kuhn and Popper as contrasting models for the education of ethnic minority pupils', *Educational Review*, 37: 119–130.

—— (1995) 'Beyond local cultures: towards a cosmopolitan art education', *Journal of Art and Design Education*, 14: 205–212.

—— (1996) 'Beyond culture: a reply to Mark Halstead', *Journal of Philosophy of Education*, 30: 295–299.

—— (1998) 'Liberalism and communitarianism: a response to two recent attempts to reconcile individual autonomy with group identity', *Educational Studies*, 24: 295–304.

—— (2000) 'Must liberal support for separate schools be subject to a condition of individual autonomy?', *British Journal of Educational Studies*, 48: 269–284.

—— (2002a) 'Anthropology, sociology, and the preparation of teachers for a culturally plural society', *Pedagogy, Culture and Society*, 10: 367–386.

—— (2002b) 'Holocaust Memorial Day in schools – context, process and content: a review of research into Holocaust education', *Educational Research*, 44: 69–82.

—— (2003a) 'Isaiah Berlin, diversity liberalism, and education', *Educational Review*, 55: 323–331.

—— (2003b) 'Social cohesion, autonomy and the liberal defence of faith schools', *Journal of Philosophy of Education*, 37: 415–425.

Burtt, S. (2003) 'Comprehensive educations and the liberal understanding of autonomy', in K. McDonough and W. Feinberg (eds) *Education and Citizenship in Liberal-Democratic Societies: Teaching for Cosmopolitan Values and Collective Identities*, Oxford: Oxford University Press.

Callan, E. (1988) 'Faith, worship and reason in religious upbringing', *Journal of Philosophy of Education*, 22: 183–193.

—— (1997a) *Creating Citizens: Political Education and Liberal Democracy*, Oxford: Clarendon Press.

—— (1997b) 'The great sphere: education against servility', *Journal of Philosophy of Education*, 31: 221–232.

—— (1999) 'A note on patriotism and utopianism: response to Schrag', *Studies in Philosophy and Education*, 18: 197–201.

—— (2000) 'Discrimination and religious schooling', in W. Kymlicka and W. Norman (eds) *Citizenship in Diverse Societies*, Oxford: Oxford University Press.

—— (2002a) 'Autonomy, child-rearing and good lives', in D. Archard and C. Macleod (eds) *The Moral and Political Status of Children*, Oxford: Oxford University Press.

—— (2002b) 'Democratic patriotism and multicultural education', *Studies in Philosophy and Education*, 21: 465–477.

—— (2005) 'The ethics of assimilation', *Ethics*, 115: 471–500.

Carens, J. H. (1997) 'Two conceptions of fairness: a response to Veit Bader', *Political Theory*, 25: 814–820.

—— (2000) *Culture, Citizenship, and Community: A Contextual Approach to Justice as Evenhandedness*, Oxford: Oxford University Press.

—— (2004) 'A contextual approach to political theory', *Ethical Theory and Moral Practice*, 7: 117–132.

Carr, D. (2003) 'Character and moral choice in the cultivation of virtue', *Philosophy*, 78: 219–232.

Carter, S. (1993) *Culture of Disbelief: How American Law and Politics Trivialize Religious Devotion*, New York: Basic Books.

Cocks, J. (2002) *Passion and Paradox: Intellectuals Confront the National Question*, Princeton, NJ: Princeton University Press.

Cohen, J., Howard, M. and Nussbaum, M. C. (eds) (1999) *Is Multiculturalism Bad For Women? Susan Moller Okin and Respondents*, Princeton, NJ: Princeton University Press.

Cohen, M. (1960) 'Berlin and the liberal tradition', *The Philosophical Quarterly*, 10: 216–227.

Coleman, J. (2002) 'Answering Susan: Liberalism, civic education, and the status of young persons', in D. Archard and C. Macleod (eds) *The Moral and Political Status of Children*, Oxford: Oxford University Press.

—— (2003) 'School choice, diversity and a life of one's own', *Theory and Research in Education*, 1: 101–120.

Collini, S. (1999) *English Pasts: Essays in History and Culture*, Oxford: Oxford University Press.

Colson, I. (2004) '"Their churches are at home": the communication and definition of values in four aided Church of England secondary schools', *British Journal of Religious Education*, 26: 73–83.

Commission for Racial Equality (1990) *Schools of Faith: Religious Schools in a Multicultural Society*, London: Commission for Racial Equality.

Cracraft, J. (2002) 'A Berlin for historians', *History and Theory*, 41: 277–300.

Crick, B. (1969) 'Freedom as politics', in P. Laslett and W. G. Runciman (eds) *Philosophy, Politics and Society: Third Series*, Oxford: Blackwell.

—— (1991) 'The English and the British', in B. Crick (ed.) *National Identities: The Constitution of the United Kingdom*, Oxford: Blackwell.

—— (1995) 'The sense of identity of the indigenous British', *New Community*, 21: 167–182.

—— (2000) *Essays On Citizenship*, London: Continuum.

—— (2001) *Crossing Borders: Political Essays*, London: Continuum.

Crowder, G. (2002) *Liberalism and Value Pluralism*, London: Continuum.

—— (2004) *Isaiah Berlin: Liberty and Pluralism*, Cambridge: Polity.

Cumper, P. (1990) 'Muslim schools: the implications of the Education Reform Act 1988', *New Community*, 16: 379–389.

Dagovitz, A. (2004) 'When choice does not matter: political liberalism, religion and the faith school debate', *Journal of Philosophy of Education*, 38: 165–180.

Day, G. and Thompson, A. (2004) *Theorizing Nationalism*, Basingstoke: Palgrave Macmillan.

Degenhardt, M. (2005) 'Hedgehogs or foxes? Some enquiries regarding educational aims arising from an essay by Isaiah Berlin.' Paper presented at the Philosophy of Education Society of Great Britain, Gregynog Conference, June.

De Jong, J. and Snik, G. (2002) 'Why should states fund denominational schools?', *Journal of Philosophy of Education*, 37: 415–426.

De Ruyter, D. J. (1999) 'Christian schools in a pluralistic society?', *Interchange*, 30/32: 213–233.

—— (2003) 'The importance of ideals in education', *Journal of Philosophy of Education*, 37: 467–482.

—— (2004a) 'Raising a beauty or a beast?' Paper presented at the Philosophy of Education Society of Great Britain Annual Conference, New College, Oxford, April.

—— (2004b) 'Is autonomy imposing education too demanding?', *Studies in Philosophy and Education*, 23: 211–221.

De Ruyter, D. J. and Miedema, S. (2000) 'Denominational schools in the Netherlands', in M. Leicester, C. Modgil and S. Modgil (eds) *Education, Culture and Values Vol. V. Spiritual and Religious Education*, London: Falmer.

Deveaux, M. (2000) *Cultural Pluralism and Dilemmas of Justice*, Ithaca, NY: Cornell University Press.

—— (2005) 'A deliberative approach to conflicts of culture', in A. Eisenberg and J. Spinner-Halev (eds) *Minorities Within Minorities, Equality, Rights and Diversity*, Cambridge: Cambridge University Press.

Dieckhoff, A. (2004) 'Introduction: new perspectives on nationalism', in A. Dieckhoff (ed.) *The Politics of Belonging: Nationalism, Liberalism, and Pluralism*, Lanham, MD: Lexington Books.

Donohoue Clyne, I. (2004) 'Educational choices for immigrant Muslim communities: secular or religious?' in B. van Driel (ed.) *Confronting Islamophobia in Educational Practice*, Stoke: Trentham Books.

Dworkin, R. (2001) 'Do liberal values conflict?', in R. Dworkin, M. Lilla and R. B. Silvers, (eds) *The Legacy of Isaiah Berlin*, New York: New York Review Books.

Dworkin, R., Lilla, M. and Silvers, R. B. (eds) (2001) *The Legacy of Isaiah Berlin*, New York: New York Review of Books.

Dwyer, J. G. (1998) *Religious Schools v. Children's Rights*, Ithaca, NY: Cornell University Press.

Eberle, C. (2002) *Religious Conviction in Liberal Politics*, Cambridge: Cambridge University Press.

Eisenberg, A. (2005) 'Identity and liberal politics: the problem of minorities within minorities', in A. Eisenberg and J. Spinner-Halev (eds) *Minorities Within Minorities: Equality, Rights and Diversity*, Cambridge: Cambridge University Press.

Eisenberg, A. and Spinner-Halev, J. (2005) 'Introduction', in A. Eisenberg and J. Spinner-Halev (eds) *Minorities Within Minorities: Equality, Rights and Diversity*, Cambridge: Cambridge University Press.

Ellett, F. S. and Ericson, D. P. (1997) 'In defence of public reason: on the nature of historical rationality', *Educational Theory*, 47: 133–161.

Ellis, V. and High, S. (2004) 'Something more to tell you: gay, lesbian or bisexual young people's experiences of secondary schooling', *British Educational Research Journal*, 30: 213–225.

Emerson, R. W. (1983) *Essays and Lectures*, New York: Library of America.

Enslin, P. (1999) 'The place of national identity in the aims of education', in R. Marples (ed.) *The Aims of Education*, London: Routledge.

—— (2003) 'Liberal feminism, diversity and education', *Theory and Research in Education*, 1: 73–87.

Fagan, A. (2004) 'Challenging the bioethical application of the autonomy principle in multicultural societies', *Journal of Applied Philosophy*, 21: 15–31.

Feinberg, W. (1995) 'Liberalism and the aims of multicultural education', *Journal of Philosophy of Education*, 29: 203–216.

—— (1998) *Common Schools/Uncommon Identities*, New Haven, CT: Yale University Press.

—— (2003) 'Religious education in liberal democratic societies: the question of accountability and autonomy', in K. McDonough and W. Feinberg (eds) *Citizenship and Education in Liberal-Democratic Societies: Teaching for Cosmopolitan Values and Collective Identities*, Oxford: Oxford University Press.

—— (2004) 'Critical reflection and religious education: how deep?' plenary paper presented at the Philosophy of Education Society of Great Britain Annual Conference, New College, Oxford, 4 April.

Forum on Islamophobia and Racism (2004) *Muslims on Education*, Richmond: Association of Muslim Social Scientists (UK).

Fortier, A. (2005) 'Pride politics and multiculturalist citizenship', *Ethnic and Racial Studies*, 28: 559–578.

Freeman, M. (1994) 'Nation-state and cosmopolis: a response to David Miller', *Journal of Applied Philosophy*, 11: 79–86.

Fullinwider, R. K. (1996) 'Patriotic history', in R. K. Fullinwider (ed.) *Public Education in a Multicultural Society: Policy, Theory, Critique*, Cambridge: Cambridge University Press.

Galipeau, C. (1994) *Isaiah Berlin's Liberalism*, Oxford: Clarendon Press.

Galston, W. (1991) *Liberal Purposes: Goods, Virtues, and Diversity in the Liberal State*, Cambridge: Cambridge University Press.

—— (1995) 'Two concepts of liberalism', *Ethics*, 105: 516–534.

—— (1999) 'Diversity, toleration, and deliberative democracy: religious minorities and public schooling', in S. Macedo (ed.) *Deliberative Politics: Essays in Democracy and Disagreement*, New York: Oxford University Press.

—— (2001) 'Who's a liberal?', *The Public Interest*, 144: 100–108.

—— (2002) *Liberal Pluralism: The Implications of Value Pluralism for Political Theory and Practice*, Cambridge: Cambridge University Press.

—— (2005) *The Practice of Liberal Pluralism*, Cambridge: Cambridge University Press.

Gans, C. (2003) *The Limits of Nationalism*, Cambridge: Cambridge University Press.

Gardiner, P. (1996) 'Introduction', in I. Berlin, *The Sense of Reality*, edited by H. Hardy, London: Pimlico.

Gardner, P. (1988) 'Religious upbringing and the liberal ideal of religious autonomy', *Journal of Philosophy of Education*, 22: 89–105

Garrard, G. (1997) 'The Counter-Enlightenment liberalism of Isaiah Berlin', *Journal of Political Ideologies*, 2: 281–296.

General Synod (1998) *Church of England Schools in the New Millennium*, London: General Synod of the Church of England.

Gillborn, D. (1997) 'Racism and reform: new ethnicities/old inequalities?', *British Educational Research Journal*, 23: 345–360.

Gilliatt, S. (2002) 'No surrender? The attachment to identity and contemporary political thought', *Contemporary Politics*, 8: 23–35.

Grace, G. (2003) 'Educational studies and faith-based schooling: moving from prejudice to evidence-based argument', *British Journal of Educational Studies*, 51: 149–167.

Gray, J. (1995) *Berlin*, London: Fontana.

—— (1998) 'Where pluralists and liberals part company', *International Journal of Philosophical Studies*, 6: 17–36.

—— (2000) *Two Faces of Liberalism*, Cambridge: Polity Press.

Great Britain: Department for Education and Employment (1999) *The National Curriculum: Handbook for Secondary Teachers in England Key Stages 3 & 4*, London: Stationery Office.

—— (2001) *Schools: Building on Success*, London: Stationery Office.

Great Britain: Department of Education and Science (1985) *Education for All (The Swann Report)*, London: HMSO.

Great Britain: Department for Education and Skills (2001) *Schools: Achieving Success*, London: Stationery Office.

Great Britain: Home Office (2001) *Community Cohesion: A Report of the Independent Review Team (The Cantle Report)*, London: Home Office.

—— (2002) *Secure Borders, Safe Haven: Integration With Diversity in Modern Britain*, London: The Stationery Office.

Great Britain, Home Office: Advisory Group on Life in the United Kingdom (2003) *The New and the Old*, London: The Stationery Office.

—— (2004) *Life in the United Kingdom: A Journey to Citizenship*, London: The Stationery Office.

Green, L. (1995) 'Internal minorities and their rights', in W. Kymlicka (ed.) *The Rights of Minority Cultures*, Oxford: Oxford University Press.

Groothius, D. (2004) 'On not abolishing faith schools: a response to Michael Hand', *Theory and Research in Education*, 2: 177–188.

Grosvenor, I. (1999) '"There's no place like home": education and the making of national identity', *History of Education*, 28: 235–250.

Gutmann, A. (1980) *Liberal Equality*, Cambridge: Cambridge University Press.

—— (1989) 'Undemocratic education', in N. Rosenblum (ed.) *Liberalism and the Moral Life*, Cambridge, MA: Harvard University Press.

—— (1995) 'Civic education and social diversity', *Ethics*, 105: 557–579.

—— (1999) 'Liberty and pluralism in the pursuit of the non-ideal', *Social Research*, 66: 1039–1062.

—— (2000) 'Religion and state in the United States: a defence of two-way protection', in N. L. Rosenblum (ed.) *Obligations of Citizenship and the Demands of Faith: Religious Accommodation in Pluralist Democracies*, Princeton, NJ: Princeton University Press.

—— (2003) *Identity in Democracy*, Princeton, NJ: Princeton University Press.

Halbertal, M. (1996) 'Autonomy, toleration, and group rights: a response to Will Kymlicka', in D. Heyd (ed.) *Toleration: An Elusive Virtue*, Princeton, NJ: Princeton University Press.

Halstead, J. M. (1990) 'Muslim schools and the ideal of autonomy', *Ethics in Education*, 9: 4–6.

—— (1995) 'Voluntary apartheid? Problems of schooling for religious and other minorities in democratic societies', *Journal of Philosophy of Education*, 29: 257–272.

—— (1996a) 'Liberal values and liberal education', in J. M. Halstead and M. Taylor (eds) *Values in Education and Education in Values*, London: Falmer.

—— (1996b) 'Values and values education in schools', in J. M. Halstead and M. Taylor (eds) *Values in Education and Education in Values*, London: Falmer.

—— (1996c) 'Liberalism, multiculturalism, and toleration', *Journal of Philosophy of Education*, 30: 307–313.

—— (1997) 'Muslims and sex education', *Journal of Moral Education*, 26: 317–329.

—— (1999a) 'Teaching about homosexuality: a response to Beck', *Cambridge Journal of Education*, 29: 131–136.

—— (1999b) 'Moral education and family life: the effects of diversity', *Journal of Moral Education*, 28: 265–281.

—— (2002) 'Faith and diversity in religious school provision', in L. Gearon (ed.) *Education in the United Kingdom: Structures and Organization*, London: David Fulton.

—— (2003) 'Schooling and cultural maintenance for religious minorities in a liberal state', in K. McDonough and W. Feinberg (eds) *Citizenship and Education in Liberal-Democratic Societies: Teaching for Cosmopolitan Values and Collective Identities*, Oxford: Oxford University Press.

—— (2005) 'Islam, homophobia and education: a reply to Michael Merry', *Journal of Moral Education*, 34: 37–42.

Halstead, J. M. and Lewicka, K. (1998) 'Should homosexuality be taught as an acceptable lifestyle? A Muslim perspective', *Cambridge Journal of Education*, 28: 49–64.

Halstead, J. M. and McLaughlin, T. (2005) 'Are faith schools divisive?', in R. Gardner, J. Cairns and D. Lawton (eds) *Faith Schools: Consensus or Conflict?* London: RoutledgeFalmer.

Halstead, J. M. and Taylor, M. (2000) *The Development of Values, Attitudes and Personal Qualities: A Review of Recent Research*, Slough: National Foundation for Educational Research.

Hampshire, S. (1991) 'Nationalism', in E. Ulmann-Margalit and A. Margalit (eds) *Isaiah Berlin: A Celebration*, Chicago, IL: Chicago University Press.

Hand, M. (2002) 'Religious upbringing reconsidered', *Journal of Philosophy of Education*, 36: 545–557.

—— (2003) 'A philosophical objection to faith schools', *Theory and Research in Education*, 1: 89–99.

—— (2004) 'The problem with faith schools: A reply to my critics', *Theory and Research in Education*, 2: 343–353.

Hanley, R. P. (2004) 'Political science and political understanding: Isaiah Berlin on the nature of political inquiry', *American Political Science Review*, 98: 327–339.

Hannerz, U. (1990) 'Cosmopolitans and locals in world culture', in M. Featherstone (ed.) *Global Culture*, London: Sage.

Hardin, R. (2000) 'Fallacies of nationalism', in I. Shapiro and S. Macedo (eds) *Designing Democratic Institutions*, New York: New York University Press.

Hardy, H. (1999) 'Introduction', in I. Berlin, *The First and Last*, London: Granta Books.

Hatier, C. (2004) 'Isaiah Berlin and the totalitarian mind', *The European Legacy*, 9: 767–782.

Hausheer, R. (1983) 'Isaiah Berlin and the emergence of liberal pluralism', in P. Manet, R. Hausheer, W. Karpinski and W. Kaiser (eds) *European Liberty*, The Hague: Martinus Nijhot.

—— (2003) 'Enlightening the Enlightenment', in J. Mali and R. Wokler (eds) *Isaiah Berlin's Counter-Enlightenment, Transactions of the American Philosophical Society*, 93, 5: 33–50.

Haydon, G. (1994) 'Conceptions of the secular in society, polity and schools', *Journal of Philosophy of Education*, 28: 65–75.

—— (1997) *Teaching About Values*, London: Cassell.

Hekma, G. (2002) 'Imams and homosexuality: a post-gay debate in The Netherlands', *Sexualities*, 5: 237–248.

Hewer, C. (2001) 'Schools for Muslims', *Oxford Review of Education*, 27: 515–527.

Hewitt, I. (1996) 'The case for Muslim schools', in Muslim Education Trust, *Issues in Islamic Education*, London: Muslim Education Trust.

Heyting, F. (2004) 'Beware of ideals in education', *Journal of Philosophy of Education*, 38: 241–247.

Hobsbawm, E. (2003) *Interesting Times: A Twentieth-Century Life*, London: Abacus.

Holmes, S. (1994) 'Liberalism for a world of ethnic passions and decaying states', *Social Research*, 61: 599–610.

Honneth, A. (1999) 'Negative freedom and cultural belonging: an unhealthy tension in the political philosophy of Isaiah Berlin', *Social Research*, 66: 1063–1077.

Horton, J. (1996) 'Toleration as virtue', in D. Heyd (ed.) *Toleration: An Elusive Virtue*, Princeton, NJ: Princeton University Press.

—— (2001) Review of B. Parekh 'Rethinking Multiculturalism' and The Runnymede Trust 'The Future of Multiethnic Britain', *Journal of Applied Philosophy*, 18: 307–311.

—— (2003) 'Liberalism and multiculturalism: once more into the breach', in B. Haddock and P. Sutch (eds) *Multiculturalism, Identity and Rights*, London: Routledge.

Hughes, M. (2005) 'The papers of Sir Isaiah Berlin at the Bodleian Library', *Twentieth Century British History*, 16: 193–205.

Ignatieff, M. (1994a) *Blood and Belonging: Journeys into the New Nationalism*, London: Vintage.

—— (1994b) *The Needs of Strangers*, London: Vintage.

—— (1998a) *Isaiah Berlin: A Life*, London: Chatto & Windus.

—— (1998b) *The Warrior's Honor: Ethnic War and the Modern Conscience*, London: Chatto & Windus.

—— (2003) *Human Rights As Politics and Idolatry*, Princeton, NJ: Princeton University Press.

Illingworth, P. and Murphy, T. (2004) 'In our best interest: meeting duties to lesbian, gay and bisexual adolescent students', *Journal of Social Philosophy*, 35: 198–210.

Ipgrave, J. (2003) 'Dialogue, citizenship and religious education', in R. Jackson (ed.) *International Perspectives on Citizenship, Education and Religious Diversity*, London: Routledge.

Iqbal, M. (1974) 'Muslims in a Christian culture', *Times Educational Supplement*, 18 January, p. 2.

—— (1977) 'Education and Islam in Britain', *New Community*, 5: 397–404.

Isin, E. F. and Wood, P. K. (1999) *Citizenship and Identity*, London: Sage.

Islamic Academy (1985) *Swann Committee Report*, Cambridge: Islamic Academy.

Jackson, R. (2003) 'Should the state fund faith based schools? A review of the arguments', *British Journal of Religious Education*, 25: 89–102.

Jahanbegloo, R. (2000) *Conversations with Isaiah Berlin*, London: Phoenix.

Jinkins, M. (2004) *Christianity, Tolerance and Pluralism: A Theological Engagement with Isaiah Berlin's Social Theory*, London: Routledge.

Katayama, K. (2003) 'Is the virtue approach to moral education viable in a pluralistic society', *Journal of Philosophy of Education*, 37: 325–338.

Kateb, G. (1994) 'Notes on pluralism', *Social Research*, 61: 511–537.

—— (1999) 'Can cultures be judged? Two defenses of cultural pluralism in Isaiah Berlin's work', *Social Research*, 66: 1009–1038.

Katznelson, I. (1999) 'Isaiah Berlin's modernity', *Social Research*, 66: 1079–1101.

Kekes, J. (1999) 'Pluralism, moral imagination and moral education', in T. McLaughlin and J. M. Halstead (eds) *Education in Morality*, London: Routledge.

Kelly, A. (1978) 'Introduction', in I. Berlin, *Russian Thinkers*, edited by H. Hardy and A. Kelly, London: Penguin.

Kelly, D. (2002) 'The political thought of Isaiah Berlin', *British Journal of Politics and International Relations*, 4: 25–48.

Kelly, P. (2001) '"Dangerous liaisons": Parekh and "Oakeshottian" multiculturalism', *The Political Quarterly*, 72: 428–436.

—— (2003) 'Contextual and non-contextual histories of political thought', in J. Hayward, B. Barry and A. Brown (eds) *The British Study of Politics in the Twentieth Century*, Oxford: Oxford University Press.

Kenny, M. (2000) 'Isaiah Berlin's contribution to modern political theory', *Political Studies*, 48: 1026–1039.

—— (2004) *The Politics of Identity: Political Theory and the Dilemma of Difference*, Cambridge: Polity.

Kirklees Ednet (2002) *Sex Education in an Islamic Framework – Lesson Plans Key Stage*

3. Available Online: www. kirklees-ednet.org.uk/subjects/pshce/sexeducation/ islam-icframeworkks3.pdf (accessed 30 December 2005).

Kittay, E. and Felder, E. K. (eds) (2002) *The Subject of Care: Feminist Perspectives on Dependency*, Lanham, MD: Rowman & Littlefield.

Kofman, E. (2005) 'Citizenship, migration and the reassertion of national identity', *Citizenship Studies*, 9: 453–467.

Kukathas, C. (1992) 'Are there any cultural rights?', *Political Theory*, 20: 105–139.

—— (2002) 'The life of Brian, or now for something completely difference-blind', in P. Kelly (ed.) *Multiculturalism Reconsidered: Culture and Equality and its Critics*, Oxford: Polity.

—— (2003) *The Liberal Archipelago: A Theory of Diversity and Freedom*, Oxford: Oxford University Press.

Kunzman, R. (2005) 'Religion, politics and civic education: a review article', *Journal of Philosophy of Education*, 39: 159–168.

Kymlicka, W. (1996a) *Multicultural Citizenship: A Liberal Theory of Minority Rights*, Oxford: Clarendon Press.

—— (1996b) 'Two models of pluralism and tolerance', in D. Heyd (ed.) *Toleration: An Elusive Virtue*, Princeton, NJ: Princeton University Press.

—— (1999) 'Education for citizenship', in J. M. Halstead and T. H. McLaughlin (eds) *Education in Morality*, London: Routledge.

—— (2001) *Politics in the Vernacular: Nationalism, Multiculturalism and Citizenship* Oxford: Oxford University Press.

—— (2003) 'Two dilemmas of citizenship education in pluralist societies', in A. Lockyer, B. Crick and J. Annette (eds) *Education for Democratic Citizenship: Issues in Theory and Practice*, Aldershot: Ashgate.

Laborde, C. (2005) 'Secular philosophy and Muslim headscarves in schools', *The Journal of Political Philosophy*, 13: 305–329.

Leach, E. R. (1975) 'Freedom and social conditioning', *Educational Review*, 27: 83–99.

Levey, G. B. (2001) 'Liberal nationalism and cultural rights', *Political Studies*, 49: 670–691.

Levinson, M. (1997) 'Liberalism vs. democracy? Schooling private citizens in the public square', *British Journal of Political Science*, 27: 333–360.

—— (1999) *The Demands of Liberal Education*, Oxford: Oxford University Press.

Levinson, S. (2003) *Wrestling With Diversity*, Durham, NC: Duke University Press.

Levy, J. T. (2000) *The Multiculturalism of Fear*, Oxford: Oxford University Press.

—— (2003) 'Liberalism's divide, after socialism and before', *Social Philosophy and Policy*, 20: 278–297.

—— (2005) 'Sexual orientation, exit and refuge', in A. Eisenberg and J. Spinner-Halev (eds) *Minorities Within Minorities: Equality, Rights and Diversity*, Cambridge: Cambridge University Press.

Lilla, M. (2001) 'Wolves and lambs', in R. Dworkin, M. Lilla and R. B. Silvers (eds) *The Legacy of Isaiah Berlin*, New York: New York Review Books.

Locke, J. (1975 [1689]) *An Essay Concerning Human Understanding*, edited by P. H. Nidditch, Oxford: Clarendon Press.

Lukes, S. (1994) 'The singular and the plural: on the distinctive liberalism of Isaiah Berlin', *Social Research*, 61: 687–717.

—— (1998) 'Isaiah Berlin: in conversation with Steven Lukes', *Salmagundi*, Fall, 1998: 52–134.

—— (2001) 'An unfashionable fox', in R. Dworkin, M. Lilla and R. B. Silvers (eds) *The Legacy of Isaiah Berlin*, New York: New York Review Books.

Mabud, S. A. (1992) 'Aims and objectives of an integrated science curriculum for a multi-faith, multi-cultural country', *Muslim Education Quarterly*, 9: 14–24.

Macedo, S. (1990) *Liberal Virtues: Citizenship, Virtue and Community in Liberal Constitutionalism*, Oxford: Clarendon Press.

—— (1995a) 'Multiculturalism for the religious right? Defending liberal civic education', *Journal of Philosophy of Education*, 29: 223–238.

—— (1995b) 'Liberal civic education and religious fundamentalism: The case of God v. John Rawls?', *Ethics*, 105: 468–496.

—— (2000) *Diversity and Distrust: Civic Education in a Multicultural Democracy*, Cambridge, MA: Harvard University Press.

—— (2003) 'Liberalism and group identities', in K. McDonough and W. Feinberg (eds) *Citizenship and Education in Liberal-Democratic Societies: Teaching for Cosmopolitan Values and Collective Identities*, Oxford: Oxford University Press.

—— (forthcoming) 'Value pluralism against liberalism?', in J. C. Espada, M. F. Plattner and A. Wolfson (eds) *Pluralism Without Relativism: Remembering Sir Isaiah Berlin*, Lanham, MD: Rowman & Littlefield.

MacIntyre, A. (1999) 'How to seem virtuous without actually being so', in T. H. McLaughlin and J. M. Halstead (eds) *Education in Morality*, London: Routledge.

Mack, E. (1993a) 'Isaiah Berlin and the quest for liberal pluralism', *Public Affairs Quarterly*, 7: 215–230.

—— (1993b) 'The limits of diversity: the new Counter-Enlightenment and Isaiah Berlin's liberal pluralism', in: H. Dickman (ed.) *The Imperiled Academy*, New Brunswick, NJ: Transaction.

MacMullen, I. (2004) 'Education for autonomy: the role of religious elementary schools', *Journal of Philosophy of Education*, 38: 601–615.

Magee, B. (1978) *Men of Ideas: Some Creators of Contemporary Philosophy*, London: British Broadcasting Company.

Mahajan, G. (2005) 'Can intra-group equality co-exist with cultural diversity? Re-examining multicultural frameworks of accommodation', in A. Eisenberg and J. Spinner-Halev (eds) *Minorities Within Minorities: Equality, Rights and Diversity*, Cambridge: Cambridge University Press.

Mali, J. and Wokler, R. (2003) 'Editors' Preface', in J. Mali and R. Wokler (eds) *Isaiah Berlin's Counter-Enlightenment, Transactions of the American Philosophical Society*, 93, 5: vii–xi.

Malik, K. (2005) 'Born in Bradford', *Prospect*, October, 54–56.

Margalit, A. (1997) 'The moral psychology of nationalism', in R. McKim and J. McMahon (eds) *The Morality of Nationalism*, Oxford: Oxford University Press.

—— (1999) 'Tribute', in I. Berlin, *The First and Last*, London: Granta.

—— (2001) 'The crooked timber of nationalism', in R. Dworkin, M. Lilla and R. B. Silvers (eds) *The Legacy of Isaiah Berlin*, New York: New York Review Books.

Margalit, A. and Halbertal, M. (1994) 'Liberalism and the right to culture', *Social Research*, 61: 491–510.

Margalit, A. and Raz, J. (1990) 'National self-determination', *The Journal of Philosophy*, 87: 439–461.

Markell, P. (2000) 'Making affect safe for democracy? On "constitutional patriotism"', *Political Theory*, 28: 38–63.

Mason, A. (2000) *Community, Solidarity and Belonging: Levels of Community and their Normative Significance*, Cambridge: Cambridge University Press.

McConnell, M. W. (2000) 'Believers as equal citizens', in N. L. Rosenblum (ed.)

Obligations of Citizenship and Obligations of Faith, Princeton, NJ: Princeton University Press.

—— (2002) 'Education disestablishment: why democratic values are ill-served by democratic control of schooling', in S. Macedo and Y. Tamir (eds) *Moral and Political Education*, New York: New York University Press.

McDonough, K. (1998) 'Can the liberal state support cultural identity schools?', *American Journal of Education*, 106: 463–499.

—— (2003) 'Multinational civic education', in K. McDonough and W. Feinberg (eds) *Citizenship and Education in Liberal-Democratic States: Teaching for Cosmopolitan Values and Collective Identities*, Oxford: Oxford University Press.

McEwan, I. (2005) *Saturday*, London: Jonathan Cape.

McLaughlin, T. H. (1984) 'Parental rights and the religious upbringing of children', *Journal of Philosophy of Education*, 18: 75–83.

—— (1990) 'Peter Gardner on religious upbringing and the liberal ideal of religious autonomy', *Journal of Philosophy of Education*, 24: 107–125.

—— (1996) 'The distinctiveness of Catholic education', in T. H. McLaughlin, J. O'Keefe and B. O'Keefe (eds) *The Contemporary Catholic School*, London: Falmer.

Merry, M. (2004) 'Islam versus (liberal) pluralism? A response to Ahmad Yousif', *Journal of Muslim Minority Affairs*, 24: 123–139.

—— (2005a) 'Should educators accommodate intolerance? Mark Halstead, homosexuality, and the Islamic case', *Journal of Moral Education*, 34: 19–36.

—— (2005b) 'Cultural coherence and the schooling for identity maintenance', *Journal of Philosophy of Education*, 39: 477–497.

—— (2005c) 'Social exclusion of Muslim youth in Flemish- and French-speaking Belgian schools', *Cambridge Journal of Education*, 49: 1–22.

Mill, J. S. (1962 [1859]) *Utilitarianism*, edited by M. Warnock, London: Fontana.

Miller, D. (1995a) *On Nationality*, Oxford: Clarendon Press.

—— (1995b) 'Reflections on British national identity', *New Community*, 21: 153–166.

—— (1997) 'Nationality: some replies', *Journal of Applied Philosophy*, 14: 69–82.

—— (2000a) *Citizenship and National Identity*, Cambridge: Polity Press.

—— (2000b) 'Citizenship: what does it mean and why is it important?', in N. Pearce and J. Hallgarten (eds) *Tomorrow's Citizens: Critical Debates in Citizenship and Education*, London: Institute of Public Policy Research.

—— (2002) 'Liberalism, equal opportunities and cultural commitments', in P. Kelly (ed.) *Multiculturalism Reconsidered*, Cambridge: Polity Press.

—— (2005) 'Crooked timber or bent twig? Isaiah Berlin's nationalism', *Political Studies*, 53: 100–123.

Miller, H. (2001) 'Meeting the challenge: the Jewish schooling phenomenon in the UK', *Oxford Review of Education*, 27: 501–513.

Mills, C. (2003) 'The child's right to an open future?', *Journal of Social Philosophy*, 34: 499–509.

Milosz, C. (1985) *The Captive Mind*, London: Penguin.

Modood, T. (1993) 'Muslims, incitement to hatred, and the law', in J. Horton (ed.) *Liberalism, Multiculturalism and Toleration*, Basingstoke: Macmillan.

—— (2000) 'Anti-essentialism, multiculturalism, and the "recognition" of religious groups', in W. Kymlicka and W. Norman (eds) *Citizenship in Diverse Societies*, Oxford: Oxford University Press.

—— (2005a) 'Remaking multiculturalism after 7/7.' Available online: www.opendemocracy.net/content/articles/PDF/2879.pdf (accessed 16 December 2005).

—— (2005b) *Multicultural Politics: Racism, Ethnicity and Muslims in Britain*, Edinburgh: Edinburgh University Press.

Modood, T., Berthoud, R., Lakey, J., Nazroo, J., Smith, P., Virdee, J. and Beishon, S. (1997) *Ethnic Minorities in Britain: Diversity and Disadvantage*, London: Policy Studies Institute.

Mott-Thornton, K. (2003) 'Spirituality, pluralism and the limits of common schooling', in D. Carr and J. Haldane (eds) *Spirituality, Philosophy and Education*, London: RoutledgeFalmer.

Mulhall, S. (1998) 'Political liberalism and civic education: the liberal state and its future', *Journal of Philosophy of Education*, 32: 161–176.

National Curriculum Council (NCC) (1993) *Spiritual and Moral Development: A Discussion Paper*, York: National Curriculum Council.

Noddings, N. (1996) 'On community', *Educational Theory*, 46: 245–267.

Norman, W. (2004) 'From nation-building to national engineering: on the ethics of shaping identities', in A. Dieckhoff (ed.) *The Politics of Belonging: Nationalism, Liberalism, and Pluralism*, Lanham, MD: Lexington Books.

Nussbaum, M. (2002) 'The future of feminist liberalism', in E. Kittay and E. K. Felder (eds) *The Subject of Care: Feminist Perspectives on Dependency*, Lanham, MD: Rowman & Littlefield.

Office for Standards in Education (OfSTED) (2005) *Annual Report of Her Majesty's Chief Inspector of Schools 2003/04*, London: The Stationery Office.

Okin, S. M. (2002) '"Mistresses of their own destiny": group rights, gender, and realistic rights of exit', *Ethics*, 112: 205–230.

—— (2005) 'Multiculturalism and feminism: no simple question, no simple answer', in A. Eisenberg and J. Spinner-Halev (eds) *Minorities Within Minorities: Equality, Rights and Diversity*, Cambridge: Cambridge University Press.

Okin, S. M. and Reich, R. (1999) 'Families and schools as compensating agents in moral development for a multicultural society', *Journal of Moral Education*, 28: 283–298.

Olivier, S. (2006) 'Moral dilemmas of participation in dangerous leisure activities', *Leisure Studies*, 25: 95–109.

Olssen, M. (2004) 'From the Crick Report to the Parekh Report: Multiculturalism, cultural difference, and democracy – the re-visioning of citizenship education', *British Journal of Sociology of Education*, 25: 179–192.

Osler, A. and Starkey, H. (2001) 'Citizenship education and national identities in France and England: inclusive or exclusive?', *Oxford Review of Education*, 27: 287–305.

O'Sullivan, N. (2003) 'Visions of freedom: the response to totalitarianism', in J. Hayward, B. Barry and A. Brown (eds) *The British Study of Politics in the Twentieth Century*, Oxford: Oxford University Press.

Pardales, M. J. (2002) '"So, how did you arrive at that decision?" Connecting moral imagination and moral judgement', *Journal of Moral Education*, 31: 423–437.

Parekh, B. (1982) *Contemporary Political Thinkers*, Oxford: Martin Robertson.

—— (1995) 'The concept of national identity', *New Community*, 21: 255–268.

—— (2000) *Rethinking Multiculturalism: Cultural Diversity and Political Theory*, London: Macmillan Press.

Park, R. E. (1928) 'Human migration and the marginal man', *American Journal of Sociology*, 33: 881–93.

Parker-Jenkins, M. (2002) 'Equal access to state funding: the case of Muslim schools in Britain', *Race, Equality, and Schooling*, 5: 274–289.

Peters, S. F. (2003) *The Yoder Case: Religious Freedom, Education, and Parental Rights*, Lawrence, KS: University Press of Kansas.

Petrovic, J. E. (1999) 'Moral democratic education and homosexuality: censoring morality', *Journal of Moral Education*, 28: 201–214.

Plaisance, P. L. (2002) 'The journalist as moral witness: Michael Ignatieff's pluralistic philosophy for a global media culture', *Journalism*, 3: 205–222.

Pogge, T. W. (1992) 'Cosmopolitanism and sovereignty', *Ethics*, 103: 48–75.

Popper, K. (1976) *Unended Quest*, London: Fontana.

Pring, R. (2005) 'Faith schools: can they be justified?', in R. Gardner, J. Cairns and D. Lawton (eds) *Faith Schools: Consensus or Conflict?* London: RoutledgeFalmer.

Qualifications and Curriculum Authority (QCA) (1998) *Education for Citizenship and the Teaching of Democracy in Schools (The Crick Report)*, London: QCA.

Quong, J. (2004) 'The rights of unreasonable citizens', *The Journal of Political Philosophy*, 12: 314–335.

Rawls, J. (1988) 'The priority of the right and ideas of the good', *Philosophy and Public Affairs*, 17: 251–276.

—— (1993) *Political Liberalism*, New York: Columbia University Press.

—— (1999) 'The idea of public reason revisited', in J. Rawls, *The Law of Peoples*, Cambridge, MA: Harvard University Press.

Raz, J. (1986) *The Morality of Freedom*, Oxford: Oxford University Press.

—— (1999) 'How perfect should we be? And whose culture is?', in J. Cohen, M. Howard and M. C. Nussbaum (eds) *Is Multiculturalism Bad for Women?* Princeton, NJ: Princeton University Press.

Reich, R. (2002) *Bridging Liberalism and Multiculturalism in American Education*, Chicago, IL: University of Chicago Press.

—— (2003) 'Multicultural accommodations in education', in K. McDonough and W. Feinberg (eds) *Citizenship and Education in Liberal-Democratic Societies: Teaching for Cosmopolitan Values and Collective Identities*, Oxford: Oxford University Press.

Reitman, O. (2005) 'On exit', in A. Eisenberg and J. Spinner-Halev (eds) *Minorities Within Minorities: Equality, Rights and Diversity*, Cambridge: Cambridge University Press.

Rescher, N. (1993) *Pluralism: Against the Demand for Consensus*, Oxford: Clarendon Press.

Riley, J. (2000) 'Crooked timber and liberal culture', in M. Baghramian and A. Ingram (eds) *Pluralism: The Philosophy and Politics of Diversity*, London: Routledge.

—— (2001) 'Interpreting Berlin's liberalism', *American Political Science Review*, 95: 283–295.

—— (2002) 'Defending cultural pluralism: within liberal limits', *Political Theory*, 30: 68–96.

Roach, S. C. (2005) 'Value pluralism, liberalism, and the cosmopolitan intent of the International Criminal Court', *Journal of Human Rights*, 4: 475–490.

Roberts, P. (2003) 'Identity, reflection and justification', in B. Haddock and P. Sutch (eds) *Multiculturalism, Identity and Rights*, London: Routledge.

Runnymede Trust (2000) *The Future of Multi-Ethnic Britain: The Parekh Report*, London: Profile Books.

Rushdie, S. (1988) *The Satanic Verses*, London: Viking.

—— (1992) *Imaginary Homelands: Essays and Criticism 1981–1991*, London: Granta Books.

Ryan, A. (1998) 'Mill in a liberal landscape', in J. Skorupski (ed.) *The Cambridge Companion to Mill*, Cambridge: Cambridge University Press.

—— (1999) 'Isaiah Berlin: Political theory and liberal culture', *Annual Review of Political Science*, 2: 345–362.

Sacks, J. (1994) *Will We Have Jewish Grandchildren?*, London: Valentine Mitchell.

—— (2002) *The Dignity of Difference: How to Avoid the Clash of Civilizations*, London: Continuum.

Saharso, S. (2000) 'Female autonomy and cultural imperative: two hearts beating together', in W. Kymlicka and W. Norman (eds) *Citizenship in Diverse Societies*, Oxford: Oxford University Press.

Said, E. (1994) *Culture and Imperialism*, London: Vintage.

Said, E. (2001) *The End of the Peace Process: Oslo and After*, New York: Vintage.

Salomone, R. C. (2000) *Visions of Schooling: Conscience, Community, and Common Education*, New Haven, CT: Yale University Press.

Sandel, M. (1982) *Liberalism and the Limits of Justice*, Cambridge: Cambridge University Press.

Sanjakdar, F. (2004) 'Developing an appropriate sexual health education curriculum framework for Muslim students', in B. van Driel (ed.) *Confronting Islamophobia in Educational Practice*, Stoke: Trentham.

Sarwar, G. (1996) *Sex Education: The Muslim Perspective*, London: The Muslim Educational Trust.

Schagen, S. , Davies, D. , Rudd, P. and Schagen, I. (2002) *The Impact of Specialist and Faith Schools on Performance*, Slough: National Foundation for Educational Research.

Scholefield, L. (2001) 'The spiritual, moral, social and cultural values of students in a Jewish and a Catholic secondary school', *International Journal of Children's Spirituality*, 6: 41–53.

School Curriculum and Assessment Authority (SCAA) (1995) *Spiritual and Moral Development: SCAA Discussion Papers No. 3*, London: SCAA.

—— (1996a) *Education for Adult Life: The Spiritual and Moral Development of Young People: SCAA Discussion Papers No. 6*, London: SCAA.

—— (1996b) *National Forum for Values in Education and the Community: Consultation on Values in Education and the Community*, London: SCAA COM/96/608.

—— (1996c) *The National Forum for Values in Education and the Community, Final Report and Recommendations*, London: SCAA 96/43.

Schrag, F. (1998) 'Diversity, schooling, and the liberal state', *Studies in Philosophy and Education*, 17: 29–46.

—— (1999) 'Review article', *Studies in Philosophy and Education*, 18: 189–195.

Schwartzmantel, J. (2003) *Citizenship and Identity: Towards A New Republic*, London: Routledge.

Seglow, J. (1998) 'Universals and particulars: the case of liberal cultural nationalism', *Political Studies*, 46: 963–977.

Shachar, A. (1999) 'The paradox of multicultural vulnerability', in C. Joppke and S. Lukes (eds) *Multicultural Questions*, Oxford: Oxford University Press.

—— (2001) *Multicultural Jurisdictions: Cultural Differences and Women's Rights*, Cambridge: Cambridge University Press.

Shklar, J. (1996) 'A life in learning', in B. Yack (ed.) *Liberalism Without Illusions*, Chicago, IL: Chicago University Press.

—— (1998) *Political Thought and Political Thinkers*, edited by S. Hoffman, Chicago, IL: University of Chicago Press.

Short, G. (1993) 'Prejudice reduction in schools: the value of inter-racial contact', *British Journal of Sociology of Education*, 14: 159–168.

—— (1994) 'Teaching the Holocaust: the relevance of children's perceptions of Jewish culture and identity', *British Educational Research Journal*, 20: 393–405.

—— (2002) 'Faith-based schools: a threat to social cohesion?', *Journal of Philosophy of Education*, 36: 559–572.

—— (2003) 'Faith schools and indoctrination: a response to Michael Hand', *Theory and Research in Education*, 1: 331–341.

Short, G. and Lenga, R. (2002) 'Jewish primary schools in a multicultural society: responding to diversity?', *Journal of Beliefs and Values*, 23: 43–54.

Siame, C. N. (2000) '"Two concepts of liberty" through African eyes', *Journal of Political Philosophy*, 8: 53–67.

Siddiqui, A. (1997) 'Ethics in Islam: key concepts and contemporary challenges', *Journal of Moral Education*, 26: 423–431.

Siegal, H. (2004) 'Faith, knowledge and indoctrination: A friendly response to Hand', *Theory and Research in Education*, 2: 75–83.

Simmel, G. (1908) 'The stranger', in G. Simmel (1971) *On Individuality and Social Forms*, edited by D. N. Levine, Chicago, IL: Chicago University Press.

Skinner, G. (2002) 'Religious pluralism and school provision in Britain', *Intercultural Education*, 13: 171–181.

Snik, G. and De Jong, J. (1995) 'Liberalism and denominational schools', *Journal of Moral Education*, 24: 395–408.

—— (2005) 'Why liberal state funding of denominational schools cannot be unconditional: a reply to Neil Burtonwood', *Journal of Philosophy of Education*, 39: 113–122.

Spiecker, B. and De Ruyter, D. (2005) 'Taking the right to exit seriously.' Paper presented at the Philosophy of Education Society of Great Britain Annual Conference, New College, Oxford, April.

Spinner, J. (1994) *Boundaries of Citizenship: Race, Ethnicity and Nationality in the Liberal State*, Baltimore, MD: Johns Hopkins University Press.

Spinner-Halev, J. (1999) 'Cultural pluralism and partial citizenship', in C. Joppke and S. Lukes (eds) *Multicultural Questions*, Oxford: Oxford University Press.

—— (2000) *Surviving Diversity: Religion and Democratic Citizenship*, Baltimore, MD: Johns Hopkins University Press.

—— (2001) 'Feminism, multiculturalism, oppression, and the state', *Ethics*, 112: 84–113.

—— (2005) 'Hinduism, Christianity, and liberal religious toleration', *Political Theory*, 33: 28–57.

Spinner-Halev, J. and Theiss-Morse, E. (2003) 'National identity and self-esteem', *American Political Science Review*, 1: 515–532.

Steinberg, J. (1996) 'The burdens of Berlin's modernity', *History of European Ideas*, 22: 369–383.

Steutel, J. and Spiecker, B. (1999) 'Liberalism and critical thinking', in R. Marples (ed.) *The Aims of Education*, London: Routledge.

—— (2004) 'Sex education, state policy and the principle of mutual consent', *Sex Education*, 4: 49–62.

Stolzenberg, N. M. (1993) '"He drew a circle that shut me out": assimilation, indoctrination and the paradox of liberal education', *Harvard Law Review*, 106: 581–667.

Strike, K. (1999) 'Liberalism, citizenship and the private interest in schooling', in R. Marples (ed.) *The Aims of Education*, London: Routledge.

—— (2000) 'Schools as communities: four metaphors, three models, and a dilemma or two', *Journal of Philosophy of Education*, 34: 617–642.

Sunstein, C. (1999) 'Should sex equality law apply to religious institutions?', in J. Cohen,

M. Howard and M. C. Nussbaum (eds) *Is Multiculturalism Bad For Women?* Princeton, NJ: Princeton University Press.

Swaine, L. (2001) 'How ought liberal democracies to treat theocratic communities?', *Ethics*, 111: 302–343.

Talbot, M. and Tate, N. (1997) 'Shared values in a pluralist society?', in R. Smith and P. Standish (eds) *Teaching Right and Wrong: Moral Education in the Balance*, Stoke: Trentham.

Talisse, R. B. (2004) 'Can value pluralists be comprehensive liberals? Galston's liberal pluralism', *Contemporary Political Theory*, 3: 127–139.

Tamir, Y. (1991) 'Whose history? What ideas?', in E. Ullmann-Margalit and A. Margalit (eds) *Isaiah Berlin: A Celebration*, Chicago, IL: Chicago University Press.

—— (1992) 'Democracy, nationalism, and education', *Educational Philosophy and Theory*, 24: 17–27.

—— (1993a) *Liberal Nationalism*, Princeton, NJ: Princeton University Press.

—— (1993b) 'United we stand? The educational implications of the politics of difference', *Studies in Philosophy and Education*, 12: 57–70.

—— (1995a) 'The enigma of nationalism', *World Politics*, 47: 418–440.

—— (1995b) 'Two concepts of multiculturalism', *Journal of Philosophy of Education*, 29: 161–172.

—— (1996) 'Reconstructing the language of imagination', in S. Caney, D. George and P. Jones (eds) *National Rights, International Obligations*, Boulder: CO: Westview Press.

—— (1997) '*Pro Patria Mori!* Death and the state', in R. McKim and J. McMahon (eds) *The Morality of Nationalism*, Oxford: Oxford University Press.

—— (1998) 'A strange alliance: Isaiah Berlin and the liberalism of the fringes', *Ethical Theory and Moral Practice*, 2: 279–289.

Tate, N. (1995) Untitled speech given to Shropshire Secondary Headteachers Annual Conference, 13 July.

—— (1997a) 'National identity and the school curriculum.' Paper presented at Centre for Policy Studies in Education Seminar, University of Leeds, 30 January.

—— (1997b) 'Ethics in the workplace.' Speech given to Royal Society of Arts, London, 3 July

—— (1997c) 'Making sense of values in learning.' Speech given to Careers Research and Advisory Council Conference, May.

Taylor, C. (1994a) *Multiculturalism: Examining the Politics of Recognition*, edited by A. Gutmann, Princeton, NJ: Princeton University Press.

—— (1994b) 'Reply and re-articulation', in J. Tully (ed.) *Philosophy in an Age of Pluralism*, Cambridge: Cambridge University Press.

Thiessen, E. T. (1987) 'Two concepts or two phases of liberal education?', *Journal of Philosophy of Education*, 21: 223–234.

Thomas, G. and Glenny, G. (2002) 'Thinking about inclusion. Whose reason? What evidence?', *International Journal of Inclusive Education*, 6: 345–369.

Tomasi, J. (2001) *Liberalism Beyond Justice: Citizens, Society, and the Boundaries of Political Theory*, Princeton, NJ: Princeton University Press.

Ulmann-Margalit, E. and Margalit, A. (1991) (eds) *Isaiah Berlin: A Celebration*, Chicago, IL: University of Chicago Press.

Underkuffler, L. S. (2001) 'Public funding for religious schools: difficulties and dangers in a pluralist society', *Oxford Review of Education*, 27: 577–592.

Ungoed-Thomas, J. (1996) 'Vision, values and virtues', in J. M. Halstead and M. Taylor (eds) *Values in Education and Education in Values*, London: Falmer.

Verhaar, O. and Saharso, S. (2004) 'The weight of context: headscarves in Holland', *Ethical Theory and Moral Practice*, 7: 179–195.

Vincent, A. (1997) 'Liberal nationalism: an irresponsible compound?', *Political Studies*, 45: 275–295.

—— (2002) *Nationalism and Particularity*, Cambridge: Cambridge University Press.

Vojak, C. (2003) '*Mozert v. Hawkins:* A look at self-knowledge and the best interests of the child', *Educational Theory*, 53: 401–419.

Waldron, J. (1993) *Liberal Rights: Collected Papers 1981–1991*, Cambridge: Cambridge University Press.

—— (1995) 'Minority cultures and the cosmopolitan alternative', in W. Kymlicka (ed.) *The Rights of Minority Cultures*, Oxford: Oxford University Press.

—— (1996) 'Multiculturalism and melange', in R. K. Fullinwider (ed.) *Public Education in a Multicultural Society*, Cambridge: Cambridge University Press.

—— (2003a) 'Teaching cosmopolitan right', in K. McDonough and W. Feinberg (eds) *Citizenship and Education in Liberal-Democratic Societies: Teaching for Cosmopolitan Values and Collective Identities*, Oxford: Oxford University Press.

—— (2003b) 'Security and liberty: the image of balance', *The Journal of Political Philosophy*, 11: 191–210.

Walford, G. (2000) 'A policy adventure: sponsored grant-maintained schools', *Educational Studies*, 26: 247–261.

—— (2001) 'Funding for religious schools in England and the Netherlands: can the piper call the tune?', *Research Papers in Education*, 16: 359–380.

—— (2002) 'Classification and framing of the curriculum in evangelical Christian and Muslim schools in England and the Netherlands', *Educational Studies*, 28: 403–419.

—— (2003) 'Separate schools for religious minorities in England and the Netherlands: using a framework for the comparison and evaluation of policy', *Research Papers in Education*, 18: 281–299.

Wallace, J. D. (1999) 'Virtues of benevolence and justice', in D. Carr and J. Steutel (eds) *Virtue Ethics and Moral Education*, London: RoutledgeFalmer.

Walzer, M. (2001) 'Liberalism, nationalism, reform', in R. Dworkin, M. Lilla and R. B. Silvers (eds) *The Legacy of Isaiah Berlin*, New York: New York Review Books.

—— (2003) 'What rights for illiberal communities?', in D. Bell and A. De Shalit (eds) *Forms of Justice: Critical Perspectives on David Miller's Political Philosophy*, Lanham, MD: Rowman and Littlefield.

Weinstein, J. R. (2004) 'Neutrality, pluralism, and education: civic education as learning about the other', *Studies in Philosophy and Education*, 23: 235–263.

Weinstock, D. (1997) 'The Graying of Berlin', *Critical Review*, 11: 481–501.

—— (1998) 'How can collective rights and liberalism be reconciled?', in R. Baucock and J. Rundell (eds) *Blurred Boundaries: Migration, Ethnicity, Citizenship*, Aldershot: Ashgate.

—— (1999) 'Building trust in divided societies', *Journal of Political Philosophy*, 7: 287–307.

—— (2001) 'Constitutionalizing the right to secede', *Journal of Political Philosophy*, 9: 182–203.

—— (2004a) 'The problem of civic education in multicultural societies', in A. Dieckhoff (ed.) *The Politics of Belonging: Nationalism, Liberalism, and Pluralism*, Lanham: MD: Lexington Books.

—— (2004b) 'Four kinds of (post-) nation-building', in M. Seymour (ed.) *The Fate of the Nation-state*, Montreal: McGill-Queen's University Press.

—— (2005) 'Beyond exit rights: reframing the debate', in A. Eisenberg and J. Spinner-

Halev (eds) *Minorities Within Minorities: Equality, Rights and Diversity*, Cambridge: Cambridge University Press.

Weisse, W. (2003) 'Difference without discrimination: religious education as a field of learning for social understanding?', in R. Jackson (ed.) *International Perspectives on Citizenship, Education and Religious Diversity*, London: Routledge.

White, J. (1996) 'Education and nationality', *Journal of Philosophy of Education*, 30: 328–343.

—— (1999) 'In defence of liberal aims of education', in R. Marples (ed.) *The Aims of Education*, London: Routledge.

—— (2001) 'Patriotism without obligation', *Journal of Philosophy of Education*, 35: 141–150.

—— (2003) 'Five critical stances towards liberal philosophy of education in Britain', *Journal of Philosophy of Education*, 37: 147–184.

Williams, B. (1978) 'Introduction', in I. Berlin, *Concepts and Categories: Philosophical Essays*, edited by H. Hardy, London: Hogarth Press.

—— (1996) 'Toleration: an impossible virtue?' in D. Heyd (ed.) *Toleration: An Elusive Virtue*, Princeton, NJ: Princeton University Press.

Williams, K. (1998) 'Education and human diversity: the ethics of separate schooling revisited', *British Journal of Educational Studies*, 46: 26–39.

Willinsky, J. (1998) 'The educational politics of identity and category', *Interchange*, 29: 385–402.

Wokler, R. (2003) 'Isaiah Berlin's Enlightenment and Counter-Enlightenment', in J. Mali and R. Wokler (eds) *Isaiah Berlin's Counter-Enlightenment, Transactions of the American Philosophical Society*, 93, 5: 13–32.

Wollheim, R. (1991) 'The idea of a common human nature', in E. Ulmann-Margalit and A. Margalit (eds) *Isaiah Berlin: A Celebration*, Chicago, IL: Chicago University Press.

—— (2001) 'Berlin and Zionism', in R. Dworkin, M. Lilla and R. B. Silvers (eds) *The Legacy of Isaiah Berlin*, New York: New York Review of Books.

—— (2004) *Germs: A Memoir of Childhood*, London: The Waywiser Press.

Wolterstorff, N. (1993) 'The grace that shaped my life', in K. J. Clark (ed.) *Philosophers Who Believe*, Downers Grove, IL: Intervarsity Press.

Wright, A. (2003) 'Freedom, equality, fraternity? Towards a liberal defence of faith community schools', *British Journal of Religious Education*, 25: 142–152.

—— (2004) 'The politics of multiculturalism: a review essay', *Studies in Philosophy and Education*, 23: 299–311.

Wringe, C. (1998) 'Reasons, rules and virtues in moral education', *Journal of Philosophy of Education*, 32: 225–237.

—— (2000) 'The diversity of moral education', *Journal of Philosophy of Education*, 34: 659–672.

Yack, B. (1996) *Liberalism Without Illusions*, Chicago, IL: Chicago University Press.

Young, I. M. (1997) 'Polity and group difference: a politics of presence?', in R. E. Goodin and P. Pettit (eds) *Contemporary Political Philosophy*, Oxford: Blackwell.

—— (2000) 'Self-determination and global democracy: a critique of liberal nationalism', in I. Shapiro and S. Macedo (eds) *Designing Democratic Institutions*, New York: New York University Press.

Zakaras, A. (2003) 'Isaiah Berlin's cosmopolitan ethics', *Political Theory*, 32: 495–518.

Index